VIOLENCE—A TRAGIC AMERICAN LEGACY

Every six minutes somewhere in the United States, a woman is raped and a child is a victim of violent abuse. Every twenty-eight minutes a person is murdered. Every minute a victim is added to the list of crime statistics. This year one of every three American families will be touched by some act of violent crime.

In *The Killers Next Door* I take an in-depth look at seven killers—serial killers, spree murderers, a mass murderer, and a ritualistic killer—all of whom gave off clear warning signs of danger. Each of these killers might have been stopped before the killing began had he or she or the people around the killer recognized the warning signs and intervened.

What you are about to read will shock, sadden, terrify, and enrage you. I hope it will stimulate all of you to reach out and to intervene in the tragic lives of the walking time bombs amongst us.

—From the Introduction

BOOK YOUR PLACE ON OUR WEBSITE AND MAKE THE READING CONNECTION!

We've created a customized website just for our very special readers, where you can get the inside scoop on everything that's going on with Zebra, Pinnacle and Kensington books.

When you come online, you'll have the exciting opportunity to:

- View covers of upcoming books
- Read sample chapters
- Learn about our future publishing schedule (listed by publication month *and author*)
- Find out when your favorite authors will be visiting a city near you
- Search for and order backlist books from our online catalog
- Check out author bios and background information
- Send e-mail to your favorite authors
- Meet the Kensington staff online
- Join us in weekly chats with authors, readers and other guests
- Get writing guidelines
- AND MUCH MORE!

Visit our website at
http://www.kensingtonbooks.com

THE KILLERS NEXT DOOR

JOEL NORRIS, Ph.D.

Revised and Updated by William J. Birnes

PINNACLE BOOKS
Kensington Publishing Corp.
http://www.kensingtonbooks.com

PINNACLE BOOKS are published by

Kensington Publishing Corp.
850 Third Avenue
New York, NY 10022

All Kensington Titles, Imprints, and Distributed Lines are available at special quantity discounts for bulk purchases for sales prmotions, premiums, fund-raising, and educational or institutional use. Special book excerpts or customized printings can also be created to fit specific needs. For details, write or phone the office of the Kensington special sales manager: Kensington Publishing Corp., 850 Third Avenue, New York, NY 10022, attn: Special Sales Department, Phone: 1-800-221-2647.

Pinnacle and the P logo Reg. U.S. Pat. & TM Off.

First Pinnacle Books Printing: October 2002

10 9 8 7 6 5 4 3

Printed in the United States of America

Dedicated to Margurite Jones McKinney and
Melvin David Maurer.
And to the memory of Dr. Joel Norris

The author wishes to acknowledge his appreciation to the following individuals who assist him with his research:
Joe Fischer, Bobby Joe Long, Jr., Louella Long, Charles Gervais, Jackie Beaver, William Walsh, Nan Cuba for Henry Lee Lucas, Captain Bob Prince for Henry Lee Lucas, Sheriff Jim Boutwell for Henry Lee Lucas, Ron Valentine, Esq., for Arthur Shawcross, John Libretti, Esq., for Joe Fischer, Parole Officer Steve Daniels for Daniel Rakowitz, Howard Schaefer, Esq., for the estate of Nicholas Corwin in re Laurie Dann, Veronica Porteous Martzell for Charles Gervais. He would like to acknowledge the investigative reporting of Joel Kaplan, George Papajohn, and Eric Zorn in the *Chicago Tribune* Sunday Supplement and in their subsequent book *Murder of Innocence* (Warner) as one of his primary sources for the background of the Laurie Dann story.

The name Dr. David Schwartz, one of Laurie Dann's victims, is a pseudonym.

TABLE OF CONTENTS

INTRODUCTION

The killer next door is a human time bomb about to go off. He could be anyone: an unbalanced person seething away at every real or imagined grievance, a serial killer living a completely camouflaged life as he trolls for victims, a high-school or middle-school student plotting revenge, or even a terrorist in a sleeper cell waiting for his suicide mission. There are human time bombs all around us, people who are on the very knife-edge of violence, needing only a single spark to set off a reaction deep within their psyches that propels them into a violent murder spree, a sudden explosion of mass murder, or a chillingly relentless skein of serial murder.

Human time bombs are people who are programmed—in some cases, even from conception—by a complex interaction of biological, psychological, social, and spiritual forces to commit crimes so heinous and bloody that even the police are confounded by the depth of hatred the killers display toward their victims. Yet, these killers give off clear warning signs about the impending danger long before they erupt. The problem is that, even today, twenty-five years after the cases of Ted Bundy and the Atlanta Child Murders, and some twenty years after the Green River Murders began, most professionals don't understand what the early warning signs of violence are or where the violence begins. The consequences of missing these warning signs—as school officials from Littleton, Colorado, to Little Rock, Arkansas, to San Diego, California, now know—can be fatal.

When a human time bomb erupts into violence, whether it be the methodical repeat violence of a serial killer or the apocalyptic self-destructiveness of a mass murderer, no one is untouched. For some communities, it's the death of innocence, while for others, it's the nightmare of an unseen terror that stalks the streets. When the story breaks in banner headlines, our sympathy spontaneously goes out to the victims and their survivors. After seeing the photographs of the crime scene and hearing the descriptions of battered and dismembered bodies, and then understanding the brutal terror endured by the victims prior to their deaths, we are simultaneously enraged and terrified that someone should die in such a way. No matter who the victims are or from what walks of life, we realize that each of them has the absolute right not to be murdered.

The horror that one of these creatures can inflict on his victims doesn't simply end with the murder. The horror doesn't simply stop there at all. A ripple effect exists. As we've seen from the recent spate of school shootings, the mass murder at Luby's in Killeen, Texas, and from the televised trial of serial killer Jeffrey Dahmer, the shock and pain that a malevolent killer causes will be felt by the loved ones of the victims for the rest of their lives, no matter what the outcome of the public investigation and the subsequent trial may be. The victims can never be brought back to life, and entire communities often share the grief of the families and loved ones who must survive and undergo their own healing processes. How many more wreaths do we have to see laid at the site of a workplace massacre or a racist killer's shooting spree, such as the one in Northridge, California, to understand the level of grief a human time bomb can inflict on a community?

Most people don't understand that families and loved ones are also victims of mass murderers and serial killers because the loved ones of victims must experience a host of long-term physical and emotional symptoms, not the least of which is post-traumatic stress. Most people don't realize either that perhaps a similarly severe grief is felt by the loved ones of the killers, who are sometimes victims in their own way. I have seen that sometimes the grief felt by the killers' families is even more stressful than the grief felt by the victims' families because the killers' families bear the added burden of guilt. It's a vicious web, and there's no easy way out of it.

With each new explosion of a human time bomb into violence, all of us, families and loved ones, acquaintances and members of the community, know that we will never be the same again. More of our collective innocence is gone, and in its place are terms and issues to be dealt with. Such terms as: "multiple homicide offender," a person who kills three or more people with a lapse in the violent episode; a "spree murderer," a person who commits bursts of murder over a couple of hours or days with no lapse in the episode; "the mass murderer," the explosive, apocalyptic, and often suicidal killer who wreaks some hidden revenge hidden in his soul on multiple victims at the same time before he turns the weapon on himself; and the newest category, the "ritualistic killer," who kills according to a script—maybe even that of a video game or the lyrics of a death-rock anthem—laid out for him by a perverted belief system, ritualistic or obsessive delusion, or self-destructive fantasies.

Add to this, serial and ritualistic rape, along with child, spouse, and elder abuse, and the implications are almost overwhelming. Even though crime rates have dropped consistently through the 1990s and into the twenty-first century, these sensational mass, spree, serial, and ritualistic murders still occur and scream at us for attention in front-page headlines and riveting images on the late-night news.

Include also the crack-baby generation now working its

way through our public school system and the potential of crime rates spiking again if the economy collapses and no longer supports the safety net that's been woven together over the past decade. If these things come to pass, the nation will witness even more school and workplace shootings, more mass murders and shooting sprees, and possibly new breeds of predatory repeat sexual offenders and killers.

Where will it all end? What can we do about it? Every six minutes somewhere in the United States, a woman is raped and a child is a victim of violent abuse. Every twenty-eight minutes a person is murdered. Every minute, a defenseless person or victim is added to the list of crime statistics. Although our economy is supposed to be returning to good times, it's predicted that by the year 2003, one out of every three American families will be touched by some act of violent crime. Think about it. That's a staggering statistic. Even in a family's moments of grief and terror, the epidemic of violence continues to tear away at our society and endangers the sanctity of other families.

In *The Killers Next Door,* I will take an in-depth look at ten killers—serial killers, spree murderers, mass murderers, a schoolyard-shooting suspect, and even a ritualistic killer—all of whom gave off clear warning signs of danger before they exploded. Each of these killers might have been stopped before the killing began had he or she or the people around the killer been able to recognize the nature of the warning signs and been able to intervene in their lives. In every instance, the cases of these killers typify what happens when opportunities are missed to short-circuit a killer's career before the homicides begin.

The ten cases of human time bombs presented in this book are part of a body of research I have compiled for the past twenty years. I am a counseling psychologist, originally from Georgia, where I worked as an educator to the defense and appeals teams of several convicted killers. I have worked with hundreds of episodic killers and walking time bombs and have helped their lawyers and medical specialists understand the nature of the syndrome that compels them to kill while they consume themselves in misery and self-loathing.

For most of my professional career, I have studied the biological, social, and psychological underpinnings of violent behavior, and the particular manifestation of episodic violence. For over twenty years, I was a consultant to the capital-murder defense and appeals of cases in Georgia, Florida, Texas, California, Michigan, and New York. Since 1984, I have researched and interviewed some of the most infamous killers of our time, including Charles Manson, Henry Lee Lucas, Arthur Shawcross, Joe Fischer, and others. Even though their personal stories from a literary perspective are quite different, clinically they are remarkably similar. This book will document and explain those clinical, medical, psychological, and social issues that walking human time bombs typically display and the triggers that unleash the pent-up violence these individuals are ready to unleash on those around them.

All of these time bombs do have a common denominator, which comes to the attention of the public every time one of them breaks into the headlines after a spectacular crime. As each case unfolds, it becomes more and more obvious that there were serious incidents of missed opportunities for intervention in the killers' lives on the parts of the courts, parole officers, police departments, and even doctors, teachers, and parents. Many people seemed to sense, for example, that the Illinois killer Laurie Dann was a walking time bomb, but nobody seemed able to do anything about it. Even the FBI got there too late to arrest her. She had already left town to begin her killing spree on the very morning an agent turned up in her University of Wisconsin dormitory.

Similarly, the parole officer who watched the accused Genesee River killer Arthur Shawcross walk out of Green Haven Correctional Facility knew that New York State had released a violent criminal back into society. Although he warned others about Shawcross's release, there was nothing he could do about changing the entire parole system. The legal process had made Arthur Shawcross a free man, even though the underlying causes of Shawcross's violent behavior had not only *not* been remedied—in fact, they had not even been adequately addressed. As the local newspapers have reported, despite the safeguards that were supposed to have been built into the New York State Correctional and Probation system, Shawcross killed again and again and kept on killing until he was finally spotted by a state police helicopter on stakeout when he returned to the crime scene to eat his lunch. He followed almost the exact psychological pattern fifteen years earlier when he was apprehended for child murder. Only fifteen years before, his victim profile was children. Now his victims were prostitutes, although his psychological behavior was the same: return to the crime scene of his latest victim to eat his lunch and demonstrate his control over the victim's body.

The frustrating nature of some of what you will read requires at least some explanation. First you will read of many things that are reported from the killer's individual perspective. You will read over and over again that "he or she claims . . . but that so and so emphatically denies." This may become repetitious, but it's important because, many times, time bombs begin fantasizing about their vision of truth so obsessively that the fantasy actually becomes reality for the subject. It is as if your worst nightmare repeats itself again and again, so many times, that you now react during your waking hours to the nightmare instead of to reality. Better still, it is as if you have walked around in a violent dream state for so much of your life that you have lost the ability to differentiate what happens in the dream from what happens in reality. When you are finally shaken out of your dream, your memories of reality are completely folded into the memories, images, and emotions of your dream—like swirls of chocolate in a marble cake—and have lost their separate identities.

Therefore, for a counseling psychologist like myself, the killer's fantasies have "become" reality, and he or she acts upon them as if they are real. In order to deal with the killer's story, his or her confession, or his or her memories of the victims and their locations, I have to treat the killer's delusions or fantasies as real so as to communicate on the same wavelength. Sometimes I even have to make sure that the killer understands my empathy for the life he's led, no matter what that life entails. That is why it is scientifically necessary to examine the killer's recollections in his stories.

It is ultimately important to make a vigorous effort to document everything the killer says. If a killer says that a relative abused him, we must ask whether this is true. And if the relative emphatically denies that he or she abused the child, then, in the absence of any evidence to the contrary, the denial must stand. When the relative is dead, as in the case of Henry Lee Lucas, all we have is the killer's own story, and the consistency of that story from interview to interview and from interviewer to interviewer.

In Henry Lee Lucas's case, that story has remained remarkably consistent, even though Lucas himself seemed to have undergone a remarkable transformation over the final years of his life. In his story, you will hear about his confession to the murder of a hapless hitchhiker the police nicknamed "Orange Socks." It was her murder that put him on death row in Huntsville, Texas. But it was a subsequent investigation into that murder by the Texas courts that found enough evidence to cast doubt on Lucas's confession to the murder that prompted then-governor George W. Bush, a strong death-penalty advocate, to lift the death sentence and spare Lucas's life. Much of Lucas's other confessions were thrown into doubt as well. Thus, he resided in Huntsville until the day he died as a kind of cult figure who was either one of this country's most prolific serial killers or its greatest confabulator. This self-confessed killer of his own mother as well as Otis Toole's niece, Becky, and his own benefactor, Granny Rich, was a recipient of one of the only reprieves George Bush ever granted to anyone on the Texas death row.

You will read other stories from killers that describe unspeakable horrors of abuse, trauma, and molestation. It is important to remember that in the absence of any verifiable facts, these are only stories, fantasies, delusions, and clouded recollections. We are not suggesting you take these as absolute facts of reality, only as facts as seen through the eyes of killers, facts that exist only in the killers' minds. Take them as we psychological investigators do: we utilize these stories as points of entry into the killers' pasts, voices from inside the minds of serial killers and mass murderers. They are the beginnings of our investigations. They are the scripts of the dramas the killers are acting out. In terms of the following stories, the killers' narratives—when they're available—often told in their very own words, are the hyperlinks to their own versions of madness.

We cite these stories here and describe them not to point any finger of culpability at anyone else, even though the killers may do so, but rather to understand better the psychology of the killers. Therefore, nothing in the following narratives should be construed in any way as an accusation against any individuals or the institutions they work for. They are the killers' words, and we specifically do not endorse their reality, only the reality as the killers may have perceived it. Where available, we have included denials from any parties named by the killers as somehow contributing to his or her frame of mind.

Similarly, the concept of "linkage blindness" may be misleading. You will read stories in which a convicted killer passes through a correctional system within which he receives therapy, is interviewed by mental health professionals, is evaluated by probation and parole officials, and is judged capable of being released on probation. Yet, the forces inside that individual still continue to rage. The tightly controlled universe inside a prison system may have become the killer's external neuroskeleton, regulating the killer's every moment so that he appeared rehabilitated, but nothing whatsoever changed on the inside. Accordingly, upon his release, the killer very quickly snaps back to his old ways, resorting to a violent lifestyle within a very short time. This is what both Henry Lee Lucas and Arthur Shawcross said they did. And Jeffrey Dahmer told the Milwaukee police who interrogated him after the discovery of his victims' remains in his apartment that he was even able to keep on stalking and killing victims while serving a work-release jail sentence for a sexual offense against a minor.

You will also read of cases in which a killer had been in therapy for months or even years before he or she seemed to explode into fatal violence. You may be tempted to blame the parole system, the social caseworkers, or the psychologists for the violence. In fact, nothing in the descriptions of the cases that follow should be construed as an implication that the professionals involved in the cases were in any way responsible for the crimes that followed. If they were not aware of what warning signs might have been present in their subjects, it only reinforces my beliefs that there is still a great deal of education that needs to be undertaken.

Some of these cases will be frustrating because we're examining them in hindsight, particularly the cases of George Jo Hennard, the mass murderer who gunned down innocent diners in Luby's Cafeteria; Laurie Dann, who took a class of nursery-school children hostage; and Daniel Rakowitz, who announced to street people in Tompkins Square Park that he was going to kill his roommate, Monika Berle, before he did murder her, boiled her remains into soup, which he served to the street people in the park, then told police about it. Nobody believed him. People laughed at him until they actually found Monika Berle's remains. Similarly, nobody seemed to realize just how dangerous Laurie Dann actually was. And nobody stepped in to stop Hennard, even though he threatened people in the community and vowed revenge on those he thought were plotting against him. Yet after the crimes and the carnage, hindsight always turns up the clues that seemed to have been neglected along the way.

The fact is, psychology is still an inexact and subjective type of science. Different therapists will honestly disagree with one another on the diagnoses and prognoses and predictions for violence. The best we can do in many cases is to educate lay people and professional people alike in what those cases and warnings are so that fewer opportunities are missed in the future. What can we say about the clear warnings the perpetrators of schoolyard and classroom shootings gave off well in advance of the crimes? Didn't Charles "Andy" Williams in San Diego and Eric Harris and Dylan Klebold in Littleton, Colorado, make it perfectly clear to friends, and even on the Internet, that they were about to exact their own revenge upon what they saw as a hostile society? How seriously can we take threats that seem to be uttered more out of frustration than anything else? Yet, it's only when the unheeded threats actually turn into violence that the finger-pointing starts.

I, therefore, have highlighted the most important of these warning signs and critical symptoms in the final chapter. This, I hope, will serve the purpose of raising the reader's awareness to the nature of the warning signs and the deceptive and sometimes insidious ways they can be camouflaged as normal behavior. Remember, people usually want to believe the best and not the worst about their friends, relatives, spouses, or colleagues. That's why even the most obvious of warnings—such as an overt threat of violence or a cry for help—can easily, even after recent workplace shootings in Massachusetts, Atlanta, and California, be misread as the reaction of an overwrought person who will quickly straighten out after the crisis has passed. Too many times we're all too willing to deny the prospect of a severely disturbed individual in our presence because it makes us fearful and forces us to scrutinize our own basis of reality. Hence, denial is sometimes much easier. I hope the warning signs in this book will increase the reader's awareness so as to make denial that much harder.

In the epilogue, we briefly look at the November 2001 arrest of Gary Leon Ridgway, who is accused by King County Sheriff's authorities of being responsible for the killings of the early victims in the twenty-year-old Green River Murders. The investigation into his background and behavior, as described in the release of information from the King County district attorney to the public, documents the intense scrutiny Ridgway was under from 1983, when local police first contacted him, to 2001. This release is one of the most interesting stories of a police investigation into a serial homicide case ever made public.

THE TERRORIST NEXT DOOR

But what of the warning signs of the terrorist next door, the seemingly private individual who rarely talks to neighbors and appears to fade into the background so as not to attract attention? Are there warning signs that identify a potential terrorist, like Mohammed Atta and the other suspects the FBI identified in their investigation of the September 11, 2001, attack on the World Trade Center? Unfortunately, whatever warning signs there are rarely make themselves obvious to anyone outside of law enforcement agencies.

Maybe FBI or BATF undercover informants knew who Oklahoma City bomber Tim McVeigh was and what he was planning to do, but, outside his small circle of confidants, very few could have guessed that McVeigh was planning to blow up the Murrah Federal Building. Only after he had been caught and charged and an investigation begun did the road map of his conspiracy appear to make any sense. And even then, actually weeks before his execution, the FBI was still turning up documents that seemed to indicate that McVeigh might have been part of a larger plot, or even an unwitting pawn of the federal law enforcement investigators, who had set him up to lead them to others. Only, it's been alleged, they lost track of McVeigh, who carried out his own plans and left federal investigators to figure out what happened.

Similarly, no one who crossed paths with "Unabomber" Ted Kaczinski would have guessed that he was one of the few individuals capable of eluding a nationwide FBI manhunt for over thirteen years. For the final few years of his career as the dreaded bomber, Kaczinski lived completely off the grid in a tiny shed in Montana and commuted into his nearby town on a bicycle, built his bombs meticulously by hand, and traveled to distant post offices to mail them to his intended targets. Although witnesses had spotted him years earlier and even helped police artists develop a composite sketch, the FBI had no way to catch him because he left no trail. He defied any attempts to track him down: by living off the grid, he was living off the radar. He used the weight of the FBI's reliance on technology and computer tracking as a form of bureaucratic judo to stay invisible. Kaczinski, a Harvard Ph.D. in mathematics, is a perfect example of how to hide in plain sight and continue to perpetrate violence even when some of the best criminal investigators in the world on your tail.

Kaczinski might have continued to prey on the targets of his own delusion had not his own stronger self-destructive tendencies tripped him up in the end. Frustrated that the message he was trying to send with each of his bomb packages was unheard, he contacted newspapers in a desperate gambit to have his memoirs published. These were the memoirs of a psycho-terrorist, inveighing against global corporate interests, government in general, and anyone he perceived as destroying the environment. What no one knew about Ted Kaczinski, not even his own brother, perhaps, was that this private war might have begun as a struggle against a younger brother who came along and, in Ted's eyes, usurped his position as the favorite son. In the end, it was this younger brother and Kaczinski's own mother who turned him in, acting out their roles in Ted's self-fulfilling prophecy that they were allied against him. But, looking at the frail, grisly, and unkempt stick figure on a bicycle, unsteadily pedaling along a dirt road in rural Montana, who would have even thought that he was one of the FBI's "Most Wanted"?

The World Trade Center bombers were successful, we believe, because they operated much like Kaczinski. These terrorists, who launched their plan in Europe amongst communities of foreign students where they would not stand out, used America's own social systems against their targets in much the same way as they used hijacked commercial airliners filled with explosive jet fuel as suicide cruise missiles. They espoused visions of suicidal violence. They participated actively in denouncing the United States and its allies. They were known within their own communities as religious zealots, if not fanatics. And they left a clear trail of culpability for all to see. Yet, it was the simplicity of their plans that made them undetectable until the very last moments of their respective flights. And by then it was too late to prevent the disaster, even though U.S. Air Force fighters had been launched to intercept the last of the airliners.

But, just like the Santee Shooter, the Columbine Shooters, George Hennard, and countless serial killers, once the hijackers were identified, not only did the road map of their conspiracy become obvious to federal investigators, the very warning signs of the attack became clear as well. What federal law enforcement and intelligence agencies discovered as the investigation into the Twin Towers bombing proceeded and the United States girded for war was that the warning signs of an impending terrorist attack were in plain sight for months, if not years, earlier. In fact just months before the attack, intelligence warnings had reached President Bush.

First, at least two previous airline hijackings fifteen years earlier—one over Algeria and aimed at Paris and the other aimed to explode over Tel Aviv—were so similar to the plans to bomb the World Trade Center that, when looked at in retrospect, they were practice runs for what happened in New York. Anyone looking at these two hijackings would almost have been able to see how the terrorists were trying to refine what they were doing so as to score a major success. Second, not only did Israel's Mossad warn U.S. intelligence services of an impending terrorist attack, but CIA informants also sent many warnings, warnings that were also picked up in NSA intercepts. However, the information was buried amidst other intelligence, and it took NSA analysts many weeks to find the warnings that were sent.

Like school and workplace shootings, particularly at post offices, even though the authorities know how these incidents happen and what the profiles of mass shooters often are, it doesn't prevent the attacks from taking place. What we know about why school and workplace shooters attack schoolmates and coworkers has made each subsequent event even more frustrating because what we know doesn't help people prevent the crimes. In the same way, even though we knew that some of the terrorists had false documentation, that Mohammed Atta had come into the United States on an expired visa, and that Atta had an arrest warrant filed against him in Florida, the terrorists still managed to hide in plain sight until the crime. In fact, six months after the deaths of the hijackers and their victims aboard the planes, at the World Trade Center, and at the Pentagon, the Immigration and Naturalization Service issued visas for some of the hijackers. It was incredible but true.

But one rule that applies to the potential of workplace and schoolyard violence also applies to the terrorists next door. Most of the school shooters announced their intentions. Most of the workplace shooters made threats long in advance of their crimes. And, in the same way, the terrorists, in unguarded moments, made some of the same threats and promises. They criticized America and gave indications that they were about to exact revenge. They were even specific about the violence they were going to perpetrate. However, no one believed them. When it comes to figuring out whether a killer or terrorist lives next door, it's a safe bet to believe a threat when it is made, even if the person seems incapable of carrying it out.

As a case in point, Andy WIlliam's friends called him a wimp who was only blowing smoke when he threatened to shoot up Santana High. After it was all over, those same friends regretted that their refusal to believe a threat made in earnest resulted in the deaths of two students. Similarly, when Mohammed Atta bragged in a Florida bar that America was about to experience something dreadful, people who heard him only thought it was the liquor talking. A few days later, they watched the terrible threat play itself out on CNN. The killer next door almost always reveals his intentions. We either don't listen or don't believe what we hear.

What you are about to read will shock, sadden, terrify, and enrage you. I hope it will stimulate all of you as individuals—but also as concerned professionals within institutions if that's where you are—to reach out and intervene in the tragic lives of the human time bombs and terrorists, who live next door, walk among us, work in the adjoining cubicle, ride the school bus with our children, sit next to us on trains and planes, but who are ticking away right now and can explode at any moment.

1

LUCAS JOHN HELDER: THE SMILEY FACE BOMBER

Lucas Helder, for all outward appearances, was a silent, non-aggressive third-year art student specializing in industrial design. When he played his music too loud in the dorm, he was told to turn it down and he apologized. When he was in high school, he followed Nirvana and had his own band, "Apathy." But no one would have believed that Lucas Helder would seize the nation's attention during three days in May when, on an Odyssey across the Midwest, he planted pipe bombs in mailboxes. In college, Luke had been the roommate next door, a kid even his college dean felt was quiet and acquiescent. In his small Minnesota town, he was the kid next door who liked grunge bands and kept to himself. Yet, his adoptive father said, there came a point in his son's life when he took a religion course and was introduced to such concepts as astral projection, out of body experiences, and, what may have been a vision of an alternate reality that challenged to his very core his concepts about life on earth.

Then, one day, Luke Helder was arrested for possession of marijuana and came into contact, for the first time, with the criminal justice system. Perhaps the confrontation was enough to turn what was the kid next door, already on the edge, into the bomber next door who went to extreme lengths to announce his message to the world. At least that's what his adoptive father, Cameron Helder, believed when he read the following mysterious note that Luke had placed victims' mailboxes in Iowa, Indiana, Texas, Colorado, and Nebraska as part of the suspicious pipe bomb packages he'd left inside on his way across the American heartland:

May 07, 2002

    Mailboxes are exploding! Why, you ask?

    Attention people.

    You do things because you can and want (desire) to

    If the government controls what you want to do, they control what you can do.

    If you are under the impression that death exists, and you fear it, you do anything to avoid it. (This is the same way pain operates. Naturally we strive to avoid negative emotion/pain.)

    You allow yourself to fear death!

    World authorities allowed, and still allow you to fear death!

    In avoiding death you are forced to conform, if you fail to conform, you suffer mentally and physically. (Are world powers utilizing the natural survival instinct in a way that allows them to capitalize on the people?)

    To "live" (avoid death) in this society you are forced to conform/slave away.

    I'm here to help you realize/ understand that you will live no matter what! It is up to you people to open your hearts and minds. There is no such thing as death. The people I've dismissed from this reality are not at all dead.

    Conforming to the boundaries, and restrictions imposed by the government only reduces the substance in your lives. When 1% of the nation controls 99% of the nations total wealth, is it a wonder why there are control problems?

The United States strives to provide freedom for their people. Do we really have personal freedom? I've lived here for many years, and I see much limitation. Does the definition of freedom include limitation? I've learned about the history of various civilizations in history, and I see more and more limitation. Do you people enjoy this trend of limitation? If not, change it!

As long as you are uninformed about death you will continue to say "how high", when the government tells you to "jump". As long as the government is uninformed about death they will continue tell you to "jump" Is the government uninformed about death, or are they pretending?

You have been missing how things are, for very long. I'm obtaining your attention in the only way I can. More info is on its way. More "attention getters" are on the way. If I could, I would change only one person, unfortunately the resources are not accessible. It seems killing a single famous person would get the same media attention as killing numerous un-famous humans. There is less risk of being detained, associated with dismissing certain people.

> *Sincerely,*
> *Someone Who Cares*

PS. More info. will be delivered to various locations around the country.

Then, on May 7, 2002, in the wake of news stories about explosives that had been planted in rural mailboxes across Nebraska, Illinois, Iowa, Colorado, and Texas, the University of Wisconsin-Madison student newspaper, "The Badger-Herald," received a strange letter from an art student who admitted he was setting off bombs in the mailboxes. The self-confessed bomber, twenty-one-year-old Lucas John

Helder, wrote a treatise in which he set forth his views on the interrelationship of life on earth and his own revelations about what he discovered about the shared consciousness of all life.

"What do you suppose would logically proceed humans?" Helder asked. He answered, "I'm happy because I know . . . I was raised to believe. All of my family and friends were raised to believe. . . . to be gullible . . . to be materialistic . . . to fear authority . . . to blindly follow . . . you can't forget greed, and god forbid they would understand themselves!" In other words, the writer suggested, humans were willfully blind to the realities of their own existence, they were sheep merely following those ahead of them rather than thinking for themselves or attempting to understand the infinite universe to which they belonged.

Yet, he suggested, "Humans have been striving for thousands and thousands of years to understand. From complex math equations, microscopes, and telescopes, to scientists, psychologists, governments (world leaders), and priests, all are designed to allow us all to understand. What the teachers/leaders understand is what the mass understands. Now wouldn't it be wise to question authority?"

Because society was becoming more complex, it was clearly doing so because of a collective search for comfort and to "avoid suffering." However, Helder asked in his treatise, was that really happening? Were people gaining a greater comfort by making their society more complex? "Look around," he said and ask yourself, now that the future had arrived, "Is the pain easing? Are the wars calming? Is EVERYONE happy? Clearly NOT!" In fact, it was just the opposite. Because people had failed to see what problems actually existed, they missed the point that the suffering of all life on earth would continue. Regardless of the technology-driven world people live in, the demands of work-a-day life, or the inherent complexities of a growing society, suffering continues.

Worse, he suggested, the direction society was taking was

all wrong because technology and the growing complexity of life would not ease any suffering. It was just the reverse. They were making life more difficult. However, in a frustratingly perverse statement, Helder suggested that he was here to help resolve the problem. "I'm here to help you," he wrote. "To expose you, to inform you, to provide for you the answers for where to look, so the 'spiritually sleepy mass' can transform themselves from believing to knowing, to have an awareness to life, and to begin understanding. Understand you have no reason to fear anything, ever, everything will be perfect, and the answers are much closer than you think! You will find answers that will allow everyone to find happiness, to know, and to understand. It's time you people open your minds to a new train of thought. You are on a journey, a very exciting one at that!"

Helder's comments were perverse because they arrived at the newspaper to explain his depositing pipe bombs in mailboxes on his odyssey across the Midwest. Like Ted Kaczinski years earlier, also protesting the mindlessness of destroying the environment and the attempt by large companies to control the masses, Helder's attention-getter was the placement of bombs. By exploding mailboxes in people's faces, Helder had hoped to transform his frustration into a message for society to reform. Those who were in the know, he said, understood what the reality of the universe was and would help others understand, even at the cost of injuries.

And what was the message Helder was bringing? "There is NO SUCH THING AS DEATH/VOID/END/NO MORE." And when people understood, as he did, that life existed on multiple planes, that individuals could learn, as he had learned, that they had the capacity to project themselves out of body so as to experience an alternate reality, death would be just another fairy tale like the existence of the "tooth fairy, the Easter Bunny, or Santa Claus.", and Death would all be categorized as fairy tales.

The concept of death exists and causes fear among the unknowing, Helder said, because people don't understand death. Driven by a survival instinct, people see death as an end, not a transition. "World powers," were capitalizing on this misunderstanding of death to suffocate the spirituality of people and keep them striving for more. The world powers were the providers, the masses their consumers.

What's especially interesting about what Helder was saying is certainly not that he was original. He wasn't. His vision of multiple planes of existence realizable through an out-of-body experience that governments and corporations derided is a vision shared not just by believers in the paranormal, but by an entire UFO culture which claims that extraterrestrials already possess this power and want to share it with us, but are kept from it by our own governments. If this was what Luke Helder had been taught, it fueled his rage at those who would deny the masses the freedom of their own spirituality.

He was especially outraged at organized religions, which were created to funnel or channel people along specific paths, herding them like sheep and shutting down creativity, while providing them with a false sense of spiritual well-being. Religions actually taught people to fear death, Helder wrote. And in fearing death, "You are forced to work (in turn providing for the government), and conform to society. You work to buy food, provide shelter, entertainment, etc. You conform to society because you will receive negative emotion/pain/death (jail/death penalty) if you don't. You fear, therefor you conform."

By seeking money as their only relief, people give themselves over to a power structure created by governments so as to enslave themselves. However, if people understood life, they would eliminate greed. But how could they accomplish this and understand true love and spirituality?

Helder saw himself as a prophet whose message was to awaken people. He began by explaining that dreams weren't simply everyday phenomena, they were a "key element" of understanding, the doorways to an alternate reality. And it was through the process of dreaming, lucid dreaming, that the discovery of multiple planes of existence would take place. Through a shared consciousness, only reachable during a dream state, individuals could participate in a collective of other minds so as to become one with all life. When this shared consciousness is reached by the individual, suddenly all fear of death vanishes and with it the power of the government and world's powers to control the masses. That was Helder's message.

"What happens when the body dies?" He asks. "Imagine how confusing is must be to be taken away from everything that you have known. When your body dies, you are simply, out of your body. Problems arise when individuals 'get out' and they aren't aware of what to do next. Many conciousnesses linger around on earth, clutching to material things; this is what ghosts are."

But understanding the nature of death implies a complete freedom. Thus, to understand death before death, releases individuals from the fear of death and liberates them. This is what Helder said he discovered and what he felt he had to bring to society.

In his treatise, he asked how people can grow to a new stage of consciousness from simple belief in something by actual knowledge. It is by practice, he said, by following a methodology that opens one's mind to spirituality people can actually "know" what it will be like for them after death. He, himself, had experienced exactly what he was talking about. "Like I said," he wrote. "I've been there. I was curious about the existence of ghosts, and my curiosity lead me to further investigation, which in turn allowed me to KNOW ghosts truly do exist. Needless to say, it was an exciting occasion to finally see one! When I got my film developed to find orbs, the week was even more exciting!"

Helder had achieved all of this as part of a course he had taken in religion, his father said, in which he learned astral projection. It was after this experience that he had undergone a fundamental change. Now, perhaps, he wanted to announce that change to a world of nonbelievers.

Thus his message delivered in a series of pipe bombs, he explained, was his way of showing people a new truth. "I'm doing this because I care, and have one in you people. If this doesn't work then so be it. In the end you will KNOW I was telling you the truth anyway. Imagine the sigh of relief you will have to KNOW you go on when you die." In other words, part of his message was to transmit death, to show his victims that if they had died as a result of his pipe bombs, the experience of death would be enlightening and an opening for them to a new world.

Helder also believed that marijuana should not be an illegal drug. He had been busted for a misdemeanor drug possession months earlier and fined. Maybe that had exposed him to an aspect of the criminal justice system he was not prepared to encounter. So he translated his outrage at the criminal justice system into part of his treatise, his diatribe against what he called the oppressiveness of government by arguing that there was a rationale for marijuana. He wrote, "Marijuana was placed here for a reason people. You spend billions per year on drug prohibition and the only thing being accomplished is the spending of billions of dollars. Alcohol is a motor skill impairment; marijuana is a mental stimulation, yet the impairing agent is legal? Is this yet another governmental agenda utilized as a tool for order?"

But what did all this have to do with causing injuries and even deaths to innocent people? This was, he said, a series of "very drastic measures" he was taking so as to provide "information" to an uninformed audience of victims. Society, "you people," have failed he said. But he would be the Christ figure for all of his victims. "I will die/change in the end for this, but that's ok, hahaha paradise awaits! I'm dismissing a few individuals from reality, to change all of you for the better, surely you can understand my logic."

It was a delusional logic, his father believed and so told the police. It was a logic borne out of frustration and a misunderstood message from a religion course. It was not a desire to hurt people. But the police were on Luke Helder's trail and would eventually catch up to him on a remote stretch of a Nevada Interstate.

When he was finally tracked down after a high-speed chase outside of Las Vegas, Lucas Helder told the police, he was planting pipe bombs in a pattern to show a happy face during his five-state weekend cross-country spree. Helder told this to one of the police officers at his arrest, according to Lt. Thom Bjerke of the Pershing County, Nevada, Sheriff's Department. "He seemed kind of carefree or amused about what was going on," Bjerke said during a CNN interview.

After his arrest, Helder confessed to planting eighteen pipe bombs in five states, knowing that people would be injured when they exploded, according to interviews assistant U.S. Attorney Craig Denney gave the press. During the first court appearance for the clean-cut, 21-year-old college student and one-time rock band member, Denney told the papers, police who had arrested him seized a shotgun loaded with a single round from Helder's car following a high-speed chase on a highway in Nevada. Denny revealed that Helder had told police he bought the gun to commit his suicide, an act, according to Helder's father, Cameron Helder, that was prevented in a phone conversation between Lucas Helder and FBI agent Paul McCabe. McCabe told Lucas Helder "If you blow yourself away, there is no way that message will get out."

It was Lucas Helder's father who eventually turned his son, calling Menomonie, Wisconsin, Police Chief Dennis Beety at 11:10 PM to tell him, in Beety's words, "he had received a letter from his son and the contents led him to believe his son may be involved." After receiving the tip from the police, the FBI issued an all-points-bulletin for Helder, describing him as "armed and dangerous."

The search for the mysterious mailbox bomber who was terrorizing rural residents across the upper American Midwest had actually begun on May, 3, 2002, when, according to FBI Agent Scott B. French's affidavit, "Mrs. And Mrs.

Bryce Werling drove to their mailbox located east of the intersection of Highway 38 and 201st Street in Tipton, Iowa. While still seated in the vehicle, Mrs. Werling opened the mailbox and retrieved mail from inside the box. Mrs. Werling then reached to the back of the box in order to remove another object she observed in the box. Mrs. Werling later described the object as in the shape of a long tube approximately one to two inches in diameter with strings or wires protruding from the device. Mrs. Werling also observed a plastic zip lock-type bag in the mailbox. Mrs. Werling reached into the mailbox with her right hand and grabbed the item. Before she completely removed the item, it exploded. Mrs. Werling sustained injuries to her forehead, face, arms, and hands. In addition, a tooth was knocked out and her eardrums were ruptured."

Law enforcement officers, alerted to the device in the Werling mailbox after Mrs. Werling's husband drove her to the hospitals, recovered a piece of pipe several inches long, remains of metal end caps, a residue of what seemed to be black powder, black electrical tape, remnants of a clear plastic bag, a nine-volt battery, and other remnants of the device. The mailbox, the affidavit asserts, was completely destroyed with such force that parts of the mailbox were found more than eighty feet away from the box's original location.

"Law enforcement officers also recovered the remains of a typewritten letter," Agent French testifies. "This letter appears to be identical to letters recovered from several other mailboxes in which the pipe bombs have been discovered in the Midwest between about May 3, 2002, and May 7, 2002."

Across five states, Agent French's affidavit attests, pipe bombs were discovered in rural mailboxes. In Iowa, Illinois, Nebraska, Colorado, and Texas, devices similar to the one found in the Werling's mailbox were discovered by residents, and some of these devices actually exploded, injuring several people. Law enforcement believed, as a result of the similar MO, the nature of the explosive devices, and the similarity of letters at the different locations that the same person was responsible for all of the bombings.

As the news about the mystery bomber—in a nation already traumatized by the September 11, 2001, terrorist attacks—spread across the news media, the police caught a break.

"On May 6, 2002," Cameron Helder, "the adoptive father of Lucas John Helder," contacted Lt. Wendy Stelter, Menomonie Police Department. He told Stelter that he "received a letter from Helder earlier on May 6 and was disturbed over the contents of the letter. Helder's adoptive father said he believed that his son was responsible for the pipe bombings recently reported in various states." Cameron Helder said that the letter he'd received referred to death and dying as well as "anti-government" comments. "Addition-ally," the affidavit reads, "Helder referred to an elaborate plan that he was prepared to carry out and that he was willing to die for it or go to prison for it. According to Helder's adoptive father, Helder also said, 'Mailboxes are exploding.'"

Later in the evening on May 6, Cameron Helder told police, his son's roommate called to say that he'd found possible bomb-making materials under Luke Helder's bed in his Menomonie apartment. While he was on the telephone with his son's roommate, Cameron Helder learned that Luke was on the phone with a neighbor and learned further from that conversation that he was in Colorado. He forwarded that information to police.

The following day, FBI Special Agent Scott Pulver interviewed Helder's roommate and two other persons and reported that twenty-one-year-old Lucas J. Helder, an industrial engineering major is a junior at the University of Wisconsin-Stout, living in a two-bedroom apartment in Menomonie with a roommate. On May 2, 2002, Helder's roommate, who was gone from the apartment for most of the afternoon, returned at about 4:30 to find a note from Lucas saying he was going to Madison, Wisconsin, to "party for the weekend." The note said, "Fuck work, just kidding. I'll call in sick." This struck Helder's roommate as odd because Lucas had not skipped work before and did not unexpectedly take off for the weekend unless it was to return to his parents' home in Minnesota.

On May 4, between 2 and 3 PM, according to Agent Pulver's report in the affidavit, Helder's roommate checked his answering machine and heard a message from Lucas, saying he would not be home that night and might not be home the next night, (May 5) either. Helder also told his roommate in the message to check the news and act accordingly. Two days later on May 6, Cameron Helder left two messages on Luke's roommate's answering machine. When Helder's roommate returned the call to Cameron Helder, Mr. Helder told the roommate that he was disturbed by a note received from his son, which he read to the roommate, that said that Lucas thought his parents were strong enough to deal with his beliefs. Cameron Helder also said something about pipe bombs and Helder's roommate believed this had something to do with some pages printed off the Internet that Lucas had sent with the note.

That Monday night, May 6, between ten and eleven, Helder's roommate along with two other people went into Lucas's bedroom to find out if he could be responsible for the pipe bombs being left in the mailboxes. One person found a white plastic shopping bag under the bed containing a large box of nails, a box of paperclips, and two black plastic bottles that said "gunpowder" and "extremely flammable." One of the bottles was light, as if it were almost empty. The roommate and his friends also found a blue plastic funnel and a receipt dated "4/17/02, 8:30 PM," that detailed the purchase of fifteen to twenty pipe casings along with the other items. None of the people had ever seen these items before in the apartment.

The FBI affidavit reveals that a friend of Helder's roommate recently read a note to him, which he had pulled off the Internet, that he believed was connected to the pipe bombings, which echoed Helder's beliefs about his being sick of the government's controlling people. According to Helder's roommate, within the previous year Lucas Helder had developed a strong interest in astro projection and out-of-body experiences. Helder had told him that death was the way of going on to another life and said that he was looking forward to that experience.

Helder's roommate told the FBI that Helder had purchased a cell phone within the previous week and had been carrying around two to three hundred dollars in twenty-dollar bills. Normally, Helder would carry only about ten bucks and pay for whatever he needed with either checks or his ATM card. He deposited his paychecks, which amounted to approximately two or three hundred dollars every two weeks, into his checking account.

The next day, in an interview with the FBI, Cameron Helder said that the letter from his son he received on May 6, which he talked about with his son's roommate, had been addressed to him, his wife, and his daughter at their home in Minnesota, had been postmarked from Omaha, Nebraska, and, in the words of the affidavit, "contained numerous papers including one typewritten letter signed 'Luke Helder,' a two-page handwritten letter signed 'Luke,' a single-page cover sheet entitled 'Explosions,' and a six-page article titled 'Life on Earth' and signed 'Lucas Helder.' The handwritten letter contained the following language, 'If I don't make it through this ordeal (if the gov't doesn't realize I can help) then I'll have to get out of here for awhile.'" Cameron Helder told the FBI agent who interviewed him that his son was driving a 1992 gray Honda Accord. Cameron Helder also said that his son had called his best friend, who told Helder subsequently that Lucas said there had a been a "change of plans," and he spoke of dying if "this" doesn't work and "I have to blow myself away."

On his deadly route across the Midwest, Lucas Helder was stopped three times for traffic violations. His first stop was for speeding on May 4 shortly after midnight near St.

Edward, Nebraska, about twelve miles away from Albion, Nebraska, where a pipe bomb was found in a mailbox later in the morning. When the police officer approached Helder's car, Helder said, "I didn't mean to hurt anybody." But the officer told him that he'd only been stopped for speeding.

Later that same day Helder was stopped again near Watonga, Oklahoma, by a state trooper for failure to wear a seatbelt. Helder told the trooper that he spent Friday in a small hotel outside of Omaha and that he was on his way to Arizona. The trooper wrote Helder a citation for an expired driver's license. Helder said he was tired and was looking for a motel room.

The next day, May 5, Helder was stopped for speeding by a Colorado State Trooper near Fowler, Colorado. The trooper remembered that Helder seemed very nervous and had "watery eyes like he was going to cry." The next day, May 6, a pipe bomb was discovered in a mailbox in rural Colorado.

The case against Helder began to build when, on May 7, FBI agents in Minnesota received information from the Goodhue County Sheriff's Office that in May, 1998, Lucas Helder was accused of threatening to blow up a mailbox belonging to a friend. That same day, a handwritten letter recovered from a Scotia, Nebraska, bombing crime scene was delivered to the FBI Laboratory for analysis and was compared against the handwritten letter received by Cameron Helder the day before. The FBI document expert concluded that the two letters had strong similarities.

Late in the afternoon of May 7, Helder contacted two friends in Minnesota by phone and admitted responsibility for the mailbox bombings. With this admission, the evidence uncovered by Helder's roommate, and the similarities between the letters found at crime scene and the letter Lucas Helder sent to his family, the police chase began for the Honda Helder was driving.

Tracked after he'd made the cell phone calls to his friends, police located Helder's Honda in rural Nevada and began the chase, which, at times, reached speeds of over

eighty-five to a hundred miles an hour while his father negotiated with him to surrender. He finally pulled over on Interstate 80 near Reno and held off police by threatening to kill
himself. In a tense series of negotiations during which time
Helder placed another phone call, this time to his father,
threatened to kill himself with a loaded handgun he had in
the car. While police remained at distance before a hostage
negotiator arrived at the scene, Paul McCabe talked Helder
out of shooting himself. The police agreed not to tackle
Helder, who, in turn, agreed to allow himself to be taken into
custody without resistance. Put under suicide watch in the
Washoe County, Nevada, jail before his hearing, Helder, according to the FBI, admitted to the bombings. Judge Robert
McQuaid said he believed that Helder suffered from "apparent mental health problems," although Helder answered questions at his hearing and told the judge he was aware that
anything he said could be used against him in court.

Who was Lucas Helder and what prompted an otherwise
mild and friendly all-American college student to take off on
a multi-state bombing spree that, for a few days in the middle of spring, captured the attention of the nation? One
teacher told the Washington Post that Luke Helder as an average student who was "attentive in class and willing to
challenge authority if he saw fit." A fellow student who had
known Helder since freshman year told an interviewer that
Lucas Helder was a music lover who didn't "warm quickly
to strangers." And still other students described Helder a
young man who'd rather stay by himself than go out with
groups of other students.

A member of a three-person rock band called "Apathy,"
Helder was also a fan of the grunge band Nirvana and, according to statements friends gave newspapers, was "preoccupied" with singer Kurt Cobain who committed suicide in
1994. While he was quiet and laid back, he also liked to play
his electric guitar and jam with other students. His dormitory advisor told the Washington Post that at times Helder
would turn his amplifier up so loud, other residents "couldn't

hear themselves think." But when told to turn it down, he would do so and apologize for disturbing the other students.

It what has become an almost too typical set of statements from friends of young violent offenders, most people from the small town where Helder grew up were amazed that he could have pulled off this bombing spree. The town of Pine Island, Minnesota, about a ninety-minute drive south of Minneapolis, was stunned by the news that one of their own carried such strong beliefs and went to such lengths to capture national attention. Cameron Helder, a former commander of the local American Legion post, is respected in town as is Luke's mother. Friends also know Helder's younger sister, Jenna, who is still in high school. No one believed that his family even know how strong Luke's beliefs were. However, his father told newspapers that after taking a religion course, Luke changed and seemed to see things in a different perspective. Maybe it was his experience with astral projection or his belief in his ability to experience an out-of-body reality that caused him to change so dramatically. At least that's what his letter suggested.

Helder said his bombings were "attention-getters," he called them, to jar people out of a conformist and materialistic mental state. They were devices to teach people not to fear death and to overcome, as he suggested he had, the limitations of their physical bodies. Helder referred to the states of lucid dreaming, a process during which the dreamer controls is thought process and, according to some religions, actually escapes his body and is able to travel on a completely different plane. The United States government—the military and the CIA—experimented with lucid dreaming and remote viewing for intelligence-gathering purposes during the 1960s, '70s, and '80s and some of the former practitioners of this ability set up their own training courses. Others claimed to have utilized the practice for corporate spying as well. Has Lucas Helder actually convinced himself that he was able to project himself out of his body, people who've gone through the training suggest, he would, indeed, have discovered an entirely different plane of existence. But would that be the cause of his violent behavior?

Sometimes it's the tiny things that set people off, little explosions deep in one's psyche that go unnoticed until they surface at a moment of crisis. In Helder's case, could it have been his arrest for possession of a marijuana pipe, a citation that led to a hundred and fifty dollar fine? As minor as that infraction might have been, it certainly seemed to be a cause of discontent in Helder's letter, which complained of society's tolerance for alcohol and intolerance of marijuana.

Whatever the association between potentially lethal explosive devices planted in mailboxes and an admonition to his potential victims not to fear death might be, as Lucas Helder goes to trial to face federal firearms and possessions of explosives charges we may never what know what it was that turned a guitar-playing art student at a Midwestern university into "the bomber next door."

2

GEORGE JO HENNARD JR.: BLOODBATH AT LUBY'S

George Jo Hennard Jr. began the morning of October 16, 1991, with a strange sense of calm that was new to him. He liked the feeling. It was a whole lot better than the rage that had been devouring him from the inside out for as long as he could remember. Today, he said to himself, today he would finally do something to set things to rights. He was free of drugs and liquor. His former drinking-in-the-park buddy, Tim Snyder, over in Killeen, had told him that booze only made him crazy. Maybe so, but not today. "Just watch and see," he kept repeating to himself. The marijuana he'd smoked in the past wasn't doing the thinking for him anymore; his liquor wasn't talking for him today.

It was two days past his thirty-fifth birthday, which would have been eventless except for the two women who disrupted the tranquillity of the day. First there had been a phone call from his mother, Jeanne Hennard, calling from Henderson, Nevada, where she had an antiques business. She had been divorced from George's father for four years and had fought with her son for more years than he could remember. He said he pictured his mother's head on the body of a rattlesnake. Once in 1982, George had talked to his then-roommate, Jim Dunlop, about killing her because, he said, he despised her domination, her abusive tactics, and the battles that had come close to blows. He hated her, and he made no secret of it to the people he talked to.

Then there was a second woman, that lawyer on TV, who intruded into what should have been the sanctity of his birthday by breaking right into his lunch. As George sat in a local café, hunched over a hamburger and fries, and watched the University of Oklahoma College of Law professor Anita Hill testify at the Clarence Thomas confirmation hearings on the small television over the counter, he felt an uncontrollable rage overtake him when Hill began to describe her recollections to the senators. Witnesses remember him screaming, "You dumb bitch" to the television set as he stood up from the counter. "You bastards opened the door for all the women!"

People who knew Hennard said that this rage had always been with him, fueling his isolation, driving people away from him. Ever since he was a child, living with his brother, Alan Robert, and his sister, Desiree, in a family that was shuttled from one city to another by his father, army orthopedic surgeon George Hennard, he had been called strange. In particular, schoolmates at Mayfield High School remembered an incident in Las Cruces, New Mexico, a small town near the White Sands Missile Range where the elder Hennard was stationed. Young Jo-Jo Hennard had been a popular and outgoing budding musician. Girls seemed to like the good-looking, friendly young man who was quickly becoming a local hero. He wanted to be a rock drummer and he wore his hair long. Then one day, it all changed. Jo-Jo appeared at school with his hair hacked off and his smile gone. Neighbors said he had had a violent fight with his strict disciplinarian father, but Jo-Jo himself never talked about it. Instead, he began to withdraw from friends and activities.

Soon after the incident, he left his rock band. People said he couldn't play in a combo or cooperate with the other musicians. He stood outside the home of one of the band members for several weeks and shouted obscenities about a supposedly stolen hat. People became frightened of his moods and behavior. Friends faded away and his dreams of becoming a rock drummer evaporated. High-school classmates said he seemed estranged from his family. No girls would date him, and he became isolated from his classmates. For his own reasons, Jo-Jo had turned into a loner. He remained a loner for most of his youth and adult life.

But today, now that he was thirty-five, he would set it all back to rights. Just a week and a half ago, he had quit his latest temporary job at a cement company in nearby Copperas Cove. When he picked up his check, he asked people at the company what they thought would happen if he killed someone. No one listened to him. It was as if they'd heard it all before. He told them about this little town of Belton, Texas, where he lived and how it had given him problems. He told them how certain women in Belton had hurt him, but no one listened to his ravings. People rarely do because there are so many crackpots making idle threats. Why worry about a threat? "Watch and see," he told them as he left. "Just watch and see."

Now the whole world would see. Within hours, George Jo Hennard would commit the single largest mass murder in the history of the United States. He left the house very early that morning, as he always did, to buy himself some breakfast. His breakfast run was a ritual he performed almost religiously every single day. It kept the things in his life in order and helped him impose an order on his day. It reined in the otherwise chaotic emotions of his existence that might explode into violence if he failed to exert control.

He had other compulsive behaviors as well, grooves to keep him from worrying about what to do next. For example, he was obsessively devoted to maintaining his magnificent mansion of a house. He tried to repair something—anything—every day, even if the thing wasn't broken. He would clean, water, mow, weed, rake, scrape, sand, paint, and hammer down any loose siding on the redbrick white-columned house with a single-mindedness that seemed to block out the world. His neighbors in Belton described the property with its expansive grounds, large swimming pool, and grand exterior as a local tourist attraction. On a lovely street of well-kept properties, realtors always drove by it when they were showing off the area to prospective home buyers, and that attention fueled Hennard's obsession to keep it up.

The property had first been purchased by his parents in 1980 and had been his home off and on between his stints in the U.S. Merchant Marine. But when his parents divorced in 1987 and his father moved up to Houston, his mother split for Nevada and he ended up being the only one left to take care of it until it was sold. It was all he had to do, really, since the court had lifted his merchant marine papers a few years earlier and with them his entire life as a seaman. The big, empty house where Hennard ended up had become the beach where he washed ashore. And now, even that was going to be taken away.

He considered the big For Sale sign in the front yard a terrible indignity, agreeing to show the house when a realtor came by, but only under protest. There were rumors that he had driven away one very interested couple with his rudeness and increasingly bizarre attitudes. He told anyone who would listen that he felt persecuted, tormented, attacked from every side. No matter how meticulous he was in keeping up outside appearances, the city of Belton still seemed to have it in for him, he said. They were all conspiring. The city cited him for not repairing a fence around the pool. Then they sent him an outrageous water bill. He complained to City Hall, he claimed. Then he said the neighbors joined against him when they called the police because he played his music too loud and too late at night. If he argued with his own friends on his own front yard, neighbors said he was disturbing the peace.

However, when *he* needed the police, it was always a different story. Someone was calling up and harassing him. The phone calls wouldn't stop; someone was taunting him by calling, waiting for the pickup, playing music, and then hanging up. Sometimes they waited on the line just long enough to hear the message on his answering machine: "Yo, cuz. You've reached Public Street. Leave your name, number, time, and message. Hang-up phone calls are absolutely prohibited and you'll get bugged if you do so." Then they hung up. And called again. And hung up. He was going to pay them back. It wouldn't be long now.

So, on the morning of October 16, Hennard followed routine. He pedaled over to the Leon Heights Drive-In Convenience Store, about a two-block bicycle ride from his house, for breakfast. It was his morning workout. It kept him in shape, muscular, and well built. He looked physically healthy and attractive, with thick dark hair and brooding, almost piercing eyes, but he always seemed belligerent, frightening, overwhelmingly angry, fighting for control of himself. He was always ready to explode.

Mary Mead, mother-in-law of the convenience store owner, and her son Jimmy often waited on him and considered him a regular customer. They described him as a "mean-spirited loner." Hennard would flash them $100 bills and $100 traveler's checks in addition to the running tab he kept for his purchases. They had seen him treat other customers rudely, once harshly pushing aside a woman as he leaned over the counter to give Mary an ominous message. He said she was to tell everyone that if they didn't stop messing with his house, something bad was going to happen. The people where he lived knew that he was not the person one wanted to cross.

But on that morning of October 16, the people who remembered seeing him noticed that there was a slight tilt to his usual demeanor. He seemed calmer than usual, almost benign, if you didn't know who he was. He didn't spit on any of the cars as he turned his ten-speed into the parking lot at 5:30 A.M. to pick up his usual: a sausage and biscuit sandwich, orange juice, candy bars, a newspaper, and a package of Old Fashioned Dunkers Doughnuts. He put the $3.37 on his tab and promised he'd be back to pay later.

Everything was ready at the house when he returned home. His 1987 light blue Ford Ranger pickup truck was sitting in the driveway, perfectly cleaned and polished. He liked to put in a lot of work on it every day. And his two 9 mm pistols were also ready, along with at least ninety-six rounds of ammunition. He quietly ate his breakfast and wrote personal notes to himself, reminders of what he thought of the women of Belton. Vipers and bitches, he called them. Watch and see, he said again and again. Watch and see. But people had been watching for a long time, to no avail.

Jane Bugg was absolutely terrified of her strange neighbor, not so much for herself as for her two daughters, Jill Fritz, twenty-three, and Jana Jernigan, nineteen. George Hennard was stalking them, she'd told the police, and the danger was escalating. Frustrated and finally enraged by the unresponsive authorities, Jane Bugg was determined to defend the girls and herself. Eventually, this practical, hardworking forty-six-year-old medical secretary would become so fearful, she would actually go out and buy a gun.

At first, Hennard seemed more harmless than troubling. Even though some of the neighbors complained of his hostility, he would wave in a very friendly manner whenever the attractive mother or either of her two daughters drove or walked by. But his piercing dark eyes would follow them all the way down the street, and she could see that he was odd. Then things began to change after that first letter arrived in June.

At best, it was a disquieting letter that Hennard had written, a full five pages long and rambling. At worst, it was frightening. The letter was disjointed, making no logical sense, and it seemed totally divorced from reality. The confused Hennard had at first sent it to the wrong neighbor, and he had even referred to the girls as Robin and Stacee. But the letter left no doubt in Jane Bugg's mind that Hennard was insane and that her daughters' lives were at stake. In it, he said that he had first spotted them at a rock concert in Austin on January 31, 1988. He had been watching them for over 3 ½ years. He pleaded with the sisters to communicate with him, even enclosing three photos of himself. Then he began his diatribe against women in general. It was very ironic, he said, that he had found the best and the worst in women here in Belton. He said he was truly flattered in knowing that he had two teenage "groupie fans" in the girls.

He rambled on. "Did you and your sister find new flames yet?" he asked. "But unfortunately," he wrote, he knew that "mommy dear" had strong reservations about him. His exact words: "Maybe your mother saw me as the wolf in sheep's clothing. Was she afraid I would act irresponsible with her two precious gems and then run and hide? Your mother made a miscalculation in her evaluation of me. There was no place to run and hide, then or now . . . Please give me the satisfaction of someday laughing in the face of all those mostly white, treacherous female vipers from those two towns who tried to destroy me and my family. Love you George, Your Fan George."

Jane Bugg went to the police with the letter she'd received and with reports of Hennard's progressively strange behavior. She demanded action. But Belton chief of police Roy Kneese tried to explain the inherent difficulty in complaints like the one she was making. Because Hennard hadn't committed a crime and because he had rights, too, the chief said, there was nothing he could officially do. Besides, he assured the distraught mother, her daughters hadn't been harmed or defamed in any way in the letter, nor were they even threatened.

"There was nothing in that letter," the chief said. "It seemed like he had a crush on the girls, but there was nothing that in any way discredited them or embarrassed them. It was just a letter." And that was his assessment. Jane Bugg had never been more outraged in her life. Chief Kneese assured her there was nothing more she could do. "Just be careful," he said as she left.

Bugg was more than careful, she was vigilant. She discussed the problem at length with her daughters and reassured them that things would be all right. But there was no way to be with them twenty-four hours a day. Jill was married and often came for lunch. Jana was a student at the local Temple Junior College and was often home alone at night. Every time Jane left her daughters there was only one thing on her mind: Would George Hennard pick that night to explode? What horror might she find when she came home?

Life became increasingly unbearable for the women as Hennard seemed to move closer and closer with complete impunity. Yet, he was committing no crime. He stalked Jill at the bank where she worked as a bookkeeper. He would saunter in, stare at her for a while from a corner, smile sometimes, or stand there with an insolent smirk at other times. But he was always watching her, watching her and grinning as if he knew something she didn't. Just a week before he snapped, they spotted him as he trailed them through the aisles of the grocery store. He raced to the checkout to stand behind them. He ran out of the store ahead of them to reach his truck, which he had parked next to their car. He even joked that he had beaten them, all the while staring and glaring as they pulled out of the parking lot. Still, Jane Bugg would not give up. Time and time again through that long, terrible summer, she went back to the police station. Time and time again, they told her she was overreacting. Finally, feeling like a fool, she stopped reporting incidents. She decided she would just watch and pray. And she bought a gun.

Then on a quiet Sunday a week before the truck incident, a loud argument broke out on the Hennard lawn in the middle of the night. George was heard up and down the street screaming at an anonymous woman whom the neighbors had taken to describing as "the tall blonde." Nobody knew her name or her connection with Hennard, only that she was a strange, nameless girl who would arrive at the house at odd hours of the night in her Camaro. That evening, Hennard was bellowing at her, and the neighbors could even make out some of the words. He was yelling something about how could she have gone into Killeen to dance with the GIs? How could she have done that to him? "You're my wife," they heard him scream. After a while, the police were called and a squad car arrived.

Jane Bugg watched the entire fracas until the police arrived; then she told her daughters, "Thank God. They'll take care of him now." But nothing happened; he wasn't arrested, and he was still there, smiling and smirking at them. When Bugg called Chief Kneese the next week, she was told that Hennard, the man named in the complaint, wasn't even in town at the time. Although she had seen the police car pull up with her own eyes, the officer on the phone said he had no record of the incident. He told her Hennard was probably in Nevada.

Hennard's behavior changed from bad to worse. Now, whenever the Bugg women drove or walked by his house, he greeted them with obscenities and ugly gestures. He turned up everywhere they went, following them full-time and so efficiently that Jane Bugg could look over her shoulder in any store and he would be right behind her. If she and her daughters were walking on a strange street and turned around, there would be Hennard just staring at them. There was no doubt about it: this man was a stalker bent on violence.

Jane Bugg further secured her house and stopped leaving Jana alone at night. She hadn't been able to get help on her own and she was now prepared to bypass the local police and go directly to the county sheriff, to the FBI, or, even to her cousin, Governor Ann Richards of Texas. Meanwhile, all she could do was pray that he would not come storming through her front door at three in the morning during one of his nightly rages.

Other people became his targets, too. He had threatened

the local garbagemen, cursing them for leaving behind litter after their pickups. Another neighbor, Judy Beach, recalls coming up to his door when she and her small son were searching for a lost baseball glove. Hennard appeared suddenly, as if from the shadows, brandishing a garden hose and threatening the woman and her child. He screamed, "Bitch! Bitch! Bitch!" at her as she and the little boy ran away in terror.

Hennard's grip on reality was steadily becoming more fragile and his behavior more illogical. He traveled from place to place in his truck within an envelope of excessively loud and pounding rap music. It accompanied him wherever he went. He might have openly said he hated blacks during the last weeks he worked at the cement company in Copperas Cove, but privately he blasted the rap album *Short Dogs in the House* by Too Short and Ice T over and over again. He said that the song "Ain't Nothin' But a Word to Me" perfectly expressed his personal philosophy of women. They were bitches, he said, and the lyrics explained exactly what a man should expect from a bitch. She was good for one thing and one thing only, according to the lyrics. Soon he would show them all.

Hennard didn't seem to have any relationships with women at all. There was speculation—only speculation—that he was intimate with the mysterious blonde who visited him late at night, or that he had occasionally visited a prostitute when he was stationed with the merchant marine. For the most part, however, there seemed to be no women in his life. And despite whatever he screamed at the tall blonde in front of his mansion for all the neighbors to hear, county records listed him as unmarried.

To observers, he seemed to live alone in a dreamworld. He often spent hours at the Heart Of Texas Music in Temple, trying out the equipment, sometimes buying an expensive cymbal or something for his drum set. He told anybody who would listen that he still had what it takes to play in a rock and roll band. He might not be technically perfect, he would say, but he had the passion. He said he identified with Too Short, the black artist who had written his favorite song. Ironically, the little rap musician had been shot in the head the year before when a man burst into a party he was attending. After lying in a coma for two months, he wrote the songs on the album, including the song, another personal favorite of Hennard's, an anthem to that shot in the head called "Dead or Alive."

Hennard obsessively believed he had already endured a psychological shot to the head: his untimely and, in his mind, unfair discharge from the U.S. Merchant Marine. He had always loved the ocean, and he enlisted in the navy right after high school as soon as he turned eighteen. He left the service in 1977 with an honorable discharge, worked the military Sealift command for nine months, and then late that same year, joined the merchant marine. His first several assignments were out of the Gulf of Mexico, and in 1981 he transferred to California.

He had thirty-seven sea voyages out of San Pedro in the next eight years, during which time his problems with drinking and marijuana got out of control. Soon after he arrived in California, Hennard began to complain about his shipmates and caused enough trouble aboard ship to earn a reputation as a strange, hostile, angry young man. Finally, there was an incident in 1982 aboard the SS *John Lykes* with a black shipmate. Hennard, who admitted throwing the first punch, was suspended for six months and got a year's probation.

It was not his first offense. In 1981, he had pleaded guilty to a single count of marijuana possession in El Paso, Texas, and had received a $25 fine with $65 in court fees and six months' probation. Then on May 11, 1989, half a gram of marijuana was found in his possession aboard the SS *Green Wave* while it was in port in Oakland, California. Hennard tried to appeal to the judge by telling him that the sea meant everything to him. "It means a way of life; it means my livelihood. It means all I've got. It's all I know," he said. His words did not sway the judge; his papers were confiscated by the Coast Guard and his seaman's credentials were lifted. His merchant marine career was over.

Although Dr. George Hennard arranged for his son to enter a $15,000 drug treatment program in July at St. Joseph's Hospital in Houston—the hospital where he had a practice—the Coast Guard did not reverse its decision. The revocation was upheld in February 1991, when an administrative judge affirmed that George Hennard Jr., by his own admission, had been addicted to marijuana for "a long time."

That same month, Hennard bought his first gun at Mike's Gun House in Henderson, Nevada. He had been working itinerant jobs from Texas to South Dakota and living part-time with his mother. He had no trouble purchasing the $400 gun, the first of his "Super Nines," even with his growing police record.

Hennard, like many of the customers who collected weapons, was an expert on the minute details of the guns he purchased. The Super Nines were the best of the 9mm guns, he thought. His first, the Glock 17, was developed in 1982 by Gaston Glock, an Austrian bayonet and shovel manufacturing company, at the request of the Austrian army. It has a barrel and slide of steel, but the entire gun, including the nonmetallic polymer parts in the handle, frame, and magazine, weighs a total of only twenty-three ounces. It is a gun with no exterior hammer and a cocking button that only engages when the pistol is being properly operated for fire. It is angular and futuristic, with a dull matte finish. It is a gun with mystique.

The Glock had caused an uproar when it was first introduced because officials feared its plastic parts would make it invisible to airport detection machines and thus make it a weapon of choice for hijackers and terrorists. The New York City Police Department banned the Glock in the mid-1980s, but the gun, with an extended magazine capable of holding up to thirty-two rounds, quickly became a favorite with both street-level and syndicate-level drug dealers and enforcers. New York lifted the ban in 1988 after it was learned that the police commissioner at the time, Benjamin Ward, was himself carrying a Glock, which he described as a "machine gun."

The Glock was found to be no less detectable than any other firearm by a congressional subcommittee in 1986, and it is now used by the FBI, U.S. Customs agents, the Secret Service, and more than four thousand other federal, state, and local law enforcement agencies. It is feared and respected because of its lightweight handling abilities, its high velocity, and its near pinpoint accuracy. It is also extremely durable. Gun aficionados say that you can bury it for a year or drop it three hundred feet from a plane and it will still fire. As one of the best-selling pistols in the United States, it is currently being used by about two hundred thousand law enforcement officials. George Hennard would soon write this weapon into history.

Hennard was caught in possession of the Glock and a Ruger P-89 in a national park in Nevada soon after he had made his second purchase. The guns, however, were not confiscated and he did not appear on the charge when it came up. And although there was a federal warrant out on the case, no law enforcement official picked up on it when the neighbors began complaining about the noise and the harassment he was subjecting them to in Belton. For whatever reason, the warrant wasn't served, and it was a tragically missed opportunity to avert the oncoming disaster.

Therefore, in the early morning of October 16, Hennard was free to load the guns, along with three 17-shot clips for the Ruger, into his shiny Ford Ranger and head out to Killeen, Texas, about seventeen miles away on U.S. Route 190. It was just about lunchtime when he checked his green shirt pocket for his cigarettes and turned the key in the ignition. It was a route he had driven a million times before. It was a town he knew well.

Killeen, population 46,000, had grown up with the three other towns that were adjacent to Fort Hood, the country's largest military base. Starting in World War II, the city had begun as a military town that used to be notable only for its bars, its tattoo parlors, and for the busloads of prostitutes who were routinely brought in to service the soldiers. But the town had eventually grown into a respectable little center of small businesses, modest shopping areas, and booming family restaurants like Luby's Cafeteria, the most popular place to eat in Killeen.

Fort Hood and the communities around it are geared for war and for the sacrifices families have to make in the name of service to one's country. The base had just recently sent 25,000 troops to the Persian Gulf, but on this particular day, in the space of just over eleven minutes, George Jo Hennard would pull into town and kill twice as many loved ones from the Fort Hood area than Saddam Hussein's army had killed during the entire Gulf War. Killeen, Texas, was not prepared for this; no communities ever are. For the nearly two hundred patrons and forty workers at Luby's Cafeteria, the imminent massacre was the furthest thing from their minds.

Luby's, according to those who visited Killeen, was a really friendly place to eat. The restaurant was just 1 1/2 years old, one of the newer additions to the 151-member chain of restaurants in Texas and its surrounding states, Florida, Tennessee, Arizona, and Missouri. This particular Luby's was an eleven-thousand-square-foot brick building on a frontage road just off the highway. There was a large parking lot and a sheltered drive-up to protect customers from the driving Texas rains. All in all, along with the good-old-boy food and the warm family atmosphere, this Luby's was usually packed with lunchtime regulars. Luby's has big Texas cooking: large servings of steaming okra and huge sweating pitchers of sweetened iced tea and the kinds of desserts you'd expect to see in a Norman Rockwell painting.

October 16 was National Boss's Day and the restaurant was busy with nearly two hundred people; festive, boisterous, the room was full of happy conversation and the clatter of lunch trays along the serving line. Round tables were packed solid with employees bearing gifts. By 12:30 P.M., the place was so full that some of the regular customers simply turned away when they approached the full-to-capacity parking lot. Those lucky individuals would always thank God for that small inconvenience, because it was just about then that George Hennard's blue Ford was approaching the restaurant like a deadly storm, coming in fast from the east on Route 190. It hadn't taken him more than ten minutes to drive in from his house in Belton.

Hazel Holley, Betty May, sixty-seven, and Evelyn Seales, sixty, had arrived at Luby's promptly at noon, just as they did every third Wednesday of the month. The three old friends from the East Side Baptist Church Sunday School in Killeen always liked to sit in the corner and eat and visit. No one ever bothered them and they loved the food and the camaraderie. That afternoon, they went through the serving line as usual and took their customary table in the northeast corner. They had a month's worth of conversation all saved up and ready to go.

At about the same time, Juanita Williams, sixty-four, parked her brand-new 1992 Buick in the lot and went inside. A domino player, art lover, and devout Baptist, Williams was president of the Heart of Texas Federal Credit Union. She was en route from a Copperas Cove branch office to the headquarters in Waco, and as she so often did, she stopped that afternoon at Luby's to get a quick diet-food lunch and still have plenty of time to make her two o'clock meeting.

There were also several members of two different school-district groups meeting at Luby's that afternoon. Sam Wink, an attendance officer for the Killeen public-school system, was eating fish and mashed potatoes and chatting with five of his coworkers, including Patricia Carney, who had been an employee of the district for twenty-seven years. She had just been named director of elementary curriculum. These, and nearly two hundred other diners just like them, expected nothing special from lunch that afternoon beyond the hour or so it would take them to eat, chat, and be on their respective ways. But within ten minutes, some would die, some would become heroes, and some would lie on the ground critically injured and gasping shallow breaths. Some would be miraculously spared that day, but no one would be untouched, and absolutely no one would ever be the same again.

Al and Ursula Gratia were an inseparable couple who had just celebrated their forty-first wedding anniversary. They were having lunch with their daughter Suzanna, a chiropractor. Eddie Sanchez, thirty-one, was rushing to get his twenty-four-year-old pregnant girlfriend, Angie Wilson, into the cafeteria kitchen, where she worked as a baker. They were running about forty minutes late. Tommy Vaughn and several fellow mechanics were treating Paul La Bombard to a birthday lunch.

Lee Whitney, forty-one, and his thirty-one-year old wife, Brenda, worked at the Centel telephone office and ate at Luby's three days a week. Delbert Smith, an auto parts distributor, and his wife, Charlene, were entering the long buffet line, along with their thirty-four-year-old daughter. At a nearby table, Anicia McNeil was sitting with her four-year-old daughter and her mother, Olgica Taylor. At another table, Lieutenant Colonel Steven Dody was discussing retirement plans with his wife.

It was 12:40 P.M. when the light blue pickup came barreling into the parking lot. George Hennard lit another cigarette and pressed the accelerator all the way down to the floor. The truck hurtled into the eight-foot front wall of glass with all the force of an explosion. At first, some thought it was a tornado. Texas twisters routinely cut swaths through Waco and Austin, spewing death and destruction right through the center of the state, collapsing plate glass windows, overturning trailers, and sucking up barns into their vortices. From the parking lot, it looked at first like a freak traffic accident, and some of the people outside ran to help anybody who still might be caught in the truck that had just seemed to careen off the road and bounce through the restaurant window.

No one realized what was happening until Hennard

jumped out, cigarette still dangling from his lips, eyes cold as the dull steel of his drawn pistol, and began to gun them down. His green shirt and pants were bulging with extra ammo clips. He had the Glock in his right hand, the Ruger in his left, and he began to fire.

His eye caught an old man, knocked down by the truck, who had risen up on his knees, holding up his hands. Hennard aimed and killed him first. Immediately, Delbert and Charlene Smith, along with their daughter, dived to the floor under the buffet line. They lay next to each other, too terrified to move. Mrs. Smith's feet touched her daughter's shoulders. Hennard advanced toward them, firing. A bullet slammed into Delbert Smith's lower back, smashing through his wallet, and fragments of credit cards and family pictures sprayed his daughter's hair. The bullet, deflected, ripped through Smith's body and lodged in his wife's foot. No one moved or screamed or whimpered. Hennard stood stock-still over them.

The only sound was the slam and click of another clip, another round, loaded above them. "Our Father, who art in Heaven, hallowed be thy name," Delbert Smith prayed under his breath. Suddenly, he saw Hennard's feet turn away and he heard Luby's echo with the *pop, pop, pop* of more and more shots as the madman continued his human target practice farther down the line.

Eddie Sanchez had just left the building when the shots began to ring out. He ran back into the restaurant, jumping through the broken glass, calling out, "Angie! Angie!" Hennard had just shot a second man. He whirled toward Sanchez and fired, and missed. Then he walked calmly into the dining room, firing again and again. All that could be heard were the echoes of gunfire, the screams of the victims as they were hit, the sharp clicks as new clips were slammed home, and Hennard bellowing above it all like a Cyclops on his island: "This is what Bell County did to me! Was it worth it? Wait till those fucking women in Belton see this! Tell me! Was it worth it?"

He kept repeating, "Bitch! Bitch! Bitch!" and "This is payback day!" as he walked down the serving line and shot woman after woman. Or, looking under the tables, he yelled before firing, "You hiding from me, bitch?" In all, fourteen women would be dead before he was finished.

Eddie Sanchez managed to escape from the building with his girlfriend. And as Hennard reloaded, assistant manager John Marr took a chance and ran to the back, struggled with the locked doors and opened them so that the kitchen help could get safely away before Hennard got to them. Meanwhile, Hennard had finished reloading. He discovered Anicia McNeil, her four-year-old, and her mother cowering near a table. He pointed the gun at the older woman and shot Olgica Taylor once, then shot her again. Then he turned the gun on Anicia and her little girl. "You get that baby and get out of here!" he yelled. "Run outside and tell everybody that Bell County was bad!" Anicia ran, not knowing whether her mother was alive or dead.

Lee and Brenda Whitney had dropped to the floor. He lay on top of her to shield her. Hennard walked past them, his foot just brushing Mrs. Whitney. He fired. Another woman, lying just a foot off Whitney's head, lay dead. Zombielike, Hennard marched on as if he were caught in a subprocedure loop of a program buried deep within his neural circuitry. Hazel Holley, Betty May, and Evelyn Seales lay hidden under their table, their chairs pulled up in a puny attempt at a protective fortress. Firing and walking slowly, Hennard advanced, shooting victims to the left and right of them point-blank in the face or chest.

Firing as he came, Hennard moved toward Tommy Vaughn and the other auto mechanics. They knew it was either escape now or die. Attempts to break the plate glass with chairs had failed, and in a last-ditch attempt, Tommy hurled his entire six-foot four-inch, three-hundred-pound frame against the eight-foot-high window. It shattered, and several grateful people poured out from under their tables and jumped to freedom through the slashing shards of glass.

Al Gratia knelt by his wife. As was his way, he just wouldn't stand for this. He rose up, despite his daughter's efforts to hold him back, and confronted Hennard. The killer shot Gratia in the head, point-blank. Their daughter tried to drag Mrs. Gratia through the window, but she returned to comfort her husband. Always together in life, they would be together that moment in death. Hennard looked straight at her and shot her, point-blank, in the head.

Odene Huron, seventy-four, was pushed to the floor in the human stampede, cut, and trampled. Still, she crawled out the broken window on her hands and knees and survived. Mark Mathews, a nineteen-year-old kitchen employee, forced his body into an industrial dishwasher and waited as the footsteps came closer. He was so frightened that he did not come out until the next day. Maria Serna, forty-one, had to be treated for hypothermia after she hid in the freezer for 2½ hours, unable to know when the siege was over. Hazel Holley and her friends ran out from under their table and dived through the shattered window as Hennard moved toward them. Thanks to Tommy Vaughn's escape route, they would live to have another Wednesday luncheon.

Outside, Sam Wink, who had miraculously been passed over by the gunman, tried to taunt Hennard into coming out. "Hey, sucker! You missed me! You're a bad shot! If you don't have the balls to shoot me, come on out and get me!" Hennard turned at the sound, ready to fire at Wink, but the rush of people out the door stopped him and he turned back inside the restaurant to kill whomever else he could find.

The Hi-Lo auto parts store next door was suddenly filling up with screaming victims crying for help. A man came running in, asking if any of the employees had a gun he could use before he went back to the restaurant to try to save his cousin who was still trapped inside. Two blocks away, children in school looked up at the *pop-pop-pop* of gunfire.

The next person turning into the Luby's parking lot after the truck crashed into the window was Richard Bone, a public works employee from Harker Heights, who saw the carnage and immediately punched his cell phone's speed dial to call the Harker Heights police. The call was relayed to the Killeen station, and two undercover narcotics officers at a nearby city maintenance facility were alerted and sped to the scene. "But today was not a good day for him to do this," a Bell County Sheriff's Department dispatcher said in wonderment. "We had everybody at the range, taking target practice."

A hundred and fifty yards away in the Sheraton Hotel parking lot, four officers from the Texas Department of Public Safety were holding an auto-theft seminar for several Killeen police officers. Suddenly, a woman ran up to them, covered in blood and screaming, "He's crazy! He's got a gun! He's killing everybody." They ran to their cars, retrieved their weapons, and were at Luby's in seconds.

Nothing on this earth could have prepared them for what they saw. The scene was one of total pandemonium, with blood, glass, spent bullets, spilled food, and bodies everywhere. The policemen could see Hennard in the back of the restaurant, still killing. They had no clear shot at him as his victims screamed, begged, and clawed at the officers for help. The officers tried shouting at the people in the way to get down so they could take aim, but there was no way to control the chaos. They kept their eyes trained on Hennard as they fought their way through the bewildered, hysterical crowd.

"Police! Surrender and drop your weapons!" they shouted at Hennard. But he answered them with a volley of shots. Then he managed to sweep back through the restaurant twice as the frustrated police tried to get into firing position. An elderly man screamed to DPS Officer Bill Cooper for help. Hennard turned and shot the old man in the head. Cooper and Sergeant Jody Fore could not shoot Hennard without hitting someone else. Everywhere they looked, there was a confused mass of bloody and injured victims. Finally, Officer Kenneth Olson got off a shot and caught Hennard in the chest. Officer Alex Morris, firing from the side of the restaurant, through the shattered escape window, also wounded Hennard. Other officers went around the back and rushed in through the opened kitchen door.

Hennard must have known that his own time was close at hand. His Ruger was now empty and he left it lying on the serving counter. Then the Glock jammed. He stopped firing. He took two more shots in the chest and the air rushed out of him as his lungs began to collapse. At first, he tried to hide behind his truck, and then he ran to the back of the restaurant. He found the last possible place he could run: down the narrow hallway leading to the bathrooms. He screamed with whatever breath he had left that he had taken hostages, but he was alone. Cornered by Morris, Olson, and Charles Longwell, his eyes wide with fear, Hennard lay on his back. Slamming a clip into the Glock, he unjammed the round, put the gun to his temple, and pulled the trigger for the last time.

There was a total of twenty-three people dead. Twenty-three more were injured, some critically. It was the largest mass murder in the history of the United States. The total time it took: just over eleven minutes. In a replay of scenes from the Vietnam War, several olive green Hueys swooped in from Fort Hood to medevac the wounded out. Seven of the victims were taken to Metroplex Hospital in Killeen; eleven to Darnall Army Community Hospital in Fort Hood; five to Scott and White Hospital in Temple. Suddenly, it was a triage situation: wounded rolling on the ground, dazed victims wandering around in shock, ambulances everywhere with their lightbars flashing red and blue, plasma bags swinging over unconscious victims, and gurneys with screaming patients rolling through a war zone. There were bloodied, shaken men and women crying and holding each other on the curbs, people hiding their faces in terror, and the heavy smoke of burned sulfur hanging over the center of town.

Reverend Jack G. Birkmeyer, the sixty-seven-year-old pastor of the St. Joseph Catholic Church in Killeen and the Police Department chaplain, had arrived and begun to work his way through the litter of glass, overturned tables, and bodies to pray over the more seriously wounded victims and to perform the Last Rites. He found Hennard lying with his eyes still open. He anointed the gunman last.

The dead were taken away in a line of white hearses to Parkland Memorial, carried out between rows of twenty law enforcement officers. Pat Carney died; Sam Wink, who had been lying right next to her, lived. The Gratias died; the Whitneys lived. The Smiths lived. Anicia McNeil and her little girl were spared; her mother was killed.

As soon as the news crews hurried to the scene and began to broadcast, Jill Fritz turned on her television and saw the carnage. She called her mother, Jane Bugg, at work. "It's him. They haven't announced the killer, but it's him. I recognized his truck sticking out of Luby's." Jane Bugg started for home, horrified but finally relieved that her worst fears were over. She turned onto her street and saw Police Chief Kneese in front of the Hennard mansion. Bugg pulled over. "It was him, wasn't it?" she asked the officer. Kneese replied that there was no official word yet. "Then why are you here?" she asked, and he shrugged as he had so many times before at questions she kept asking about Hennard.

The truck was towed, back-end first, from the littered front of Luby's at four o'clock the next morning. Drapes were pulled over the broken windows in the front and back and secured with chairs. The strong Texas wind pulled the curtains aside from time to time and allowed the curious a view of the blood-spattered gray carpet and beige walls, the overturned tables and chairs, and the chaos that filled the rooms from wall to wall. Gawkers and lookie-loos brought camcorders and cameras, and some, with their children in the car, drove slowly by, taping, snapping, trying to take it all in. Wreaths and flowers were quietly placed where the truck had entered. Yellow police crime-scene ribbons flapped in the same breeze that had animated the patriotic yellow ribbons for the returning heroes of Desert Storm just a short time before.

George Jo Hennard's body was transported to Parkland Memorial Hospital in Dallas for an autopsy. His father stated to the press that he thought his son might have had an aneurysm. That might have accounted for his bizarre behavior. But neither an aneurysm nor a brain tumor was found. The toxicology screen detected no drugs or alcohol in Hennard's system.

All of this carnage might have been prevented had the federal warrant been served on George Jo Hennard before he headed into Killeen on his day of rage. Had he been prevented from buying a gun because of a previous criminal conviction, the crime might have been averted. And there are many other factors that can help to identify potentially dangerous individuals bent on mass murder/suicide. For example, Hennard led a life of profound frustration in which the tensions had been building ever since high school. Most mass murderers and serial killers exhibit some warning signs even in their early teens. Hennard's withdrawal from everyone around him was one of those warning signs.

He also gave clear warnings that he was going to commit some kind of public crime. Most mass murderers give direct threats immediately before their killing sprees, and in almost every case of mass murder, someone has reported that the killer revealed his intentions weeks or even months before the crime. These threats have to be taken seriously.

Hennard also had a previous criminal record and was the subject of an outstanding arrest warrant. Most mass murderers and serial killers are either fugitives or the subjects of outstanding warrants. Almost all mass murderers and serial killers have been arrested previously in their lives or have served time in jail. In Hennard's case, there was a singular precipitating event—the loss of his U.S. Merchant Marine status—which set the mass-murdering event into motion. Most such murderers begin their sprees after a catastrophic run-in with the law, the loss of a loved one, the loss of a job, or an event they perceive as so unjust that they have no means to cope with it.

Hennard had access to firearms and had received training in their use. He understood the effectiveness of his weapons and knew that more people can be killed at one time with a gun than a knife, more still with a semiautomatic weapon, and even more still with a machine gun. The amassing of a personal arsenal is always a clear indicator that the person buying the weapons is bent on violence, even if he is unaware of just how dangerous he really is at the time.

Hennard was a social isolate who had no place to turn and no one to talk to. Most mass murderers are social outcasts who live lives of unbearable frustration and rage. Their final act of suicide is also an act of punishing the society they believe inflicted the pain on them.

Finally, Hennard was identified as potentially dangerous by his earlier harassment and stalking incidents. The majority of mass murderers do not suddenly wake up one day and decide to kill. Their crime is almost always preceded by months or sometimes years of threats, crimes, and conflicts with the law. In Hennard's case, at least one person understood how dangerous he was, even though she was not able to persuade the authorities that a crime was about to be committed.

No one had ever seen George Hennard at Luby's before that day; the people he killed were strangers to him. Like other mass murderers before him, he had chosen to commit a public suicide, taking a score of innocent people with him. The dead: Pat Carney, fifty-seven; Al Gratia, seventy-one; Ursula Kunath Gratia, sixty-seven; Lieutenant Colonel Steven Charles Dody, forty-three; Dr. Michael Griffith, forty-eight; Sylvia Mathilde King, thirty; Ruth Pujol, fifty-five; Suzann Neal Rashett, thirty-six; John Raymond Romero Jr., thirty; Glen Arval Spivey, fifty-five; Connie Deen Miller, forty-one; Zona Hunnicut Lynn, sixty-four; Juanita Williams, sixty-four; Venice Ellen Henehan, seventy; Clodine Humphrey, sixty-four; Lula Belle Welsh, seventy-five; James Welsh, seventy-five; Debra Gray, thirty-three; Olgica Andonovsk Taylor, forty-five; Jimmie Eugene Carruthers, forty-nine; Thomas Earl Simmons, thirty-four; Nancy Hedgepeth Stansbury, forty-four; and George Hennard.

3

ARTHUR SHAWCROSS, THE CANNIBAL OF GENESEE

Parole Officer Bob Kent began his May 1987 memo to the Elmira area office of the New York State Division of Parole with a terse but urgent warning: "At the risk of being dramatic, the writer considers this man to be possibly the most dangerous individual to have been released to the community in many years." Kent was describing Arthur Shawcross, who was about to be transferred from Vestal, New York, just outside Binghamton. The parolee was a convicted burglar and child murderer and a confessed arsonist. Sixteen years earlier, a psychologist at Auburn, where Shawcross was serving time for burglary, had warned the parole board that although he was a "fair parole risk," Shawcross was nonetheless a "schizoid arsonist" who required "supervision, emotional support and psychiatric treatment" and whose "latent projected homicidal intent" should not be underestimated.

Only a few weeks after his release, Shawcross beat a ten-year-old boy to death with his hands. A few weeks after that, he returned to the burial site, cut off the boy's decomposing genitals, and ate them. "God help me, I was a sick fool," he later wrote in his journal. Four months later he raped an eight-year-old girl, beat her, and strangled her. She was still alive when he buried her facedown in a shallow grave, forcing her into the soft mud, and covering her with rocks, loose dirt, and bark. He filled her mouth and nostrils with dirt until she stopped breathing. Then he left her in an unmarked tomb, returning to it time and again to eat his lunch and make sure it was still undisturbed.

After plea-bargaining his way out of the first homicide and getting a reduced sentence on the second homicide, Shawcross was free again, and Bob Kent was worried. As he pointed out to the Elmira district office, Shawcross had still been on parole from a previous burglary conviction when he murdered the two children, and whatever had driven him to commit those murders had not been addressed in prison. If anything, Shawcross was probably more at risk than he had been back in 1972 when he was first charged with the murders. And now he was free.

"Shawcross is 41 years of age, He is currently serving a 25–0–0 year term for manslaughter in the first degree, having been sentenced out of Jefferson County after what appears to be an incredible plea-bargaining arrangement. Shawcross admits the murder of two young children in two separate incidents . . . he was on parole supervision at the time serving a prison term for burglary in the third degree. His criminal history dates back to 1963."

At the point of Kent's memo, Shawcross was already a full-blown homicide sociopath. Despite previous warnings from doctors, numerous encounters with the criminal justice system, and loud cries for help and intervention from Shawcross himself from the time he was discharged from the army, he had been allowed to slip right through the system and into society.

THE SHAWCROSS SYMPTOMS

Bob Kent wasn't being overly dramatic. Kent was aware that the system was dealing with a severely psychotic killer who was getting out of jail only because of a plea bargain that effectively covered up Shawcross's gruesome crime of killing a small boy and burying him in a desolate area. But Kent was only a voice in the wilderness. Kent's memo reveals that he believed Shawcross was a time bomb who could explode into homicidal rage at the slightest provocation, and he knew that psychologists in prison had warned of the possibility of reoccurrence of "poor impulse control" and the likelihood of sexual drives surfacing "in a manner which will be found socially abhorrent." But nobody listened to the parole officer. A time bomb had been released back into the innocent and unsuspecting community, and nobody was going to do anything about it. Shawcross was going to kill again, Kent feared, and he was right.

Arthur Shawcross was a crucible of violence within whom explosive and homicidal rage had been building since he was a child. In his own journal, written for prison psychologists after his arrest for the murder of eleven women in the Lake Avenue area of Rochester, New York, during this second parole, he claimed to have been abused by his mother when he was a child, something that his mother has emphatically denied. He wrote of being sodomized repeatedly by girls in his neighborhood. And he vividly described an incident that occurred when he was a fourteen-year-old when he was violently raped by an older man who beat him during a prolonged session of anal intercourse. Shawcross wrote that after that event, he was unable to achieve an erection unless he was inflicting pain on himself. This rape was among the ingredients that taught Shawcross to hate, and in his mind, to associate sexual gratification with the inflicting of pain. These ingredients can often arm a human psyche and begin a person's devolution into a walking time bomb fueled by pentup rage, and a propensity for violence. The process is set into motion by violent experiences that distort normal childhood development on a primal level and turn what should be childhood pleasure into prolonged and traumatic childhood pain. As adults, these individuals are potential time bombs. What happened to them during the rest of their lives determines whether they will defuse, keep on smoking indefinitely, or go off in an explosion of violence. Arthur Shawcross was just such an individual whose head injuries, experiences in Vietnam, battles with the police and courts, and years in prison turned him into a human predator.

Was Shawcross legally insane? Not according to a Rochester jury that found him guilty of ten murders. Nothing they heard as testimony—not the opinion that he was a multiple personality, not the descriptions of his mother's personality rising up within him, not the videotape of Shawcross acting out the personality of a thirteenth-century vampire—was enough to convince a jury that Shawcross was insane. However, there was another side to Shawcross, a side even more frightening than the jury could have realized. Shawcross was a violent human time bomb.

THE BEGINNING OF THE TIME BOMB SYNDROME—SHAWCROSS'S CHILDHOOD

"Something happened to my mom and dad when I was nine," Shawcross claims. According to him, there were intense arguments in his home when he was a kid—arguments over things that eventually created a running tension between his parents and especially between himself and his mother.

Shawcross believed these ruptures in his household turned his mother against him. He felt that she equated him with something evil, something that didn't deserve to live. Suddenly there was what psychiatrists call a "loss of bliss." The childhood innocence and freedom from guilt that most children take for granted was withdrawn from Shawcross, and in his mind he became an enemy in his own family. This sentence of shame and guilt began Shawcross's deadly rejection of life, a rejection that continues to this day. Despite all of the horrors of his life, this is the one subject that he cannot talk about without displaying obvious symptoms of frustration and rage. Shawcross told Dr. James Clark, another clinical psychologist, that he believed he was a "doorstep baby," a child conceived out of wedlock; this belief contributed to his spending much of his life feeling different from his other siblings and feeling rejected by the family. "Loss of bliss" has different effects on different individuals depending upon their family structures. At some point, even if everything else were equal in his life and there were no subsequent traumas, he would out of his frustration and anger have found the means to strike back. This need to satisfy the pent-up rage is a critical component of most criminals who are discovered to be walking time bombs.

Shawcross was already severely damaged by his self-perceptions and by his feelings of family rejection when, he claimed, he was molested by an older woman. He was nine when it happened, he says, and it paralyzed him. This type of sexual molestation, or fantasy that includes sexual molestation, is a universal element in the violent symptomology of serial killers. It destroys a child's sense of self, turns victims into sex abusers in later life, and prompts children to equate sex with rage and pain.

Shawcross claims that when this older woman taught him how to give her oral sex, it so stimulated him that he sought to have oral sex with a variety of older women. As a preadolescent, who was especially vulnerable to any form of female interest because of the rejection he felt he was experiencing with his mother, his perceived violation of his sexual privacy had a stronger than usual impact. The nine-year-old Shawcross was already coping with a withdrawal of trust and security, and instant sexual gratification became a kind of security blanket. He was becoming hypersexual and soon began offering oral sex to a variety of women in his surroundings. He was gradually developing a lust and a need for stimulation and gratification that would not be easily satisfied.

"I became obsessed with sex after that," Shawcross remembers. A few months later Shawcross almost drowned in a swamp near his house. "I was up to my neck in muck and was screaming my head off for help. A little while later all I could do was cry." Shawcross says he doesn't remember how long he screamed. He remembers that after he had given up and was only trying to conserve his last air, another boy passed by, saw him, and pulled him out of the swamp hole with a long tree branch. He and Shawcross walked to a nearby stream to wash off the mud. The two of them took off their clothing, jumped in the stream, and then lay down on the flat rocks alongside the banks to sun themselves. "After a while, I started to jack off. No reason. Just did it. [A friend named John] [Ed. Note: A pseudonym] did it too. Then we would touch each other. Then we had oral sex. John and I soon got to be good friends. Only once in a while did we have touching sessions." At this point, already compulsive about his need to have orgasms, Shawcross discovered that he could have sex with animals. "One time on a farm nearby, John and I started playing with sheep. We didn't know that sheep had organs like a woman. It felt good at the time."

Bestiality and childhood molestation are two more common themes in the lives of violent sex offenders, and Shawcross revealed to his prison doctors that he was no exception. Shawcross felt that he had to accept being routinely violated. He believed that he wasn't worth respect or dignity, that he was simply damaged goods. He, in turn, learned to associate sex with the violation of someone else's dignity and integrity. But because he was a child, he had no other human victims in his immediate vicinity that he could dominate. Therefore, Shawcross turned to farm animals. By subduing and violating them, Shawcross, as have other serial killers during their childhoods, worked out his need to sexually violate others as a way of working out the rage and violence he was feeling. Shawcross's almost emotionless revelation of his childhood sexual encounters and molestation at the hands of people he trusted are typical of the confessions of most serial killers.

Shawcross had experienced homosexual feelings, had sexually molested farm animals, and claims he had been the victim of child sex abuse. But human beings are resilient and can cope with almost any situation, even those that are threatening or dangerous. Shawcross might not have crossed the threshold into brutal violence, he claims, had he not been raped, beaten, and threatened with death by a stranger. An older man had enticed him into his car, Shawcross remembers. "I didn't think about it at the time, I just got in. Then he grabbed me by the throat and told me to take my pants down. I did. Then he held onto my balls and sucked me off. I was scared and crying. Then the guy got mad because I couldn't come. He raped me. I was left off near home. I couldn't tell anyone what happened either." The experience was so terrifying that for a long time af:terward, he was unable to have an orgasm unless he was feeling pain. "After that, when I masturbated, I could not come until I inserted a finger in my ass. Why, I didn't know." And then he began to experience even more aberrant sexual behavior. "One day I did it to a chicken. It died. Then a cow, dog, and a horse. I didn't know where this was leading up to." Are his claims real or fantastic? His psychologists cannot confirm them but say it doesn't matter, because his perceptions of violence are real even if the events were not.

Rape is another critical symptom of an evolving time bomb. There is no way to deny or dispose of the anger at being violated. In resilient people, the anger must be accepted and eventually integrated. Rape victims themselves have reported that the shame they feel, the guilt that they were powerless to defend themselves, and the threat of imminent death result in a type of stress trauma that saps them of their resiliency. They can lose the ability to cope for a period of time and become hair-trigger violent unless the stress is relieved. In Shawcross's case, not only could he not relieve the trauma because he felt rejected in his household, he was also working out his fury by brutalizing other creatures. He began to obsess over his frustrations. Eventually, his sexual obsessions and fantasies completely took him over and he became hypergonadal and paraphilitic, symptoms neurologists often associate with severe neurological disorders and biochemical imbalances.

If even half his claims are true, Shawcross, by the time he was an adolescent, was clearly antisocial, sexually impaired, and on the same track of sexual violence that many other serial killer time bombs routinely take. And there was nothing anybody could do about it, because Shawcross was too ashamed to ask for help. He perceived himself to be the victim even as he was becoming the aggressor, another feature common to violent sexual aggressors.

"When I was seventeen I had sex with a girl that lived near us. Only oral sex. She wouldn't do the other. Then I went and did the same thing with another girl nearby who lived on a farm. I got to like going down on girls. When I was eighteen I had sex with a girl of twenty-seven. She was a waitress at a bar. I learned everything that night. After that I got a job doing construction. At this place, I met my first wife, Sarah Chatterton. We got married in 1964. Had a baby boy, Michael, on October 2, 1965. Everything was okay for a while; then I started doing strange things. I'd pick up girls near where we lived. We'd have sex. Sometimes with others as well. I couldn't stop myself—just the desire to have more. Then I got drafted in 1967." Sharah Chatterton and Arthur Shawcross were divorced in 1968.

VIETNAM

Whatever traumas Shawcross had experienced in the past would pale in comparison with what he claimed he saw and did on his tour of duty in Vietnam. Yet, twenty years after

Vietnam, Shawcross would describe his tour of duty as some of the best times of his life. It was in South Vietnam, he claims, that he was transformed into a full-blown serial killer. In a breakthrough to new levels of terror, Shawcross found the key to staying alive: He would be more cruel and more violent than his enemy; he would violate all boundaries of human behavior; he would penetrate the heart of darkness. He trolled for sex partners among the streetwalkers, ages nine to twelve, who haunted the strip bars near American bases or who called out to passing servicemen from the back-alley doorways in Saigon. Was this where he first became fascinated with preadolescent children like eight-year-old Karen Ann Miller, whom he was convicted of killing after he was separated from the service? Shawcross claims that he killed women and children from small villages indiscriminately. He says he not only tortured, mutilated, and dismembered his victims, but he was a cannibal who roasted their dead carcasses and ate them. Vietnam became a living fantasy of horror and sadomasochistic delight for Shawcross, an impenetrable jungle of the spirit that reduced him to the most base levels of existence. He says, "I was never happier."

"The VC put razor blades up whores' vaginas," Shawcross explains. "Shoved them inside a rubber cup deep in where you'd never know until it was too late. When the GIs would fuck 'em they would slit their penises to shreds or cut 'em clean off." Hookers were dangerous, Shawcross says, like his mother.

In Vietnam, Shawcross claims, Americans learned to kill hookers in ways that told every other hooker that the GIs knew what they did. "I was with some guys, ROK Koreans, who took a whore and put a firehose inside her and turned the water on. She died almost instantly. Her neck jumped about a foot from her body. Another time we took another prostitute and tied her to two small trees, legs to the trees, bent down. She had a razor blade inside her vagina. She was cut from her anus to her chin. Then the trees were let go. She slit in half. Left her there hanging between the trees. This may be why I did what I did to those girls. Vietnam was a haunting experience."

For someone already traumatized by repeated violence performed on him since he was nine, Shawcross lost all control in Vietnam. He quickly became worse than the enemy, so violent toward the peasants that they feared him more than they feared the VC. "They would wire up little kids or babies like land mines and put them where we would pick them up. Once you touched a baby, it would blow you to pieces. Fingers and teeth everywhere. I remember one time in Pleiku a small little girl about six walked into a bunch of GIs and exploded. Another time there was a fat little girl sitting on a pile of dirt and was not moving; crying, yes, but not moving. We did not get too close, but we walked around her. Good thing, too, she had a wire around her waist going down the crack of her ass into the ground. We had a jeep with us. Put a loop under her arms and a good hundred feet of rope between her and the jeep. That jeep took off and that girl came off that pile in two ways, pulled and pushed. She left a thirty-foot crater and lost one foot also." When the GIs saw abandoned babies they often didn't ask questions. They just gave them a wide berth and blew them up. "One time I ate part of one. That scared the mama-sans all to hell. There is so much I can't shake. I lay here, don't sleep. When sleep does come I dream . . . It hurts."

This sounds unbelieveable and may well be part of the mythology veterans suffering from posttraumatic stress endure, but if Shawcross perceived it, he was reacting to it as if it were true. This phantom zone between reality and fantasy is a real place for individuals like Shawcross who cannot differentiate between what has happened in the world and what has happened in their own minds. Reality is only an extension of themselves and not a separate entity. As the human time bomb changes, so does his or her reality.

Even while he was in Vietnam, Shawcross knew he was changing, that his personality was going through severe fluctuations and splitting off from itself. "I was like hot and cold water, on and off at will. I could turn something aside at will and forget. I can't hide the fact that something was wrong with me. I ate human flesh over there. Same thing I did here. I couldn't help it. The urge was too strong, couldn't stop or didn't want to . . . I was becoming a monster of sorts."

One incident in particular during his Vietnam tour of duty made such an impression on Shawcross that it came to the surface immediately during his postindictment interviews in jail. It concerned two Vietcong women that Shawcross claims to have tortured for secreting away ammunition in an arms cache near a village. It haunts him to this day, and he describes it with a hypermnesic intensity. "I shot one woman who was hiding some ammo in a tree. She didn't die right off. I tied her up, gagged her, then searched the area. Found the hut with another girl inside of it who was about sixteen. Knocked her out with the butt of a gun and carried her to where the other girl was. There was a lot of rice, ammo, and other stuff in the hut. I tied the young girl to a tree, still gagged. Tied her legs, too. They didn't say anything to me at all. I had a machete that was very sharp. I cut that first girl's throat. Then took off her head and placed it on a pole in front of that hut. Then I took and cut the ham section of the body and roasted it. Didn't smell too good, but when about burnt, I began to eat it. That girl at the tree peed, then fainted. I stripped her then. When she came to, I had taken the body away. Flesh cooked over a fire tasted like pork, like monkey. I raped that girl at the tree, but first gave her oral sex. I untied her, then retied her to two smaller trees. Afterwards, I ate some more. She fainted several times. I cut her slightly from the neck to the crotch. She screamed and shit herself. I took out my M16, pulled on a nipple, then put the gun to her forehead and pulled the trigger. Cut off her head and placed it on a pole where they got water. The superstitious NVA would not go near those two spots.

"The other girl in the jungle I killed where I had taken her head and placed it on a pole by a creek; I butchered her like a steer, neck down. I used the machete and cut her body down the middle. Then cleaved the backbone and washed the blood out. Why? I wish I knew for sure. The same way you cut a deer I did to the body. Back in 1965 I had a job at a meat market just south of Watertown. This is where I learned to butcher. Nineteen cows and bulls a day. It was nothing new to me. Once the outside skin is taken off, who can tell? Yes, I did roast half the body to about the way a well-done roast beef is cooked. Almost dry. The meat lasts for days that way. The rest of what I did not take I placed on a goodsized anthill. The ants will do the rest. The body of the other woman was placed on another ant mound. I was a sick fool. Maybe what bugs me is those two women and these I butchered. I lay here and wake up crying. Why? All these years I've tried to forget and now it haunts me." Shawcross, in his own mind at least, had become the "Ghost of Vietnam."

The incident that Shawcross described is part of the common apocrypha retold by many seriously traumatized Vietnam veterans, most of whom felt themselves powerless in a hostile country. Shawcross's own reliability in this point is in question. The Shawcross defense team in New York after the Rochester murders asked several Vietnam combat veterans to give their opinions of Shawcross's Vietnam claims. The unanimous opinion was that while Shawcross's story could have taken place, veterans that make such grandiose claims are usually attempting to cope with their own terror and rage through fantasies.

Similarly, many doctors who have treated Vietnam veterans suffering from posttraumatic stress have suggested that violent sexual fantasies involving the enemy were just that—fantasies. They represented attempts to work through a hostility that most GIs felt but were unable to accept, even though there were real atrocities committed by both sides during the war. Whether Shawcross's descriptions of Vietnam are real or perceived, they nevertheless represent his reactions to violence and his inability to deal with it.

Violent sexual fantasies are shared reactions among all serial killers. Shawcross, thus, was developing true to form as he was gradually transformed into a violent lust killer.

READJUSTMENT TO CIVILIAN LIFE, BURGLARY, ARSON, AND JAIL

When his tour was over, Shawcross boarded a plane and flew away. In 1969, that's what it took . . . But for him, the war was not over. There was no deprogramming, no required postcombat counseling, no period of decompression. He was transferred from the intensity of the South Vietnamese theater of war to the business-as-usual United States in less than a week. "When I left Vietnam, I wasn't ready for the States—I was too keyed up, too hyper. I should have stayed another six months. I left Vietnam and flew to Japan, then to Alaska, then to Washington State. Stayed there twenty-four hours and then flew to Chicago. Stayed at the airport four hours; then got a ride in a private jet to Detroit; then on to Syracuse. I was taken to the bus station in Syracuse. Stayed there overnight. The next morning people started calling me names—'Baby killer.' If I'd had a gun."

His homecoming was less than celebratory. He appeared, unannounced, at his mother's job as suddenly as a ghost. He felt his mother, Bessie was ice-cold toward him when she saw him even though his left sleeve was pinned up to his shoulder as if he'd lost an arm in combat. Actually, his arm was only wounded. For the rest of the evening, he thought that his parents were ignoring him. Shawcross himself was hyperactive and couldn't stop talking. That came to a sudden halt when his mother castigated him for repeating the word "dinks," the GI racial slur for Vietnamese. His mother though he was referring to whores and rebuked him in a way that recalled all the frustration and pent-up rage from his childhood. "I was mad. I couldn't control my emotions." He stayed home for three days, forgetting he had gotten married to a woman named Linda Neary just weeks before he left the States for his tour of duty, even though the two of them had spent their honeymoon in Hawaii. He eventually drove over to see her, and the two settled down to resume a marriage they had started only a week before he'd been sent into combat.

His moods just got "darker," Neary said to reporters about her former husband, describing the period in Fort Sill, Oklahoma, while Shawcross was completing his enlistment after his return from Vietnam. She said she'd wake him up in the morning and "he'd come up with his fists like he was going to hit me." "I felt scared," Shawcross remembers. "I had nightmares about Vietnam. One night I hit Linda after having a dream. Blonde girl with two black eyes." Despite Shawcross's attempts to receive counseling from a base psychiatrist at Fort Sill, he remained uncommunicative. "He wouldn't answer the doctor's questions," Neary said about the times she accompanied him to the sessions. "He wouldn't talk about what was bothering him." Finally, the doctor suggested that the counseling be terminated. "The doctor said there was no point in him coming if he wasn't going to do anything to cooperate," Linda Neary recalled in an interview with the local newspapers.

In 1969, another door had closed on the life of Arthur Shawcross when the army's counseling was formally terminated by the army after the army psychiatrist, according to Linda Neary, approached her about signing hospitalization commitment papers for her husband that would confine him to a mental institution. The doctor evidently realized, Neary said in an interview, that Shawcross needed to be committed, but the army couldn't do it against Shawcross's will. Understandably, Linda was a young wife with little experience of what was going on in her husband's life. She says she asked Arthur Shawcross's mother about committing her son, but that Bessie declined. This was a clear intervention point that turned into a missed opportunity. It was the final opportunity for mental health intervention before Shawcross returned to civilian life. Shawcross had asked for help. Aware that he was on the road to becoming a monster, Shawcross felt that he needed attention, intervention, someone to halt the slide into chaos, and that was why he agreed to talk to the Army psychiatrist. But he didn't know how to ask for help directly. He was still feeling the pent-up shame, guilt, and rage from his childhood that he had been unable to talk about. Only now he was an adult who had killed in war and he could act on that rage. The time bomb within him had started to tick. The army psychiatrist recognized that it was ticking, but did not have the legal authority to defuse the time bomb. Like other time bombs, such as Joseph Fischer and Bobby Joe Long, who were released from the army in states of severe mental impairment, Shawcross was walking among the innocent while something inside him was set to explode.

By the end of the following year, Shawcross would begin a spree of felony, arson, rape, and murder, all the while sporadically looking for help and intervention from psychiatrists and counselors. By the time he left the army, the pattern of fantasy and violent behavior was already in place. It had been played out in Vietnam—even if it had been only in his own mind—and had emerged again in a series of fantasies and at least one domestic near-assault. Shawcross was aware of a monster growing within. Linda Neary sensed that he had changed, grown darker and more sullen than usual. Even his doctor was aware that something—he didn't know what— was wrong. I believe that had Shawcross been committed, perhaps thirteen lives might have been saved over the ensuing twenty years. This was a missed opportunity, a point of intervention that passed.

After Shawcross's enlistment was up, the couple drove home to Clayton, New York, where their lives went from bad to worse. If anything, his therapy in the army only intensified his critical psychological problems. Upon his return home, he lapsed into his pre-service compulsive cruising-and-trolling-for-sex-and-adventure patterns, and found himself in violent conflicts with his bosses at work, resulting in a series of physical confrontations. During the summer of 1969, according to police reports, Shawcross set up a string of fires in the Watertown, New York, area including a $280,000 blaze at the Knowlton Brothers paper mill where he worked, a small barn in Delafarge Corners, and finally at the Crowley Milk Company in LaFargeville. Linda Neary said in a newspaper interview that her husband reported the fires and received praise from the police for helping to extinguish them. But the praise later turned to suspicion. After he was arrested for the burglary of a Clayton gas station in October 1969, he admitted setting the fires in exchange for a combined sentence. He only vaguely explained setting the fires, a police spokesman told local newspaper reporters. According to the police, Shawcross had told them he was nervous and had been talking to himself before tossing a burning cigarette into a pile of dry paper at Knowlton Brothers. He claimed something had "told him" to start the fires. Fire starting is a clear indicator, a red flag, for predictors of future dangerousness.

Linda Neary sensed something was not right with her husband, but was unable to do anything about it. She was not a mental-health professional equipped to deal with Shawcross's problems as they manifested themselves as daily behavior—his sullenness hostility roiling right below the surface, and his need to be alone and on the road. She felt he was working out whatever was bothering him. She didn't realize that he was trolling for women even then and that he was getting into fights at work. She didn't realize he was responsible for the fires at the barn and the milk company until after her husband was arrested. She also didn't know about the burglary until after the police informed her that Shawcross had been taken into custody. She explained to the press years later that Shawcross rarely talked with her and that she suspected at the time that her husband had suffered some trauma in Vietnam.

Shawcross remembers the arson and burglary incidents

differently from the police reports. "One night I picked up two teenagers who were hitchhiking. I didn't know they broke into a gas station. But my car had what they stole in it. I got arrested and went to jail. They did not. Bullshit. I was ready to explode at any given moment. One night I burned down a barn, then set a fire at the plant." He was charged with both burglary and arson, but he was allowed to plead guilty only to the burglary charge and received a single 2½ to 5-year prison sentence.

The arson incident was a further escalation of Shawcross's growing propensity for homicidal violence. Psychologists in Shawcross's case have indicated that repeat arson offenders like him are either seeking sexual gratification or have latent homicidal personalities. Shawcross falls into both categories. His own statements reveal that both instances of arson took place after he had fought with his boss or other people at the factories and while he was unsuccessful with other women. Fire starting is a symptom shared by most serial killers at some time in their lives before they begin their killing spree.

After his conviction for burglary, Shawcross was sentenced to serve "hard time" at a state penitentiary where he claims he was involved with several violent attacks. "Got raped in Attica prison by three black guys. I was lost, threatened, and in pain. I got all three my way, their way. I hurt them like they did me, but I used a sock with soap as a blackjack. Knocked them out and screwed them and then smashed them once in the nuts. I was never bothered after that." By that time Linda Neary had already divorced him. Shortly thereafter, he was transferred to the correctional facility at Auburn where, during a prison riot, he saved a guard's life in the act of fleeing for his own life. The prison riot, Shawcross said, prompted him to have a Vietnam flashback.

The violence had erupted in a cellblock when a fight between prisoners quickly escalated to a general melee. As the unarmed guards turned to retreat from the area, one of the fleeing officers was trapped in the corridor and surrounded by inmates who were taking up defensive positions outside the cells. The inmates savagely attacked the downed officer with lead pipes and parts of bedframes, leaving him to bleed to death from a severe laceration across his temple. Meanwhile, guards had begun to re-form and charge the cellblock, trapping the fleeing Shawcross in a crossfire. He couldn't run back to the prisoners who were busy taking hostages, and he was afraid to run across the no-man's-land toward the guard's command post he could see in front of him. Fortunately, he stumbled across the officer's body as he fled the burning cellblock. He saw his chance to save his life and first staunched the man's bleeding by applying direct pressure to the wound. When the bleeding began to ebb, Shawcross half-carried, half-dragged the struggling officer through the low-hanging clouds of densely toxic, eye-stinging smoke of burning mattresses in the confined cellblock into the prison yard where the police had set up a command post. He had saved his own life, but the correctional officer's union called him a hero. Six months were lopped off his minimum sentence, and he was released on parole one and a half years later after having only spent a total of two years behind bars. No one thought of the stresses Shawcross had suffered during his "return to combat or his act of bravery," whichever it really was.

Shawcross was out of jail, but he was not free. The repressed monsters inside him were only waiting; still seething; still demanding revenge. In less than a year, they would strike again.

MURDER AND RAPE

In March 1972, only months after his release from Auburn, Shawcross got married again. Now it was to Penny Sherbino, a woman he had known since childhood who had two children from a previous marriage, and whom he had gotten pregnant. "I didn't want to shame my parents," she told a newspaper reporter years later. "I was a woman with two little kids and I saw the opportunity to get a man to support them." Less than five months later, she miscarried. "Thank God I miscarried," she said eighteen years later. She hadn't known about Shawcross's Vietnam experiences or his prior arrests and conviction. She didn't know that he was on parole. "I thought I knew him because I knew his family. But I guess I didn't know him at all." But she did notice that he was becoming increasingly violent, displaying bursts of ugly temper at the slightest provocation, and turning his rage on the children who lived in the apartment complex. One afternoon, she told a newspaper interviewer, police responded to a complaint filed by a young boy's parents who said that Shawcross had stuffed freshly cut grass down the boy's pants and spanked him. The parole officers thought it was a harmless prank because Shawcross told them and his wife that he was only playing with the boy in the yard by stuffing grass down his pants. It was only a joke, he said, but his wife had a sense of foreboding and doom. That sense was only heightened when a neighbor, Mildred Vincent, a waitress, had a bouquet of roses left on her doorstep with a note that read, "These are for your grave, Mrs. Vincent."

On June 4, 1972, Shawcross's life changed again when he had an experience that tore open the fabric of the present and confronted him with a replay of an incident that had taken place almost fifteen years earlier. He was walking across the open lots that separated his house from Penny's parents' house when he heard the voice of a child calling after him. He turned and saw ten-year-old Jack Blake, a neighborhood boy, waist-deep in one of the many muck holes that dotted the landscape. Shawcross pulled the child out of the muck and ordered him to go home and clean up. But the child wouldn't leave. "Go home," Shawcross remembers screaming at the boy. "He kept following me," Shawcross told the police months later. "Every time I turned around, there he was. When I said go home, he said he would go where he wanted to." Shawcross tried to run, he said, but he heard splashing behind him and he turned and hit Jack hard across the back of the neck with a karate chop. The boy fell face-forward in the mud and stopped moving.

"When Jack Blake followed me across a swamp and over railroad tracks plus into some woods, I couldn't take it any longer, telling him to go back. I did hit him in the throat and head, then strangled him. . . . I cut parts of him out and ate them. I took his penis, his balls, and heart and ate them. Why I did this, I don't know. I also had sex with his body. God does not want me, Satan does."

Three months later, he killed again. "She reminded me of my sister," Shawcross has said about his eight-year-old vic-tim, Karen Ann Hill, a child who fell into the waters of the Black River near where Shawcross was fishing from the Pearl Street bridge. Shawcross lifted her from the water and had oral sex with her. "She didn't scream or nothing," he re-called years later. Then he laid her on the wet grass along the riverbank and had vaginal sex with her, as he wrote to his defense team after his arrest for the Rochester murders.

Shawcross was scared as he stared down into the girl's face. As reality flooded in around him, he not only realized what he had done to Karen Ann, he also remembered what he had done to Jack Blake. He strangled the girl until she lost consciousness, caved in part of the riverbank right under the bridge, and buried her in the soft dirt. He packed her mouth and nostrils with wet mud until she suffocated, and covered her torso with large flat river stones, leaving her hair, hands, and feet exposed. "I wanted to get caught," Shawcross told the police after he finally confessed later that night.

Two state troopers had used a dog to track Shawcross from the crime scene to his house. At first he denied being at the scene. But he eventually relented after a witness reported that he had seen Shawcross and a young neighborhood boy sitting astride bicycles on the bridge above the site and eat-ing ice cream cones while they stared into the river just after

Karen Ann's body was discovered. The state troopers called sergeant John Dawley and officer Charles Kubinsky to report that a parolee in their jurisdiction was a prime suspect in the murder of Karen Ann. The local detectives picked Shawcross up and spent more than six hours interrogating him, slowly guiding him through the evidence they had assembled, and begging him for help. At first he was vague, they told reporters, almost not even in the room with them. "He would just sit there and listen," Dawley said. "When you faced him with facts, he'd say, 'Maybe so.' Then he'd say, 'What's going to happen to me if I tell you something?'"

In return for confessing to a single count of manslaughter in the first degree for the death of Karen Ann Hill and revealing the location of Jack Blake's body, Shawcross escaped convictions for the felony rape of Karen Ann Hill, a second count of manslaughter in the death of Jack Blake, and a parole violation for the sentence he was currently serving. He was convicted to a maximum term in prison of twenty-five years, in what would have been at least a fifty-year sentence had police already known about the Jack Blake murder. With time off for good behavior in prison and a clean rehabilitation record, Shawcross was up for parole fifteen years later. Career parole officials were dismayed. Shawcross would be in the community again, and there was nothing anybody could do to stop him. Some people sensed it was only a matter of time before he'd kill again. But nobody knew it would happen so fast or that he would begin killing adults.

According to parole supervisor Bob Kent's memo, Shawcross had struck an "incredible deal" with the district attorney which Kent was still talking about fifteen years later. Because he had been granted immunity for the Blake murder, that homicide wasn't allowed to be in his record when the time came to sentence him. It was as if the homicide hadn't occurred, even though it was a violent act of murder, mutilation, and sexual molestation.

This was another missed opportunity that had, by the time

of his parole hearing, formed a pattern in Arthur Shawcross's life: smoldering rage that burst into violence, and a
fortuitous array of circumstances that enabled Shawcross to
walk away from the ultimate consequences of that violence.
By rights, Shawcross should have spent the rest of his life
behind bars for the double murder. But the court missed the
opportunity to put him in jail for life because the prosecutor
needed his cooperation in admitting to the Blake murder. He
confessed to the Blake crime, under immunity, indicating
that he was in obvious need of help, but because the crime
was not allowed on his record, he did not receive the help
that might have rehabilitated him. The time bomb was allowed to fall through the system. Only, this time, it would
have fatal consequences for the eleven victims he would
soon encounter.

PAROLE

It is difficult to conclude that the parole board spent a
great amount of time considering Shawcross's voluminous
case file before releasing him into the community. The parole board's chairman later explained in a state Senate committee hearing that the board made its final decision to
release Shawcross based in large part on psychiatrists' finding no compelling reason to keep him in prison, even though
one parole officer had labeled Shawcross a "psychosexual
maniac" in the file. That assessment was buried deep inside
a folder of more detailed psychological reports that concluded that Shawcross had made a successful adjustment to
prison life, had responded positively to counseling, had
learned a trade, and had thoroughly rehabilitated himself.
The board declined to give similar weight to parole officers'
concerns that Shawcross couldn't control his rage, focusing
instead on another prison counselor's report that suggested
Shawcross was rehabilitated enough to reenter the community.

As frightening as Shawcross's claimed experiences in the Vietnamese jungles were, no less frightening was the final killing spree he conducted beginning in February 1988, only ten months after having been released on parole for his rape/murder of eight-year-old Karen Ann Hill. He had, after his release, literally split into two only-partially-complete personalities, each aware of, but neither in control of, the other. On one level, this is a prototypically severe post-traumatic stress reaction. On another level, Shawcross was experiencing what neuropsychiatrists call "limbic psychosis," a homicidally violent form of criminal behavior in which the homicide episodes are triggered by a mechanism the killer isn't even aware of. In Shawcross's case, the episode was almost always triggered by a challenge to his basic self-esteem.

Parole officers knew that they would have to contend with managing Shawcross once he was released because of the negative impact his release was bound to have on the community where he was settled. Parole Officer Gerald Szachara first attempted to resettle Shawcross in the Binghamton area, because, according to Bob Kent's memo, he would have access to the "excellent services of the Broome County Mental Health Clinic," which would coordinate his supervision. Shawcross says that he wanted to be in a rural setting because there would be less temptation, and less stimulation. But parole officials didn't want to let him out in an isolated area where he could simply disappear. Accordingly, Shawcross arrived in the Binghamton area on April 30, 1987, and was assigned to a job as a cook at the Volunteers of America offices. The Binghamton police, however, were so incensed at Shawcross's arrival in their community, especially because a sergeant on the department's vice squad was still in mourning over the death and sexual assault of his daughter, committed by another child killer, that two Binghamton city police officers located Shawcross and told him they wanted to get a close-up look at him. Two Binghamton city detectives also went to the Volunteers of America offices and told

Shawcross that they, too, wanted to see what he looked like. "The police started stopping me every day," Shawcross wrote in his journal. "So I told my parole officer I had to go somewhere else."

Shawcross was transferred to Delhi, another Southern New York Tier community, where the police again were asked to see that he be placed elsewhere. "At the end of the week, our landlady said to leave. The chief of police was going around and telling people who I was. So he moved me into a cellar of a church until another place was found." His freedom, security, home, and new wife were threatened, which flashed him back to moments of danger in Vietnam.

A short time later, Shawcross was moved to the upper Catskill community of Fleischmanns. He was only there for a week when he again smelled trouble. "I went to the post office to register for mail. The woman at the window told me that I would not be getting any mail from there. Two days later a deputy stopped by and told my wife Rose and me that there was a lynch mob coming to kick me out of town." Sure enough, two nights later, the mayor and a contingent of town leaders showed up on the front porch of Shawcross's house and threatened to throw him out of town. "I refused to move. We were scared, sure. Then the people got out front with flashlights and torches. They started screaming my name to come outside. I had all the lights out. I opened the front door and one guy started making threats. I made one statement: Whoever made one step into the yard was a dead man. Whoever! Man, woman, or child. That stopped them for a while. Then the deputy came back and told us that the parole department of Binghamton wanted to pick me up and bring me there. He only said me; not Rose. But I told him I was not going anywhere without her. So we both went to Binghamton."

From Binghamton, the newlyweds were transferred to a motel where they stayed until arrangements were made to place them in the Rochester community. This time, the Rochester police were not notified of Shawcross's presence.

He integrated into the community quickly and began dealing drugs very soon after he established his residence, he admitted to his defense team after the Rochester murders. Before a year had passed he had begun four separate relationships with four separate women to whom he gave engagement rings, he had begun a relationship with Clara Neal, and, finally, he had killed his next victim.

Shawcross's serial-murder spree was carried out while he was under the supervision of his parole officer and several mental health clinics. Prior to his first homicide and during most of the ensuing serial murders, Shawcross was undergoing intensive psychological counseling, during which time his doctors praised his adjustment, based on the information he gave to them. His counselor was especially encouraged by the way he seemed to be adapting to the hard knocks of life outside the penitentiary walls. Now, his counselor reported, he seemed to be settling in, working at the local labor pool on temporary jobs, and living with his girlfriend, Clara Neal. (He had previously been divorced from Penny and had married a woman named Rose. However, Shawcross had many different girlfriends throughout his marriages.) Neither his therapist nor his parole officer had any indication that Shawcross was sliding back into old ways, that nothing about him had ever been ultimately resolved.

He was still the same killer, waiting for the trigger that would plunge him into another violent episode that he was powerless to control. That episode began in late December 1987.

THE ROCHESTER KILLING SPREE

"In December we asked Mom and Dad to come for a visit. Never came! In January, we asked again. Still no one showed up," Shawcross wrote in his journal. Then Shawcross learned that during the period his parents were supposed to visit him in Rochester, they were in Virginia visiting his older sister. He began to brood. Then he started to get angry. Then he felt the need to get out on the road and drive. He couldn't stay inside and sit still. He had always taken long walks when he was younger, or bicycle or car rides to calm himself down. It was a reaction to stress that he had developed when he was very young. After he and his mother would have a bad argument, Shawcross had said, he would walk out into the woods and sit until he calmed down. Those same feelings of brooding and anger, of restlessness and the need to be moving, came over him again.

"Something in me was weird. I started to sweat. Why? It was chilly outside with snow on the ground." He took his girlfriend Clara's car and began driving along Lake Avenue through a red-light district along the Genesee River front. It was there, where Lake Avenue crosses Lyell, that he encountered Dorothy Blackburn. She was his first victim.

Shawcross's account of the first murder was chilling in its simplicity, lack of remorse, and lack of responsibility. He used this same detail of language and heightened memory awareness when he described each of his successive victims—most of whom were prostitutes, some of whom were homeless, some of whom laughed at his inability to perform sexually, and all of whom threatened him at the time his emotional critical mass had been reached. Some of these women reminded him of his mother, he said. They promised him love, but instead he felt humiliated. A shame welled up in him that he could not erase. Others had threatened to tell his wife, Rose, and expose his violent nature to shame and ridicule he could not withstand. Thus, he erased the victim. It was cold-blooded and methodical, feral and instinctive.

The killer transformed into an automaton whose language bleached away passion and rage. And the murder itself became a kaleidoscopic but straightforward *quid pro quo* exchange of violence for insult, love for hate, and death for pain. He strangled them while he tried to have sex with them. When it was over, Shawcross disposed of the bodies in the same matter-of-fact way he disposed of carcasses at the meat-packing plant he had worked in years earlier.

"I drove as far as the 'Tent City' and a girl stepped into the street in front of me," Shawcross writes. "I stopped. She got in and asked me if I wanted a date. I said o.k. then asked where do we go? She guided me to an area behind a warehouse. I was a dummie. Going out I thought meant to a restaurant or something. She laughed at that. Then she asked if I wanted to fuck! Point blank. I was surprised for I've never done it this way. I asked how much and she said $20 for a blow job and $30 for half and half. Half blow job; half screw. I gave her the $30 and told her I would like to give her oral sex while she did me. She agreed. I had my zipper down and my penis out. She took off her pants, and underwear, shoes, and socks. Why all that I don't know. The car was real warm though. I had my penis in her mouth and I on her. It was o.k. for about three minutes then she bit me. I screamed and pulled back. There was blood all over. I was scared. I thought I was going to die. I really did. I grabbed my penis and screamed, why did she bite me. She said not one word but had a smile on her bloody face. So I reached over and bit into her vagina. Something tore loose. I didn't care. So now she was bleeding also. But I could not stop the pain. I grabbed her by the throat with one hand, my right, and squeezed until she passed out. I got out of the car and got some Handi Wipes and wrapped myself up, then zipped up. I got back in and turned her around so she was sitting up. She was breathing o.k. I took her pants and tied her arms behind her. She came to and asked me what I was going to do. Meanwhile we were outside the city. I told her to shut up. Then she said I was not the same person she got into the car with. I pulled over and stopped. Grabbed her by the hair and asked her why she bit me. Because she felt like it! I got her shirt and tied her feet together. Then drove out to North Hampton park. Pulled in by a small bridge. Turned off the engine and sat there. This time I smacked her in the face and asked again. I took the flashlight out and inspected myself.

What a bloody mess! All Miss Blackburn said was, she felt like it! I told her I won't be able to love a woman again. Then she started calling me queer, faggot, and cursing me. I took off my pants and got out of the car and put snow on my penis. That cold stopped the bleeding. I put rubber on as slowly as I could and got back in.

"Now I told her she is going to be raped. All she did was laugh. Then I got mad and started to sweat real bad. Pulled her close to me and fondled her. Then whispered in her ear she was going to die, and what did she say now? She must have been on drugs. She just smiled at me. I took her shirt off her pants off her arms then told her to get dressed. She did, then called me 'Little Man.' I choked her for a good ten minutes, or as near as I thought. She went limp. I sat there half the night with her . . . Took her out of the car and dropped her into the creek. She was face down. Watched for about a half hour, then drove away. Came back to the city and stopped at Marks on Lake Avenue. Had coffee, calmed down, and then went back to the car. Then I drove to a parking lot to clean up the car. Her shoes, socks, and coat were still in there. Dumped them in a trash can, minus any I.D. Then went home. At daylight, I cleaned the car as best I could, but still the blood was in the seat. I was in a daze for over a week. Even Rose and Clara asked me what was wrong with me. I didn't say much to anyone. I felt I wasn't me; not the same me."

This pattern, this demonstration of homicidal violence and distorted thinking, was to repeat itself ten more times in dfflerent areas around Rochester, Wayne, and Monroe Counties. There would be ten more victims; ten more street-walkers, most of whom would be cocaine addicts and already so far beyond the protection of the law that even after their respective deaths the police would be too slow to grasp the significance of the clues that were amassing at the dump sites. Finally, in late 1989, over a year and half after the Genesee River murders began, the police recovered Shaw-cross's first six victims. As in most serial murder cases, the bodies were so badly decomposed that the causes of most of the deaths were indeterminate. Without a cause of death, the killer's MO couldn't be definitively established. And without a single MO, the police were hard-pressed to explain the large number of bodies.

In October 1989, only weeks before the police would make their discovery, Shawcross had returned to his trolling grounds near the park and encountered Frances Brown. "I found her walking on Lyle Avenue. She took me to Seth Green Drive where a lot of people go fishing, including me. She was wild and crazy, didn't act right. I gave her $30 and she took off all her clothes and got in the back of the car. The Dodge. I let down the back seat and we had 69. She asked me to deep throat her, so I did but got carried away. I didn't pull out so she could breathe." As Frances Brown began to choke, she went into convulsions and tried violently to wrench away and gasp for air. "She peed into my mouth and I kept pushing, uncontrolled reaction to doing it that way. She suffocated. I used her then also while still warm. Even to kissing her and sucking her teeth and breast. Didn't have an orgasm." She was the fifth victim.

In November, the police announced that there were three or four prostitute killers stalking the streets around Jefferson Park and burying the bodies in the soft dirt along the banks of the Genesee River. The similarities between the Genesee River dump site, the Green River dump site in Seattle, and the San Diego dump site were so strong that the media suggested that New York State had its own Green River Killer. That investigation had cost Seattle millions of dollars and still the killer hadn't been found. Would Rochester endure the same fate? And how long would the killings go on?

Early in November, even while the forensics teams were sifting the remains of his victims from the Genesee site, Shawcross met June Stotts. "She always told me her name was Jay. She was not a hooker! I stopped to talk to her on a park bench. It was a warm day. I asked her if she would like to go for a ride. She said yes, please. We went down the beach. Walked hand in hand along the pier leaning against one another, watching the boats coming in and going out. I had a loaf of bread and we fed the ducks and gulls and some minnows. When we were walking along toward the boat dock she kissed me. Why I don't know." After they had driven around again and had lunch near the docks along the river, June Stotts kissed Shawcross again. "I pulled her close and asked her where she learned to kiss like that. Jay said by watching t.v. I was smitten!"

It would not be Shawcross's day to fall in love. His infatuation with thirty-year-old June Stotts quickly turned into a violent battle when he again felt threatened by someone "good" who had turned into someone "bad." "She sat there watching me. Leaned over and kissed me the third time. I asked Jay what is the matter. She took off her shoes, socks, and pants; also her coat, shirt, and bra. Left her panties on. She asked me to teach her how to make love. That's when I thought she was a virgin . . . I took all my clothes off and laid down beside her. I kissed her and ran my hand over her body. No response at all. Kissed her neck and breast, her stomach also. Took off her underpants and she closed her eyes. She was a funny girl. Gave her oral sex. Nothing happened! So I laid next to her with one leg between her legs, looked in her eyes, and kissed her. She did know how to French kiss. But something was wrong. I kept looking at her and stroking her vagina. Her eyes showed me nothing. Then we talked. She never had a man. Jay has been with women. I tried to mount her and she screamed, "Oh my God," and fainted. I was in then. Stayed still till she came to. Then I screwed her for a good twenty minutes, fast and slow. I couldn't stop it felt that good. Then she started. She went wild on me. Couldn't get enough it seems like. When I got tired she tried to keep me up. Jay was not Jay at that moment. She turned into something else—wild, crazy. How can I explain? She used my hands, toes, and face. I could not stop her. She used her hands, both at the same time. Then she sucked me. I gave her more. I thought that I had come.

So did she. Then she sat up and said she was going to tell the police that I had raped her, I snapped once again. It was over in ten minutes. I took her clothes and dropped them next to the barge into the water. Left her laying right there. Came back to her in a week, looked around, found her jackknife and change. Tossed her glasses into the swamp. I sat there next to her and screwed her some more. Her body was limp I took her knife and cut her from chest to her ass hole. Cut out her pussy and ate it. I was one sick person. Dragged her into the swamp then put the rug over her head and left."

June Stotts was Shawcross's sixth victim. The discovery of her body later that month by the police prompted them to revise their assumptions about the Genesee Killer. There had to be more than two killers at work, they reasoned, because June Stotts, the mildly retarded girl whom people had called an introvert, was no prostitute. She didn't fit the profile. Neighbors referred to her as slow and shy, a simple, solitary person who liked to take long walks alone by the docks. She and Artie Shawcross, two loners who could not relate to others, had enjoyed picnics together along the riverbank that summer. On one or two occasions she had even been to his apartment. She knew Artie's wife, Rose. She regarded Arthur Shawcross as a gentle man—a father figure, even—who liked to fish and was willing to listen to her. She believed she had nothing to fear from the graying, quiet man who looked far older than his forty-one years.

The police were still far from the truth about the serial murders along the Genesee River on November 9 when Shawcross picked up his seventh victim, Maria Walsh. Nor were they any closer the next month when a prostitute named Trippi laughed at Shawcross because he couldn't get an erection, called him "little boy," and became number eight. By the time Shawcross saw Liz Gibson, victim number nine, sitting in his car outside Marks on Lake Avenuc "she was cold, she said. And it was warm in there"—the news stories about a serial killer on the loose in Rochester were breaking into the front pages all across the state and dominating the lead-in teasers on the local evening news. Shawcross had even killed two women in one day and was now a rampaging monster.

Would Liz Gibson have lived if the police had warned the Lake Avenue hookers that there was a prostitute killer on the loose in their area? Would she be alive today if she hadn't tried to steal Shawcross's wallet bulging with cash he'd scored from the minor drug deals along Lyle Avenue the night before? Might Shawcross not have killed her if, after he slapped her and took back his wallet, he didn't think that she looked a little bit like another woman who had humiliated him? These are moot questions now. And Shawcross asked no questions at the time. He choked her until she went limp beside him and drove around town with her body still in the front seat. Maybe he was grieving more for himself than for anything else. "I cried while driving. What was I becoming? I couldn't think right."

Even weeks later, he wasn't worried about the police units cruising along the riverfront parks when he picked up June Cicero at midnight in front of City Mattress on Lyle Avenue. He doesn't remember where he took her or what happened to trigger his savage attack. When it was all over, Shawcross dumped her in an icebound creek near Northampton Park and kicked snow over her body to conceal it. It froze solid. Three days later, he returned to the site with a small handsaw, scraped off the snow, and cut out her vagina.

"I went there for the purpose of cutting out the sex organ and giving it to Clara's son. After I sawed it out, I pulled out the hairs and wrapped it in a bar towel. Went back to the car and came back to the city. Dropped the saw off at Wegman's dumpster on Chili Avenue. Drove near Turning Point Park and sat playing with myself and that vagina. Then I put it in my mouth and ate it. I had no control at all. Why did I do this? I don't know. Couldn't taste anything either. Something is in the back of my mind that won't come out. I am scared of what may be in there."

Shaweross's returns to the dump site helped police to

catch him after a police helicopter followed him after murder number nine.

WHAT THE MENTAL HEALTH
PROFESSIONALS SAID

The capsule summary of Shawcross's psychiatric evaluations, prepared by the parole board, hardly seems to take into account the list of crimes Shawcross has confessed to since the 1960s. In May 1971, one year before he murdered Jack Blake and while he was still in prison for the burglary conviction, the Auburn Correction Facility psychiatrist wrote that Shawcross evidenced "no florid psychosis" even though he had a "schizoid personality." Shawcross has spent his life wearing a mask of sanity. Similarly, a month after the murder of Karen Ann Hill, a psychiatric evaluation compiled at Attica stated that Shawcross suffered from a weakness of his superego and had an "apparent intellectual deficiency." Their clinical evaluations are understandable since they were based on interviews with Shawcross, who did not discuss his Vietnam experiences with them or the incidents of sexual molestation that he later claimed to have occurred. Shawcross appeared almost detached and disoriented during these sessions. The Attica prison psychiatrist recommended that Shawcross receive prescribed antianxiety medications to curb his chronic depressions. Nine months later, the prison psychiatrist at Green Haven, wrote that Shawcross displayed "no clinical evidence whatsoever of depression at the present time." Apparently, Shawcross was responding to the medication. In an evaluation written four months later by a psychologist at Green Haven, Shawcross was called a "normal individual," who realized he had done wrong and wanted to help himself get back on track.

Prior to his release on parole in 1987, the board reviewed two evaluations. The first, written for the parole board in August 1985, stated that Arthur Shawcross "does not exhibit emotional disturbance." Eighteen months later and only two months before his release, the mental-status report officer for the division of parole wrote that Shawcross was "not mentally ill at present" even though he recommended ongoing therapy to resolve emotional conflicts. Four months later, a psychiatrist with Broome County Mental Health Services, which had been charged with supervising Shawcross's therapy after his release, wrote that the parolee had "no mental order requiring any specific counseling or treatment at this time" even though he was complaining about an inability to ejaculate. This is a red flag for sexual offenders who need help and are approaching the threshold of violence. The psychiatrists added that Shawcross was denying ever having had any homosexual experiences in prison, and reported a positive relationship with his minister. He summarizes his report with the following diagnosis: "No mental disorder." Six months later Shawcross murdered Dorothy Blackburn.

Even more startling were the last two psychiatric evaluations written while Shawcross was in the midst of his murder spree. In these interviews, there was unfortunately no serious confrontation with his past violence, no serious confrontation with his Vietnam experiences, nor any confrontations with his past confessions of arson. It was as if his previous crimes did not exist at the very same time he was killing women in Rochester.

The first evaluation, written by a clinical social worker at Genesee Mental Health Center in April 1988, accepts Shawcross's report of recurrences "of any impulses or inclinations toward the sort of behavior which landed him in prison for a number of years." The clinical social worker suggested further that Shawcross also "has no need for psychiatric counseling." Six weeks later he murdered prostitute Anna Stephens by crushing her to death with his own body, then he pushed her over an embankment, wrapped her dress around a large rock, and dropped it into the Genesee River. And on June 29, 1988, a clinical social worker for Family

Service of Rochester, wrote to Len De Fazio, the area parole supervisor for Rochester, to assure him that Shawcross was "cooperative and reasonably comfortable" during their interview sessions. "He is currently exhibiting no particular symptoms, discomforts, or behavior difficulties which would benefit from mental health treatment." Moreover, he states, "I find that Art is currently a well controlled and fairly stable individual. Although he continues to exhibit some discomfort or flashes related to anger, he is able to manage these episodes extremely well . . . Consequently, I see no need for pursuing counseling with Art at this time." For all intents and purposes, Arthur Shawcross was pronounced healthy, sane, rehabilitated, and fully integrated into his new life. Unfortunately, at the time this report was written, Shawcross had already killed and mutilated three women, one of whom he cannibalized, and was suspected of dealing cocaine and other drugs among the prostitute population of Rochester.

THE WARNING SIGNS
OF DANGEROUSNESS

Arthur Shawcross's personal history reads like a road map of symptoms, all of which, he claims, began with sexual molestation and rejection. With each experience of escalating violence, each new emotional and physical trauma, the pressures built until the critical mass was created. And despite numerous individual intervention points, including almost twenty years of prison—and state-supervised counseling—no one was skilled or sensitive enough to penetrate Shawcross's surface reactions. Even while he was murdering and mutilating the hookers who sidled up next to him in the front of his girlfriend's car, he was able to present an appearance of emotional stability so that doctors and counselors were giving him a clean bill of emotional health.

Shawcross's problem began early in his youth, he claims, when his mother subjected him to abusive punishment—

treatment that she has categorically denied. After Shaw-cross's childhood trust in the world was supposedly breached by his mother, an older woman molested him. However, had it not been for Shawcross's encounter with a male rapist, he might have evolved out of his preadolescent experimentation with deviant sexual activities. But the rape resulted in posttraumatic stress and sexual dysfunction and created a sense of horror and fear. By the time he had reached his later teens, he was already sexually dysfunctional, alternating between hypersexual activity, the need to inflict pain on his sexual partners, and an inability to remain sexually stable or faithful to a partner. This was the person who went to the Vietnamese killing fields.

In custody in Rochester, Shawcross described a history of four major head traumas that required hospitalization. In 1962 he was hit on the top of his head with a stone. He was taken to the hospital. In May of 1962 he received a blow to his temple from a flying discus, which knocked him unconscious and required three days' hospitalization. In 1963, he received a blow from a hammer which, again, knocked him unconscious and required hospitalization. Some time after that, he fell backward from a ladder, was again knocked out, and received a serious concussion that put him in the hospital. He was also a high school football player and wrestler and received blows to the head throughout that period. He was continually at risk for head injuries that might not have required hospitalization and might have even gone unreported. Finally, he was knocked out at the gate of Attica prison and to this day experiences severe headaches during periods that require any prolonged mental activity.

Radiological studies performed on Shawcross indicated lesions on his brain, and a magnetic resonance imaging performed on March 14, 1990, shows that there is still a cyst formation on the right side of his brain as the result of childhood injuries. Dr. Vernon Mark, a neurologist and neuropsychologist at Harvard and a neurotoxicologist at the Health Research Institute, is conducting further neurological and biochemical tests to determine the degree of impairment.

Most violent killers who have been medically evaluated have had similar head traumas. Neurologists speculate that people who display gradually evolving dangerous behavior—human time bombs— have a type of neural dysfunction that prevents the higher brain functions from mediating primal instincts of rage, fear, flight, and sexual gratification. In certain types of temporal-lobe epilepsy, these instincts emerge in an episodic fashion once or twice a month or once a week, increasing in intensity and frequency until the individual either is caught by the police or destroys himself. Human time bombs almost always destroy themselves unless they are stopped.

After his head traumas, Shawcross was subjected to the emotional and spiritual traumas of war. Shawcross's later reactions to the violence of the war were so extreme that he, whether in fact or in his own fantasies, became a rapist, murderer, and cannibal, taking some pleasure from each of these activities. These continuing assaults traumatized his system even further, diminishing his body's ability to control the flow of neurochemicals that trigger intense survival reactions. This would have turned Shawcross into a biological time bomb set to go off every time a woman inflicted pain on him or posed a threat to his manhood.

Shawcross was also a victim of toxic lead poisoning. He slept in the same tent with lead-lined ammunition boxes and cooked his food from leadlined boxes as well. This suggests that Shawcross had ingested enough lead to cause hallucinations, paranoid delusions, and diminished capacity. If too much lead had concentrated in his system, the residual affects of lead poisoning would have lasted long after the war. That would be another indicator that Shawcross was unable to control his reactions.

From biochemical and biogenetic testing, doctors discovered pyroluria, a chemical condition that at the very least produces a weakened ability to deal with stress. Shawcross's pyroluria was diagnosed because of a 200 count reading of kryptopyrolles in a blood specimen. The average kryptopyrolle count is 5 in normal people, and 10 is considered above average. Shawcross's 200 count puts him right off the scale during periods of high stress. In periods of moderate stress, his count drops to 75, still way above average. Shawcross was also discovered to have the telltale XYY chromosomal karyotype that has in the past figured in cases of time bombs predisposed to extraordinary violence. At the very least, his XYY chromosomal karyotype also predisposes him to react with hostility when confronted by stressful situations. These are all clear indicators of human time bomb dangerousness.

Shawcross has reported severe indicators of psychological and biological stress during periods preceding violent activity—an aura sensation. He has said that after he feels threatened or has become enraged, "light gets ten times brighter," "I hear little or no sound . . . sometimes I hear a woman's voice behind me, but look around and no one is there," he smells a strong urine smell "like a farmyard or barnyard," and at those moments "I don't realize anything around me. I lose all sense of feeling. I lose all sense of time . . . I forget everything." He also claims to have a tingling around his mouth, chin, lips, hands, arms, and feet.

The clearest signs of a potential time bomb, especially in an evolving serial killer, is an early set of crimes that establish sexual patterns of violence. In Shawcross's case, these were the murders of Jack Blake and Karen Ann Hill. It's safe to say that unless the motivations of violent sexual behavior are addressed, they will repeat themselves. The psychological reports from Green Haven referred to Shawcross's hostility, his suffering from posttraumatic stress syndrome, and his inability to mediate his rage, but none of them really addressed the issue of the rape and murder of Karen Ann Hill or the murder of Jake Blake. It is astounding that the state correctional authorities who knew that Shawcross had been allowed to walk away from the first killing and mutilation and who were aware of Shawcross's extensive criminal record prior to his murders allowed him to earn parole after only fifteen years in prison. There were numerous signs suggesting that Shawcross was a multiple homicide offender, a red-flag case, and a dangerous individual who should never have been released on parole. But the state had no mental health mechanism for addressing the types of symptoms that Shawcross complained of. There was no method of rehabilitation for Shawcross because, even though he had complained years earlier about being unable to control his violent urges, there was no method of understanding what Shawcross was. As a result, he was simply allowed to slip through the cracks, even though a parole officer was calling out after him that he was a walking catastrophe about to be unleashed on an unsuspecting community.

SHAWCROSS'S FUTURE

When Arthur Shawcross was released from Green Haven before his spree, he was handed $41, his compensation for seven years as the prison locksmith. With his $41, all the money Shawcross had in the world at that time, he says he bought his mother an elaborate re-creation of a German "Black Forest" clock from a mail-order catalog. Shawcross says that his mother had repeatedly refused to communicate with him while he was in prison. According to newspaper reports, she had warned each of his wives against marrying him, intimating that he had a dark side that none of them would be able to fathom. But Shawcross hoped that with his Christmas present he might be able to make amends.

He never saw his mother. The clock was delivered by Parcel Post. It was also Parcel Post that brought the clock back to him. Shaweross was devastated. He tried one last time to get his parents to visit him in Rochester over Christmas. He and Rose waited in their apartment, but his parents never came. Shortly after the first of the year, he told his psychiatrist, he had heard that his parents had traveled to

Virginia to visit his sister Jeannie. For the following month, he said, he felt a cold hostility taking hold of him until one night when he began sweating and couldn't stop. He felt "weird." He was wet with perspiration. By the time he saw Dorothy Blackburn stepping out of the shadows on Lake Avenue, his psychosis had already taken hold of him.

"I would get mad at the drop of a hat and get madder still. I have no control of my feelings. I am too sensitive and I get too emotional a lot also. I've been a loner most all of my life. I do admit that I've made a lot of friends while in Rochester and now I've got just a few of those still praying for me. I feel I am not normal. I don't think right and hardly ever did the right things in life. Whenever I got pressured in some way, I start thinking bad thoughts. God help because I can't . . . Mostly it was Vietnam. I should have died over there. Then all this would not have happened or with the two kids in Watertown. I could have put myself in a hospital. I was scared; still am. If I have to die now for these crimes that I don't figure is all my fault, then let it be with the needle. There is too much torment bottled up inside of me, too much anger that needs to be rid of. I should be castrated or have an electrode placed in my head to stop my stupidness or whatever. I am just a lost soul looking for release of my madness. Please, God, let someone help me."

Shawcross was found guilty of eleven homicides and has been sentenced to 250 years in prison. He will never again be a free man. He had told his psychiatrist that there is nothing more he wants—his life has effectively ended. However, he has asked his mother to send him one photograph of each of his family members. If he can have photographs to tape to the wall of his prison cell, he has promised his mother, he will never bother her again.

4

FISH:
THE STORY OF JOE FISCHER

"If I could dig up my mother's grave," 67-yearold serial killer Joe Fischer says in the interview room at Sing Sing. "I'd take out her bones and kill her again." Fischer still believes that much of the misfortune and violence in his life resulted from a curse his mother laid on him almost fifty years ago. "My mother was so evil she put a curse on me. She hated me as much as I hated her. I remember one day we were arguing or she was beating me, and she told me for the rest of my life on Tuesday, I would be cursed and something bad would always happen to me on Tuesday. Fifty years later I still believe this curse exists on me. I wish I could remember how many murders I committed on a Tuesday in my lifetime."

JOE FISCHER'S SYMPTOMS

Joe Fischer fits one of the basic patterns of homicidally enraged individuals that Charles Manson, Henry Lee Lucas, Bobby Joe Long, and Arthur Shawcross belong to: individuals who developed homicidal feelings of rage toward their mothers. By their sons' accounts, both Viola Lucas and Louella Long were prostitutes who brought their johns into the home and transacted business in front of the growing child. (Louella Long had emphatically and consistently denied her son's account.) Fischer describes the exact same pattern. The damage to the basic esteem of a growing child's psyche is almost immeasurable, and nearly always results in some form of moderate to severe dysfunctional behavior in later life. In the presence of other life-threatening catalysts such as head injuries, posttraumatic stress, and alcohol or drug abuse, it is usually always fatal to the adult child and his victims. To have your own nurturer turn against you— which is how the young child interprets what he sees—is devastating. It implants a basic and almost primal rage that can never be satisfied or quenched.

But Fischer's experience is similar to Shawcross's in that he believed that his mother had rejected him or threatened him. When mothers are perceived as threats by their male children, those children can develop deep hostility toward women. Both Fischer and Shawcross fit this pattern and so do their criminal careers. They were driven to violence in different wars in different generations and were subsequently examined by doctors who reported incipient violence in each of them. But the doctors, powerless to intervene, were unable to alter the courses of their lives.

Fischer's career of unremitting violence was ultimately played out during a thirteen-month period from June 1978 to July 1979. Fischer committed forty homicides and robberies in a cross-country murder spree with a killing partner reminiscent of the Depression-era Bonnie and Clyde bank holdups. Fischer was on parole at the time, having just been released from prison in New Jersey after doing twenty-five years for a murder he committed in 1953, that murder taking place just twelve days after he'd been released from prison, where he'd been since 1948. He has only spent about two years outside prison bars since then. Now, dead at sixty-eight while serving a life sentence at Sing Sing and at the

Sullivan County Correctional Facility for the murder of his wife, Claudine, in upstate New York and after having been sentenced to death by lethal injection in Oklahoma (the sentence was later reversed), Fischer was one of the oldest serial killers in the prison system. He was a long-term spree killer, a time bomb who once he began killing never stopped.

Fischer's life story has fascinated interviewers from Geraldo Rivera to Fox's Steve Dunleavy to the BBC. Countless interviewers from television stations, from newspapers, and from European magazines have sat across from him, staring into the heavily tranquilized, blank-faced, tired-looking World War II veteran who looked more like somebody's grandfather than a brutal killer. These interviews, one every two or three months, had gone on for years before Fischer died in September 1991. Occasionally during them one of his massive wreckingball hands would reach up to the tiny white cigarette usually protruding from between the giant cheeks, and the camera would linger on the huge handspread that was the murder weapon in at least ten stranglings. It didn't matter who was interviewing him, or what television station—here or abroad—carried the tape. It was the hands that have fascinated camera operators so much that they lingered on them.

How could a man so passive have been so violent? It's not a question Fischer was able to answer, and when asked by reporters, he would become detached. Fischer barely shrugged, but it was the massive doses of sedatives that kept him under control. During his previous jail terms, he was involved in prison fights and the murder of at least one prison guard. Fischer has had a long history of violence in prison, and correction officials take no chances with him.

Considering the number of murders he's committed, the close scrapes with the law and other felons, and the times he's come close to being executed, Fischer cannot figure out why he is still alive. He's told more than one interviewer that if the "Japs didn't kill me in Iwo, nobody was ever gonna get me." During a typical conversation, even with friends in prison who've known him for years, Fischer dwells on his memories of World War II in the Pacific, his one-man stand against a Japanese machine-gun nest that mowed down his squad as they tried to storm a sand hill, his lobbing hand grenades into the network of enemy tunnels that connected the pillboxes on the hill's crest, and his toe-to-toe shootout with a Japanese officer who tried to rally his men against the crazy marine who wouldn't stop shooting. He was awarded the Bronze Star and two Purple Hearts. These were vivid moments for Fischer, he has said, when killing was legal and they gave you medals for it. Fischer has also described his inability to readjust to society after the war—"killing felt too good to stop." Fischer has also described in detail, as if it were another form of war, his thirty-year prison stretch in the New Jersey system, his thirteenmonth cross-country killing spree, and his career as a hit man for an underworld organization. The times I worked for them were the only times I wasn't drunk when I did my killing."

Even to close friends, in prison, where up until very recently he has been a counselor to violent felons, Fischer has a difficult time describing the extraordinary levels of violence in his household during the 1920s when he was growing up in the "Ironbound" districts of Newark and Belleville, New Jersey. "My mother was a whore," he says. "Pure and simple. My dad would go out to work and she would have boyfriends in. They would give me a nickel or dime—which was a lot in those days—to get lost. But I was a kid. I didn't get lost. I'd watch. I'd watch her fuck them and they'd give her money. I was mad. How could she be doing this to my father? She was a whore. A whore is a whore."

Joe Fischer grew up in a combat zone. "My mother was a physically big woman. She drank and cursed like a steelworker, and she didn't spare the beatings when it came to me. She obviously didn't like my father at all as well because ever since I can remember, she always had men over the house while my father was working. These were johns who paid her good money for her sexual favors. I guess what really helped me hate the woman was that she just didn't care if me or my brothers were home when she brought her customers in. It went on for many years, and as I got older, I became more defiant towards her and she became more abusive toward me. I would have killed her ten times over, but I really believed that would have broken my father's heart. For the longest time I was convinced that my father did not know anything of her true nature. Maybe he found out towards the end, but while it was going on when we were young, I really don't think he knew. There is no doubt in my mind that I could have killed her, and I think I could have done it by the time I was ten years old."

People who are not fueled by the anger that drives human time bombs have a difficult time understanding that anger. But to people like Joe Fischer and to a similar degree Henry Lee Lucas, Bobby Joe Long, Arthur Shawcross, and even Charles Manson, the feedback loop that keeps pumping feelings of hate, self-loathing, and unremitting fury into their psyche is constant and is always threatening to send violence bubbling over the top.

Even to this day, Fischer taps into the deep well of hatred that he says has ultimately driven him to commit all of his crimes. "One cannot believe how much hatred I developed for that whore mother of mine. There is no doubt in my mind now that I do have some mental problems or psychosis and maybe that's why I reacted the way I did to my mother. But she made it really easy for me to hate her and almost every time I'd kill somebody I was trying to get back at her. But it was like I could never get at her enough for what she did and what she was. I would have to keep killing and killing and killing and even then my revenge wouldn't be satisfied."

In families where physical violence and abuse are routinely present, the children often grow up with no sense of personal physical or emotional boundaries. It is as if they are endless, respect no limits in their wants and needs, and respect no rights of other people. Fischer's criminal career reflects this. His propensities toward violence as an adult typify the behavior of a person who grew up in a family where personal boundaries were consistently violated. He describes a situation in which both parents as well as his mother's johns attacked him. Growing up in that environment, it's completely understandable that Fischer's first responses to real or perceived threats would be violence. Absent any intervention in his life and with World War II as the catalyst of his rage, it would be surprising had Fischer not turned into a violent felon. As he remembers it, "Everybody beat everybody else. The whore's boyfriend beat the shit out of me just for the sake of beating the shit out of me. Then when they left, I'd call my mom a whore and she'd beat the shit out of me. Then Dad would come home and he'd beat the shit out of her. One time, the whore grabbed me by the hair and swung me around over her head and bouncing me off the walls. There was blood all over. I must have screamed for my life because my Aunt Florence came running in and grabbed the whore. She let me go and I went flying into the wall. Then my Aunt Florence cursed the whore out terrible. She was the only person who ever watched out for me."

The stories of different time bombs, although ultimately similar in the warning signs and future indicators of dangerousness, differ in the background each had and how each background forged a unique brand of criminal. It is almost as if, in a Dantesque universe, each dysfunction resulted in a related type of serial homicide. In Manson's family it was criminal parental neglect, so Manson formed a family of killers; in Shawcross's family he claimed there was an icy coldness in place of maternal love, so Shawcross became cold and homicidal to his female victims at the point of having sex with them. Fischer grew to adolescence in a war zone. His household was a pitched and furious battle of physical fury. And he grew up just as he had been shaped in this family: violent, bitter, brutal, and mean. He didn't just murder his victims, he savaged them with his bare hands, tearing them apart and breaking their bones. He used whatever weapons were at his disposal as if they were bench tools to shape his handiwork. "I was in trouble from the time I was little. At first it was the kind of stuff any kid from a neighborhood gets into—street fights. Then I went to Catholic school where the nuns would hit you for anything. After what I seen at home, I didn't believe in any of the religion shit they pushed on me. The other kids did. I didn't. I seen the whore with her boyfriends and my dad fighting with her and I couldn't go for the God stuff. Then I began stealing money."

Fischer got into trouble with the law while he was still a juvenile, clashing repeatedly with police and school authorities. He gained a reputation as a troublemaker and was arrested for assault and petty larceny. He stole money from local stores, from other children, and finally from St. Peter's itself. His disciplinary problems became so bad that he was eventually expelled from school. "My dad was a roofer. I always wanted to work with him on the job. One day I was sent home by the nuns and told my dad that now I could work with him all the time. He asked me why. I said that I wasn't going to school no more because they threw me out. He beat the fucking shit out of me. Threw me off walls and loosened half my teeth. Then he took me to the public school and enrolled me. I was mad as hell after that."

His father's response to his son's troubles was a continuation of the same brand of violence that got Joe into trouble in the first place. It is the unremitting nature of that violence that is so appalling to anyone listening to his story. Just the story itself can set a listener on edge. His later career as a serial killer is almost fatalistic—violence begetting violence as a salve for the violence he experienced as a child. The only hope for him would have been to break the cycle of violence, but in the 1940s no one knew about how walking time bombs were created.

Fischer was prosecuted for robbing from the holy jars at St. Peter's Catholic Church and was sent to the state reformatory at Jamesburg in Middlesex County. He continually got into fights at the school, was taught to steal and fence his stolen merchandise by the older inmates there, and was able to get through his sentence without the requisite amount of counseling sessions. His hatred toward others grew more and more intense in the pseudopenitentiary environment of the Depression-era juvenile prison. "Spending time at Jamesburg certainly didn't change my outlook on life, and certainly didn't teach me a lesson, if there was a lesson for me to learn. By the same token, the correction geniuses at Jamesburg never realized what a potential time bomb they had on their hands."

WORLD WAR II

By the time Fischer was released from reform school, he was already realizing his potential for violence. War and his descent into alcoholism would launch him fully into his life as a killer.

Fischer was put on juvenile probation by the court, and he entered the merchant marine in 1938. "I was running away. I was still afraid of getting violent even though I'd already served time in prison." But Fischer went AWOL from the merchant marine a few months after his enlistment, and fled to North Carolina where he was picked up by the local police on a traffic violation and returned to New Jersey. The merchant marine never prosecuted him for being absent without leave—probably because he was underage at the time—and he was sent home to work at odd jobs, work for his father, and try to assimilate himself into adult society. But it was becoming increasingly difficult, and even Fischer soon realized that something was very wrong with him. "I believe now that I was unable to hold a job down though I did not mind working. I also recall I started drinking at that point in my youth." In fact, Fischer's problems with alcohol were becoming so severe that he was rarely able to get through the day without drinking. By the time he enlisted in the marines after the outbreak of World War II, he was on his way to becoming an alcoholic. He drank so heavily in boot camp on Parris Island that he spent his first thirty days in the marines in the brig for frequenting an off-limits saloon. Once he dried out in the tank and returned to a unit, he completed boot camp and was shipped out to California.

"Fortunately for me and unfortunately for the Japanese, World War II broke out. I must admit that my time in the marines—specifically, fighting on these Pacific islands—was one of the happiest times in my life. On several islands, I was part of the assault force, sometimes the first wave, sometimes the second wave. I fought on Kwajalein, Guam, Johnston Island, Guadalcanal, and Iwo Jima. I recall killing many Japanese at various times on these islands. On at least one occasion, it was hand-to-hand combat and, as I learned later on, I was very good with a knife. The marines taught me well."

"I recall on Kwajalein, a pillbox had us pinned down with machine-gun fire. Crawling on my stomach, I made it to nearby the pillbox and began tossing grenades in while I was still under their fire. Fire was coming at me from all directions, considering that the Japanese had tunnels dug all over the place and they could pop out at any given time. I received a medal for that bit of conduct, a Silver Star. I no longer have the medal or any other citations I received. After spending almost forty years in prison, you tend to lose such personal articles in the shuffle. By the time I was sent to China, I had gotten to know what it was like to kill, and even though I had no personal animosity toward the Japanese, they were the enemy and therefore killing them was legal, was recognized, and as a matter of fact, it was welcomed. It was a different story when I got to China. One of my assignments was to guard various trains crossing one end of China to the other—from Tinsing to Peiping. At times, civilians or militia or Communists, whatever, would either try to attack the trains or board them. I can remember on several occasions killing civilian noncombatants like this. I am sure now that there were times it was not necessary to kill these people."

The marines transferred Fischer's unit out of China as the Communists moved in to replace the retreating Japanese. Fischer, because he had been implicated in the deaths of a number of civilians as the situation in Peiping deteriorated, was assigned to Guam to undergo testing at the medical facilities there.

PSYCHIATRIC HOSPITALS AFTER THE WAR

By the end of the war, Fischer had been diagnosed a paranoid schizophrenic by the navy and was classified as extremely dangerous. "I was bugging after all that fighting. I enjoyed the killing, but I was in trouble for killing civilians . . ."

From Guam, Fischer was shipped to the naval hospital at Pearl Harbor and from there to the naval base at Mayo Island in California where he was admitted to the hospital's psychiatric wing for evaluation. But after receiving a routine pass for weekend liberty—"everybody got those passes unless they were in the brig"—Fischer went on a two-week alcoholic bender, hitched a ride east on an interstate transport truck, and woke up in Belleville, New Jersey. "'Where am I?' I think I asked when I looked around," Fischer remembers. "The guy told me, 'You said you wanted to go to New Jersey.' Sure enough, I was in Jersey. I hitched another side to Belleville and walked in on my Aunt Genovese, who was very sick and looked like she was dying."

At first Fischer's father thought he was on leave. But when Fischer told him he had gone AWOL from a mental hospital, his father took him to Newark where he forced him to surrender. "No son of mine goes AWOL," his father said to the military police in Newark when he surrendered his son. Fischer was arrested by the shore patrol and sentenced to time in the brig while the navy decided what to do with him. His pattern of sequential jail time had begun.

"There was a petty officer in charge of the brig in Newark named Chief Cooney," Fischer remembers, "who was talking to me about being in the bughouse. I told him what I'd seen and been through and how I'd got the Silver Star, and he said I belonged in a hospital." On the CPO's referral, prison psychiatrists interviewed Fischer and sent him to Philadelphia Naval Hospital for further psychiatric evaluation. He was deemed homicidally violent and transferred again to a military hospital in Fort Worth. It was here that thorough medical treatment might have helped to prevent this time bomb from turning his rage on civilian society. But the year was 1945, and hospitals were overloaded with veterans who had all types of war injuries. Fischer wasn't looked at as a "sick" person, but as a felon with a previous police record. Therefore, rather than mediating therapy, doctors saw him as a criminal, an alcoholic at a time when alcoholism was considered a moral and not a medical problem, and an unruly individual who refused to conform to the rules. Psychotic violence was not a real medical issue until the 1950s, when Fischer would become the subject of medical experiments designed to alter his behavior. At this point in his life, confining him was the issue, not "curing" him.

At each hospital, Fischer displayed violent outbursts of rage and the medical personnel, rather than try to control him, transferred him out to a different facility. He was finally discharged from the hospital at Forh Worth without having received any meaningful treatment. The marines had had as much of Joe Fischer as they could handle. He received a medical discharge under honorable conditions from the service and sent to a sanatorium in Texas for treatment. But even there, Fischer resisted doctors' attempts to impose an authority over his life. After clashes with the medical personnel and even more outbursts of violence, he was allowed to leave the hospital on his own recognizance. However, in a matter of days, he was arrested for the robbery of a jewelry store in Belleville and placed on probation. Maybe because he was a decorated veteran, maybe because of his psychiatric problems, or maybe because the country was still too flush after the war, the court was never presented a full investigation of Fischer's background. One of the final opportunities for intervening in his life medically before he began his killing spree had been lost.

This is a recurring tragedy in the lives of the time bombs. Most of them have at more than one time in their lives been in a situation where medical intervention might have turned them onto a different path. But because of a variety of reasons, most having to do with the medical profession's frequent failure to understand fully and appreciate the violent nature of individuals under treatment, the opportunity for intervention was lost. The problem in Fischer's case was—and it continues to be—that too few medical professionals actually comprehend the physical and emotional underpinnings of violence. Few medical professionals realize that violence itself is a kind of disease. Just like any other medical condition it had its causes, symptoms, prognosis, and treatment. In Fischer's case, as in the cases of Shawcross, Lucas, and Long, doctors saw these felons, treated them for symptoms related to the violence, but never fully understood the violence itself. All of them subsequently became killers.

Six months after his arrest in Belleville, Fischer was in hot water again. This time, he became charged with, and convicted for, atrocious assault and larceny when he robbed a soldier with a fake gun. At his trial, Dr. Jonathan Kesselman, a criminal psychiatrist, testified that Fischer was a probable psychopath who should remain in prison for the rest of his life. "His history of violence and antisocial attitude make him a threat to society," the psychiatrist said. This was the first clear official warning to the court that standing before a New Jersey judge was not just a thief who threatened a victim with a fake weapon, but a potentially dangerous psychopathic criminal. The psychiatrist's dire warning might have influenced the court to impose a stiff sentence on Fischer, but in the absence of any homicide or attempted murder, the testimony could serve as a warning but little else. Fischer was sentenced to fifteen years at Bordentown.

The New Jersey correctional facility at Bordentown during the 1950s was a medium-security prison where thieves and many first-time felons served their time. It was not for the hard-core violent felons sentenced to jail for much of their remaining lives. Fischer remained under these medium-security conditions for three years before he was transferred to maximum security at the notorious Trenton State Prison after beating up another inmate. From Trenton, Fischer quickly worked his way up to an even higher level of maximum security after a series of inmate fights in Trenton. Fischer had to be transferred to Rahway State penitentiary after fracturing another inmate's skull in a cellblock fight. Rahway, during the 1950s, was considered the last stop for the state's most incorrigible prisoners. At this point in his life, Fischer had become a violent psychotic with a hair-trigger temper. He was oblivious to pain inflicted on him and insensitive to the suffering of others. His wartime experiences in the Pacific and in China, the violence of his upbringing, his pathological hatred of his mother, and his years in a maximum-security prison had turned him into a career criminal. Unfortunately, after five years in one of the toughest cellblocks in the northeast with no readjustment counseling whatsoever—another missed opportunity that he shares with killers like Henry Lee Lucas—Fischer was released back into society. Like Shawcross, Fischer, in effect, went from a war zone into a peaceful society with no period of decompression. He was more a time bomb than ever after his day-to-day fights in the prison yard, but he had gone through no significant counseling to render him fit for life outside prison walls. At first, Fischer has said, he had every intention of starting his life again. But he was drinking heavily again and a new turn of events seized control of his life. What was supposed to be his reentry into society proved only to be the setup for a vicious homicide. It was Christmas, 1953.

MURDER IN NEW JERSEY

Within days after his release, he returned home to the middle of a fight between his parents that indirectly resulted in a homicide and life sentence. "I didn't wait around Rahway, but went right from prison to my parent's house in Belleville, where they were having a fight that had been going on for days. Mom was back to whoring and this time, I think, Dad must have caught her or something. But they were swinging away at each other and I walked right into it. He was beating her up like he was going to kill her, and I didn't want him to get in trouble so I broke it up. Then he turned on me. Started screaming that I hit him, and the whore even took his side. They were both yelling at me like I was a monster and trying to throw me out of the house." It was as if the war years and his years in prison had never occurred. He was right back in the same war zone that had incubated him, and his reactions were those of a violent teenager.

Fischer was horrified and seized by an intense fury when in the midst of the fighting, his mother blurted out that he was just like his father, and that by coming home alive both of them had cheated her out of the money she'd borrowed against their military life insurance. Now she'd have to pay it back herself. That got him out of the house. It was just what he didn't want to hear on the week following his Christmas parole.

Fischer described the events that took place later that night as if they had happened to someone else. Even at the time, they seemed to go by him with a blurring speed. He says that it was bitter cold in New Jersey that night. He was flush with his back pay, most of it in cash because he'd redeemed the war bonds when he got out of prison. He said he tried to get very drunk so he wouldn't go back to the house and kill his mother. Then he blacked out. He remembers getting on a bus in Belleville. And he remembers a sixteen-year-old boy named Powell sitting next to him. The Scotch and rye he'd been drinking since three that afternoon was severely affecting him, blotting out his memory, making him "act stupid like [I] always did before I hurt someone."

Fischer recognized the teenager sitting next to him because he had been around his parents' house before Fischer left for the service. "He was my brother Jackie's friend and they sent him to find me because they were afraid I'd get hurt. I was still pretty sick from all the drugs the doctors had given me in the hospital, and I guess the navy told my father that I was supposed to be a mental patient. Powell told me that my brother didn't want me wandering around in the middle of the night, especially since it was Christmas Eve." Powell stayed on the bus with Fischer until the end of the line. "He was trying to get me to stop drinking and go home and I must've told him that I would because he stayed on with me to the end of the line." Fischer was very drunk and nearly stuporous, but he said he wanted to buy one more bottle to take back with him on the bus. "The kid didn't want me to go. He kept threatening to drag me back on the bus himself. He probably thought I was too drunk to fight him, but he was wrong." Powell followed Fischer out into the night, screaming at him to get back on the bus. He was only a few feet behind Fischer as they crossed an open field, Powell still calling after him, when Fischer suddenly picked up a rock, spun, and brought it down across the top of Powell's skull. Powell fell forward and didn't move. Fischer robbed Powell of his money and personal effects and left him in the field to die.

"I wandered around downtown Newark for days before my uncle came to get me and bring me back. They told me they knew I killed Powell because he was missing and I was the last person to see him. My brother Jackie wouldn't talk to me, but my uncle said the whole thing was the whore's fault. I knew the police would be looking for me."

NEW JERSEY STATE PRISON

Fischer didn't go back to Belleville with his uncle. He stayed in Newark, hoping that his uncle was wrong and hoping that Powell wasn't really dead. When he thought about it, he wasn't sure of anything that had happened that night. He only remembered trying to get away from Powell and waking up in the Newark bus terminal late Christmas afternoon. The place was deserted. That evening, one of his friends from prison in Bordentown told him that the Belleville police wanted to question him in connection with Powell's disappearance. "They don't think he's dead," the former inmate told him. "They just want to know where he is." Fischer was picked up in Newark and interrogated by the Belleville police, and before the afternoon was out, had negotiated a plea bargain with the young Essex prosecutor and future New Jersey governor Brendon Byrne. He was arrested for manslaughter and sentenced to life.

"I began in Trenton State, which was one of the toughest prisons in the system. I was a screwup when I started, always getting into fights and never following the system." Within months after beginning his sentence, he stabbed a black inmate who tried to approach him sexually, and he spent a full year in "the box," Trenton State's isolation cell for dangerous inmates, while the man he stabbed waited for Fischer's return to his cell. There would be a score to settle. But prison officials realized that Fischer was involved in a racial attack and could never return to the general inmate population. They transferred him to Rahway where he would be somebody else's problem.

"Things didn't get no better at Rahway," Fischer says. But his reputation as a fighter had preceded him and, during the months of racial tension at New Jersey prisons, he found himself courted by Rahway's organized-crime community, inmates who were alleged to have had ties with New Jersey's vast network of underworld crime families. Fischer was an Italian from the Newark neighborhoods that were run by the local capos. He had never worked for the mob, but had never crossed them. Therefore, he was considered "good people" and recruited for the mob inside prison. "There were a lot of wise guys at Rahway in the '50s who really ran the prison. I played cards with a real big shot on the inside. One day this stooge ratted him out to federal investigators and was put in protective custody. I told the mobster, 'Never mind, I'll take care of him.' Right before his time was out, I got ahold of him in the kitchen and kept hitting him in the head and cutting his face until he stopped fighting. I wanted to give him scars to remind him what he did every time he looked in the mirror. Then I stomped on his back. I wanted to leave him a cripple so he'd always have pain. That's the best way to teach someone a lesson they'll remember." In fact, Fischer had effectively paralyzed the man from the waist down for the rest of his life.

Fischer's crime was so violent that he was transferred to the infamous Vroom Building in Trenton, the criminal psychiatric wing of Trenton State Psychiatric Hospital. Fischer claims that inmates there were routinely punished for infractions of the arbitrary and capriciously enforced rules.

THE VROOM BUILDING

Fischer spent ten years as a patient in prison rotation at Trenton Psychiatric. After the completion of each medical cycle he would be released from the psychiatric hospital and returned to the prison population, only to commit another violent crime and be returned to the hospital for more treatment. "It was like I was a guinea pig," he said. "There were times I couldn't even remember my name." As his behavior became more violent, the treatment became more and more orientated toward sedation. For much of the early 1960s, Fischer remembers walking around the eighth floor of the Vroom Building in a drug-induced state.

"I remember waking up in a hospital bed wet from my own piss and with a pain somewhere in my head. I'd be all swollen in my joints and my throat would be closed tight. I couldn't even swallow or talk. I was strapped to the bed. Sometimes an orderly would give me water and a bedpan. Sometimes, I just stayed in bed and pissed in the sheets. Sometimes, if you pissed, they'd give you something to put you asleep again."

Fischer became lethargic and no longer cared about confronting staff members and other inmates. He knew he'd been changed. "Fighting didn't matter to me no more," he remembers. "It was like waking up from a drunk and not caring much. So I did whatever they told me to do and didn't fight with anyone. If somebody pushed me around, I just walked away. If I had a cigarette and somebody else took it, I didn't fight him or nothing. They began letting me alone."

Fischer was able to maintain enough control during his interviews with the psychiatrists to convince them that his behavior had permanently changed, that their therapy had worked, that he was a docile inmate who could be processed through the system without the danger of another explosion. They assigned him to permanent duties on the ward and continued interviewing him until they were satisfied he could be transferred back to the prison population. They had made him into a permanent inmate of a high-security prison. But fortune smiled on Joe Fischer just as he was contemplating his fate. Fortune visited him, Fischer says, in the person of Dr. William King, one of the state's leading criminal psychologists.

King, one of the Vroom Building psychiatrists who had taken a particular interest in Fischer's case and who had scheduled follow-up interviews even after Fischer had been shipped back to Trenton Sate Prison, repeatedly asked that Joe consider him a friend. "I understand what happened to you," he kept telling him. According to Fischer, after months of postclinical treatment, King asked Fischer to find him someone who could fulfill a murder contract on his former wife, her husband, and her sister. In those private interviews with King, protected because King's own interests were at stake, Joe Fischer saw his way out of the maximum-security prison. He saw his way to "soft time," to a way he might even escape, to a way he could get revenge on the system. Thus, Fischer claims he continued to set up King, leading him along to the point where King was even begging him to set up the hit. Fischer knew he had King hooked.

Fischer claims he and another inmate contacted the New Jersey State Police, who agreed to recommend them for parole if they participated in a sting operation to trap the psychiatrist into giving execution money to an undercover cop. Within six months the trap was set and King had been conned into setting up a meeting with a hit man who was really a state police detective. King was caught, the case made the major newspapers, and eventually Fischer was transferred out of Trenton and into the minimum-security prison work farm known as Jones Farm. (King pleaded not guilty by reason of temporary insanity, was convicted, and then managed to get his conviction overturned because of "excesses" by prosecution.)

At Jones Farm, the rules were different. Inmates were like trustees, who accepted their incarceration and worked until the day they earned their freedom. Unlike the maximum-security prisons, there was little inmate violence or brutality. Inmates wanted to stay at Jones Farm because it was easier time. Therefore, the cardinal rule was observed: "You don't cross the line." On Fischer's first day off the prison bus, the warden pointed to a white line that separated the prison from the outside world. There was no fence. "Cross that line," the warden explained to Fischer, "and you're an escapee. We'll catch you and throw you right back in the penitentiary. Stay on this side of the line and you'll walk out of here a free man."

Two months later Fischer walked right over the line and escaped. He remembers getting drunk the first time he left the prison and fleeing to New York where he and his companions caught a northbound train out of Grand Central Station. He fled to New Hampshire where he remembers killing a man at a railroad station and stealing his wallet. He and his companions then took a bus to Portland, Maine, where he murdered a prostitute on a dark street because she reminded him of his mother. He also remembers having killed another woman in a park and a man along a waterfront. He can't remember the specific motivations for each homicide, only that he was drunk and that killing was his only reaction to encountering strangers.

Fischer eventually returned to Belleville, where he was recognized immediately, arrested, and returned to custody; extra years were added to the minimum sentence he would have to complete before becoming eligible for parole. But he was allowed to remain at Jones Farm because the state still wanted to protect him from prison officials still angry at him for his having worked to incriminate William King at Trenton. However, Fischer explains that he was an incorrigible prisoner and he escaped from Jones Farm a second time. This time he headed for San Francisco, where he believed he wouldn't be recognized, but started drinking heavily immediately upon his arrival. He blacked out again—alcohol rendered him stuporous but violent—and only vaguely remembers awakening one morning from a drunk in the Haight-Ashbury section of the city. He says that he killed one man on Howard Street, another on Heath Street, and another in a gay bar during his alcoholic bender in California. The man in the gay bar came on to him, he says. "I think I cut his penis off and stuffed it in his mouth," he has said. "But I can't be sure. I was drunk like I was for all of my killings. I remember I headed south and met up with some guys at a motel in San Diego who were staying there with a couple of girls. We got into a fight over the girls and I killed them. Then I met up with a pair of sailors and their girls and

I killed them, too. The police were after me and I headed east."

Fischer went to Florida where, again, he believed he wouldn't be recognized, but he was still drunk and violent. He says that he woke up one morning in a hotel in Jacksonville and remembered having shot and stabbed a young couple and stealing their money the night before. He claims he fled from the Florida State Police and went from Jacksonville to Pittsburgh, where he robbed another man, shot him, and dumped him in one of the three rivers that meet just south of the center of town. As his lust for drinking and killing wound down, Fischer again headed back to Belleville, New Jersey, where he knew he would be captured and probably put back in one of the state's penitentiaries, but he wanted to be free of the burden of remaining on the outside, he explains.

PAROLE; MURDER, INC.; AND FORTY-STATE KILLING SPREE

Fischer was remanded to the state prison at Clinton, where he got a job in the prison kitchen working at night and staying out of the general prison population during the day. His reputation for having exacted retribution for the mobster upon a prison snitch at Rahway also followed him to Clinton and protected him against attacks from younger inmates who had begun to show up in the prison population since 1970. Fischer was the elder statesman of the prison now, schooled in the ways of state penitentiaries since the end of World War II and a survivor of the psychiatric hospital for the criminally insane. He had already become a legend.

Joe Fischer had learned to play the game, to keep his head down and his mouth shut. He went from challenging the system at every level to accommodating himself to it, as if he understood that someday the system would spit him out the other end. His time would soon come, he told himself at the time, and the change in his behavior had become apparent. To people who knew him during that period, Fischer says, he seemed different. The homicidal rage that would spring up in him at the slightest provocation seemed abated somewhat. Actually, he says, the effects of long-term alcoholism had begun to take their toll. Even the prison psychiatrists, who had kept him at arm's length because they feared him, began to trust him just a little. For the first time in his life at Clinton, he began to talk about his mother, albeit with great difficulty. This might have been an opportunity for some of his homicidal rage to have been addressed, for an intervention that might have saved the lives of his future victims. But the prison system was inundated with new inmates, struggling to cope with the large population of drug addicts who were being sentenced, and simply did not have time for an aging old rummie who'd fought in the World War. But unlike the younger inmates, Fischer had labor skills—his father had been a roofer; he had worked in a construction company. Therefore, rather than send him for medical help, the prison officials at Clinton—a rural facility in the foothills of northwestern New Jersey near the Pennsylvania border—decided to rehabilitate him through work therapy.

Prison logic, Fischer eventually came to understand, was and continues to be unlike any other logical system. It functions under its own rules, satisfies its own political considerations, and is driven by the basic premise that no one wants to be in prision, not even the warden. Therefore, whatever relieves the pressure is implemented, even if the results are deadly. If people are killed inside the prison walls, that is the warden's fault. Therefore, if someone is going to be a killer—and in prisons, Fischer finally understood, there are always killers—it was important to make sure whoever was a killer did his killing on the outside. Prisons, Fischer will explain to anybody who will listen to him, are meant to protect the people who run them, not people on the outside. Therefore, Fischer, probably one of the most brutal killers in

the history of the New Jersey state prison system, was made
a trustee as soon as possible. Shawcross was also a trustee
during his time at Auburn, and Henry Lee Lucas was a
trustee during part of his time in his Michigan penitentiary.
This is how walking time bombs slip through the system, get
out of prison, and kill again. This will continue to happen
until the prison officials understand the medical nature of violence and appreciate that prisons in and of themselves cannot control it.

Near the end of his time at Clinton, inmate trustee Joe
Fischer was allowed to leave the prison to perform construction and yardwork for local residents. He had access to people's homes and used it to obtain liquor and other items he
could smuggle back into the prison cell to the inmates for
cash. He also began drinking heavily again. In fact, as he
made the rounds of different houses, he would systemati-
cally drink all the liquor from his employers' homes and replace it with water. What he didn't drink himself, he brought
back to prison. Prison officials discovered the large amounts
of contraband on their routine searches of inmate cells, and
Fischer was busted and thrown back in the lockup for selling
booze. Eventually, however, the people he worked for supported his parole application, and Fischer himself was able
to show that although he had access to money and guns in
the houses where he worked, he only drank and sold the alcohol. Finally, in June 1978, after having served twenty-five
years for his Belleville homicide and related charges and
having experienced ten years of drug therapy, Joe Fischer
was officially turned loose on society. He had become a free
man.

The terms of his parole required that he remain in the
state of New Jersey, and his parole board had arranged for
him to live at a Salvation Army shelter. However, Fischer
had never really been rehabilitated. He should never have
been released; even he admits that to friends and interviewers. He was incapable of adhering to a parole contract because he was incapable of following any rules that didn't

carry with them the threat of immediate punishment. Once on his own, Fischer simply reverted to his old ways. Within the month, he had left New Jersey. He married his seventy-year-old pen pal, Claudine Eggers, and went to visit her in a trailer in upstate New York. He had violated his parole and began a thirteen-month odyssey of drinking and continued violence that would end with the murder of his wife. Fischer was still a walking time bomb, still a threat to anyone who crossed his path, a threat to anyone who placed any trust in him. All the years of prison had done nothing to treat the violence, fury, and hatred that was still eating away at what was left of him. He had existed on violence and only violence; now he would make his living at it. For the first time in his life, he turned professional.

MURDER, INC.

Shortly after his marriage, Joe began working for underworld figures, carrying out contract killings that were arranged by his contacts from Rahway State Prison. They were also set up by a man named "Louie," an inmate at Rahway and Trenton State who said he worked for organized crime families in New Jersey. Louie got Joe a hotel room at an old hotel near Madison Avenue and East 29 Street in New York City and set him up with a string of prostitutes from the nearby Third Avenue strip. But because of Fischer's deep hatred of prostitutes—they all reminded him of his mother, he said—he killed most of them and dumped their bodies in upstate New York and Connecticut. When questioned by the Connecticut State Police abut the bodies of the two prostitutes that were dumped along side the Merritt Parkway, Fischer maintained that he was in New Jersey at the time the bodies were dumped. The Salvation Army, where Joe was still "living," even though he was leaving the state whenever he wanted to, didn't contradict his story. He was there, they told the Connecticut State Police, when he was supposed to be there. The state police decided that there was no further evidence that would allow them to pursue a homicide investigation even though Fischer was a convicted murderer who was suspected of violating his parole at the time. The case was dropped for lack of evidence, and Fischer's career of savagery continued. Clearly, this was another missed opportunity, another point of intervention that was allowed to slip by.

Shortly after killing the prostitutes, Fischer moved to a bungalow in Keansburg at the New Jersey shore where Louie sold drugs and Fischer contracted four more homicides. He received a contract from Louie—"Louie told me, 'These guys gotta get hit'"—for a double homicide that precipitated his flight from New Jersey. Fischer killed both men and left their bodies at the rented house. Now he was on the run from the law again, this time officially. First he fled to Cooperstown, where he stayed in the trailer with Claudine until he came back to New York City to deal drugs, rob neighborhood drug distributors in the South Bronx, and knock over cash-laden neighborhood loan companies and check-cashing services. He was making $8,000 to $10,000 per job; he was also drinking and killing, and he had a "safe house" up in Cooperstown where the elderly and lonely Claudine believed she was being supported by the pen pal who had been so kind to her after his release from jail that he married her. She never even realized he was on parole and couldn't leave New Jersey.

During this period when he was committing crimes and then fleeing to Cooperstown to hide out, Fischer says, he and Louie undertook a murder spree in the South Bronx over the course of a weekend in which they robbed drug dealers of their cash, killed them, and left their bodies in alleys. When he felt the police were closing in, he and Louie took a Greyhound bus to Oklahoma City, where Fischer found work making pizzas and took roofing jobs while he waited for Louie to scare up more contracts from the *caporegimes* he knew in the organized-crime families.

"Going to Oklahoma was like a dream," Fischer says. People in the bus didn't know about his past and didn't treat him like a monster or a geek in a carnival sideshow. After a month and a half, when he got bored, he returned to Claudine in Cooperstown. Finally Louie reappeared with money on another contract hit, and the two went off to St. Louis to murder two guys who, according to the talk on the neighborhood streets, had stolen money from one of the local syndicate bosses. Joe and Louie caught up with them just as they were trying to leave St. Louis, took them to the basement playroom of a house they had rented, shot them in the head, and left them for the police to find. He was never even suspected in this crime.

Now Joe began to move around the country, in and out of alcoholic stupors, and got himself caught up in a wave of killings and robberies. He'd described his thirteen-month drunk as an ordeal in which he'd wake up to occasional lucid blue-sky mornings with blood all over his hands only to start drinking by midday and lapse back into a black sleep that would envelop him for weeks. Once, he awoke in San Francisco with vague memories of having murdered a young man in Redwood City the night before. Or had it been the week before? Or when he escaped from Jones Farm ten years earlier? He really didn't know. He could see that the scars from the piano wire he remembered using were still fresh across his palms, but when he went to the park in Redwood City where he thought the homicide had taken place, there was no sign of a crime. Maybe he'd buried the body. Maybe he'd dumped the body somewhere else. Then he saw a familiar-looking knobby tree and remembered having tied the body to a tree trunk while it struggled. But it was all a daze.

He claimed to have been involved with the kidnappers of the missing SoHo child Etan Patz: "They were connected to the mob," he says. "And worked out of Fort Worth." But Fischer claims that his calls to Manhattan DA Robert Morgenthau did not result in any contact and that his information on the case was never pursued. Then he reversed himself and said he had told the Etan Patz story to fool the F.B.I. He claims to have raped and killed a young girl and her boyfriend in Oregon, to have shot four local Texas police officers at a roadblock set up to catch him, and to have killed a driver he hitched a ride with in Nevada. He remembers killing a wino in Seattle near a bar when they both were drunk and fighting over what was left in a bottle. He beat the man with his bare hands until he crushed his windpipe. Then he stabbed him to make sure he was dead. He remembers a night of murder in Denver when he went from bar to bar, picking up prostitutes, robbing them, and stabbing them. The third, he says, he stabbed in the park, because the bodies of his two earlier victims that night had made his hotel room too crowded. He finally recalls stabbing a prostitute in downtown St. Louis and then shooting her boyfriend who was also her pimp. Finally he remembers a lonely cabin outside Bangor, Maine, where he killed people he met at a local bar. He robbed them and buried their bodies in a mass grave which, he says, is probably still there just outside Bangor. There are at least thirteen people buried in that grave, he claims, and all of the crimes he committed there are listed as unsolved missing persons. But it is a blur, all of it, only images and impressions, memories that come to him in the early hours of the morning before he realizes who he is and where he is.

His thirteen-month spree came to an end in July 1979, when he appeared at the NYPD's 24th Precinct to surrender himself for the murder of nineteen people, including his wife. Claudine Eggers's death was the one crime, Fischer says, he never committed. He's convinced that Louie did it, but Louie is dead and his story can never be corroborated. Whether Fischer is telling the truth about his wife's death is something that only he will know for sure. His lawyer, New Jersey tax attorney John Libretti, claims that since Joe had confessed to every murder he had ever remembered, it stands to reason that he wouldn't deny a murder he has committed. Libretti's logic is persuasive. However, part of the mystery surrounding Claudine's murder is the mystery of why Fischer married her in the first place.

Claudine Eggers was a lonely old woman who had adopted Joe Fischer through the mail. They were pen pals for almost twenty years while he was in prison in New Jersey. She gave him emotional support through the mail—a very important element in the life of an inmate—and offered to help set him up if he was ever granted freedom. When he was released, she was the first person Joe turned to for help. She offered to marry him in order to stabilize him on the outside. But she let him have his freedom and he sent her money. It was a convenient arrangement. Joe feels that Louie might have killed her for the money she kept in the trailer.

Over the course of the next year, while New York State charged him with the murder of Claudine Eggers, convicted him after a lengthy psychological defense in court, and sentenced him to life in Sing Sing, Fischer confessed to over forty murders around the country—one of which resulted in his receiving a death-by-lethal-injection sentence from an Oklahoma court. He has since tried to help families of some of his victims find the bodies. In some cases, Fischer's testimony is the only evidence the police have that a crime even took place.

LIFE SENTENCE: REHABILITATION AND RESTITUTION

"Sing Sing was the first place I felt like wanted to be a human," Fischer said about the prison that he thought would be his home for the rest of his life. Fischer worked as a counselor in the prison, assisting the psychiatrist in dealing with younger, violent felons who will eventually be returned to the streets. This was the first time Fischer has ever made anything even remotely like a contribution to a system and it began having profound effects on him within a year. He claimed to have adopted three or four young offenders, helping them navigate through the prison system, and getting them jobs on the outside after they were paroled. Fischer had also been a recovering alcoholic since 1980 and reports that his memory is coming back in bits and pieces. He was even able to talk about his mother and the hatred that drove him to commit his crimes. He also realized that he could never be returned to society. Fischer was aware that what happened inside of him had been in place too long for him to return to the world. He completely adapted to life behind bars. The prison rules, the strict conformity to a military lifestyle, had become his entire world. Without the extreme regulation of prison, Fischer realized that he would be unable to survive. "I know what I feel inside," he said. "There is still too much hate. It burns inside of me. I should have been executed a long time ago. I killed people with my bare hands. I belong in jail. They should never let me out as long as I live. I'd only go back to doing what I did before."

JOE FISCHER AS A WALKING TIME BOMB

People who have seen both Joe Fischer and Arthur Shawcross are struck not only by how similar they look but by how similar their demeanors are to one another. Both appear passive, as if sullenly guilty for all of their crimes. Both move slowly, as if the processing of neuromotor impulses takes forever in their sluggish systems. But for both, the surface passivity belies an intensity of hatred that can well up at any moment they perceive threats or their invisible triggers are pulled by someone who reminds them of their mothers. Both men have been drained of their resiliency by abuse of alcohol and both have been traumatized by seeing their mothers turn on them as if they were enemies. Exactly like Henry Lee Lucas, another career serial killer and time bomb whose mother turned on him and who was reported to have engaged in prostitution, Fischer felt his deepest feelings of intense violence toward women.

When a young child's mother becomes the enemy, when the mother withdraws love and nurturing and replaces it with something as seemingly innocuous as coldness, it is a virtual guarantee that the child will grow up with a basic lack of trust and misperception of human boundaries. These are the earliest and some of the most critical steps in the development of a human time bomb.

The intervention of the educational system can help. Intervention from friends, family members, or even healthcare or community agencies can help. But the basic pattern, once established, can never be erased. It can only be overcome by an individual who recognized that basic nurturing was missing in his life and makes up for it by trying to nurture himself. However, when the individual is savaged by brutal domestic abuse, violated sexually, and taught to equate survival with pain and revenge, the child almost always turns to violence as it gets older. This is how time bombs get molded.

Joe Fischer carried this violence to exponential proportions. His adolescent reliance on alcohol impaired his neurological system early and permanently, as it does in most young heavy drinkers. Chemical damage done at this stage often impairs the resiliency of the drinker as well, making it exceedingly difficult for him to handle primal emotions of fear and rage and to respond to real or perceived threats with anything less than animal violence. This is what happened to Joe Fischer.

When this type of ticking time bomb enters into a particularly stressful life-and-death situation, such as the World War II assaults on Iwo Jima, the Marshalls, and other islands, the immediate threats to his existence combined with his lack of normal social controls turns him into a killing machine. This is what also happened to Shawcross in Vietnam. In the absence of any sort of intervention, when this person is unleashed upon society, the same reactions that he learned during the war are entirely in place. Thus, from the moment that Fischer was released from the service, he was committing crimes and escalating to homicide.

Prison was another major element in the Fischer story. The daily violence of the prison environment, the arbitrary enforcement of rules by the guards, the confrontations between inmates, and the gang rules of order that every prisoner had to adhere to kept him wary and distrustful of everything. We can only guess at the number of people who fell victim to him while he was on the loose after being paroled.

John Libretti, Fischer's lawyer and friend, reports that Fischer had begun contacting police in places he remembered he killed to locate missing persons so that he could put the facts together in his own mind. He believed by the end of his life that at least a limited amount of retribution was possible. Joe Fischer died of a heart attack at the Sullivan County Correctional Facility in September, 1991.

5

THE SHORT HOT SUMMER
OF BOBBY JOE LONG

There are two versions to the Bobby Joe Long story. Captain Gary Terry of the Hillsborough County Sheriff's Office in Tampa, Florida, tells one of them. In his task force report, he writes that the "grisly" serial murders were finally stopped by the efforts of homicide detectives who combed the crime scene for physical clues to the murders and abduction of ten women in an eight-month period of time. After they had an eyewitness, a victim who had been abducted, raped, and then released by Bobby Joe Long, the detectives were able to piece together the remaining evidence to build a case against the serial killer who is now on death row in Stark, Florida. Gary Terry's version is a description of the task force ideal, different law-enforcement agencies working together to stop a brutal serial killer on the loose.

Bobby Joe Long himself tells a different story about why his killing spree started and how it came to an end. It wasn't the detectives who caught him, he says, even though they were in such hot pursuit during the final week he could sometimes see them in his sideview mirror just down the street. The way Long characterizes it, he just plain gave up. The tension was too great, the pain too severe, the self-revulsion too powerful to withstand any longer. In the end, he hated himself more than his victims and realized that either by suicide or arrest, his homicidal career would have to come to an end. At the tail end of a killing spree that seemed like an endless strip of psychological agony, Bobby Joe Long met a victim whose own tragedy broke his fantasy. It was the tragedy of this victim that forced him to stare directly into the horror of bis own hopeless existence. At that point, he says, knowing she would run directly to the police, he decided to set her free.

When Bobby Joe Long spotted the pretty young woman bicycling home from her shift at the doughnut shop in North Tampa, he had already decided he'd killed enough. For seven months, as he described it, he'd been on a wild binge of rape and murder that loosely followed the cycle of the full moon. He picked up "whores and sluts" in the strip bars around the North Tampa strip, drove them to stretch of deserted road in the rural countryside outside town, raped them, strangled them to death, and then left their remains strewn along the side of the tarmac. The local sheriff's office was stymied and assembled a task force of state police, Florida Bureau of Law Enforcement detectives, and consultants from the Behavioral Science Unit of the FBI.

Bobby reveals that his decision to let the girl free was an act of surrender. "I knew when I let her go that it would only be a matter of time," he remembers. "I didn't even tell her not to talk to the police or anything. And before her, when I first read about the task force in Tampa, I could have gone to Fort Lauderdale or anywhere else and they would have never found me. Hell, I knew exactly what they were doing and when they were doing it. You could see the police cars all over the place. I just stayed out of sight until I let her out of my apartment. Then it was all over. I just didn't care anymore, and I wanted to stop. I was sick inside. Doesn't the fact that I could have run and didn't count for something?"

During the entire period of his skein of murders, Bobby Joe Long lived and worked among the residents of Tampa as if he were just another one of the young guys trying to scratch out a living and find a girlfriend. He dated lots of different girls, worked at whatever jobs he could, and even tried to pursue a career as an X-ray technician. He tried as best as he could to satisfy a sex drive that had gone beyond compulsion. Long knew that a part of his personality was no longer working. He knew that ever since the massive head injuries he had received in a motorcycle ten years earlier, things just weren't the same inside him. Connections had been broken, circuits had overloaded, two and two no longer equaled four. He lost his temper easily. Loud or sudden noises sent him into a fury. He became violent with little or no provocation and took his frustration and anger out on anybody around him.

BOBBY JOE LONG'S CHILDHOOD

Bobby Joe Long has said that he always had a problem with women. He has always been fearful that women would take him over. Even when he was a child he was afraid that he would turn into a woman, and that would have been the worst punishment of all because from the earliest times he could remember, Bobby Joe Long says, he hated women. That was why he became so petrified when he realized he was growing breasts.

Eleven-year-old Bobby Joe Long didn't understand it, but when he reached puberty he began turning into a girl. At least that's what it seemed like. His breasts became abnormally large, swelling up and becoming tender, and he began to feel ashamed and foolish. He could look down in the mornings before school and see his enlarged nipples filling out his shirt right through the breast pockets. When he ran in gym, his breasts would shake up and down. Other children at school teased him about it. He was in a fury about that. His clothing became tight and looked ill-fitting as it stretched around his chest and spread at the seams over his enlarged buttocks. His mother reminded him that other male members of his family had experienced this congenital dysfunction of the endocrine system when they reached puberty. She brought him to a doctor she knew, who prescribed surgery. Bobby's mother recalled that the surgeon removed more than six pounds of tissue from her son's chest. That remedied his physical appearance, but it didn't keep him from experiencing a lunar protomenstrual cycle for the rest of his life.

"Even now," he recalls, "I can always tell when it's the full moon, I get crazy when the moon is full. I can't sit still. I have to pace. Even the smallest thing sets me off."

Long's youthful fear of being transformed into a woman reinforced the many problems he had relating to women throughout his life. Like the vast majority of convicted serial killers and prostitute murderers, Bobby Joe's early life was dominated by his mother.

When he was two, his mother divorced his father and took her son to Florida. They were very poor, both Louella and Bobby Joe recall, and lived just barely at the subsistence level. They rented single-occupancy rooms in motels and boardinghouses where there was only one bed in the room. Thus they had to share the facilities that were available. But the two of them remember this period of their lives very differently.

Mother and son shared the same beds even while Bobby was growing to puberty, both Bobby and Louella explain. They never actually slept together, Louella claims, because she worked nights and he went to school during the day. They slept in shifts—he at night and she during the day—and it was as if they had different beds. Louella concedes it was different raising a growing boy in a hotel room.

"I never undressed in front of him or did anything anyone would consider indecent," Louella Long explains. "We just didn't have the money to rent two bedrooms or even put up a fold-up cot in the room." She also denies that she ever slept in the same bed with her son. "I'd get home from work at five or six in the morning. By the time I was getting undressed to go to bed, Bobby was getting dressed and ready for school."

But for Bobby Joe Long, as it might have been for any elementary-school-age boy, sharing a bed with his mother on a regular basis was inappropriate behavior. It was, as some family therapists such as John Bradshaw and Jim Mastrich have written, the inappropriate crossing of personal and sexual boundaries. Children don't make distinctions about who is tired and who isn't, they only know when boundaries are crossed at the wrong time for what they perceive are the wrong reasons. Today, child psychologists refer to the problem as emotional incest. Bobby himself didn't know what to feel except uncomfortable and then angry. It might have been from just this perceived violation of boundaries that Bobby Joe's problems began. In his mind he thought he had been violated. He thought he had become the victim of a type of emotional abuse. As a child, a time bomb mechanism had been put into place.

Bobby claims that his mother also brought her boyfriends home with her from time to time. He says that she would stay out all night with different men. Other times, he says, Louella entertained men at home. Louella Long, however, denies ever bringing men over to where the two lived.

The most unfortunate aspect of Bobby Joe Long's perceptions of his childhood is that they don't have to be accurate to be real. Louella Long may have been a lonely woman living on the absolute precipice of poverty and desperately trying to preserve the little bit of family she had left. She may have been overprotective, and in her steps to scrimp wherever possible, she may have inadvertently breached an invisible boundary set up by Bobby Joe. What for Bobby Joe was sexually inappropriate behavior may have been for Louella simply a way to save money—double duty for a single bed. If this were the only troubling event in Bobby Joe's disastrous life, he might have never turned violent. But it wasn't. The child within him had been lost—whether in truth or in his screen memory—and the subsequent and consequent loss of personal resiliency made him vulnerable to the accidents and catastrophes that later befell him.

For her part Louella Long denies that she ever did anything sexually inappropriate. But again, it may not even matter at all, because only Bobby's perceptions of his mother's presence and his fear of his mother's encroachment need be active for a child to feel violated. But the reality of their family situation was that they were always on the move as she changed jobs frequently and kept them one step ahead of the bill collectors and the sheriff.

"We were very poor and had to live on the tips I could make waitressing or carhopping," she says. "There were times when I didn't even know where I would get the money, afraid we'd be living in the street. But no matter what Bobby Joe or anyone says, I was never a prostitute, and I tried to be a good mother." She was always looking for new work, especially where she could get a few more bucks for food and better lodging. As a result, Bobby was never in one place long enough to make real friends or establish any relationships with peers. He learned not to expect anything from friends, because he knew he would have to leave them. He learned not to trust in any situation, because he was always transitory, a member of a migrant family, a child who had fallen through the bottom of the social fabric while America enjoyed its affluent sixties. He was always the new kid in the neighborhood and was forced to rely on his mother for any companionship and friendship. Eventually this situation aroused extreme rage in him when his mother navigated in and out of relationships with older men who only saw Bobby as a nuisance and a distraction.

Thus two important components of a "time bomb" syndrome were present in Bobby Joe's psychology while he was still too young to do anything about them: He felt encroached upon by his mother and felt shame as a result; and he was completely rootless, a child without a home. He had no basis to establish community or identity, and became ashamed of that as well. A third component had to do with

Bobby Joe's developing sexuality, a time bomb in any family that the family itself defuses as part of its natural development. However, because Bobby Joe had no family, his sexuality was more difficult for him to understand and it was exacerbated by his hormonal condition which, in effect, made him feel like he was a young pubescent girl.

As Bobby began to realize his own sexuality, he faced men who were not his father, men who he perceived were taking away his mother's loyalty, men to whom Louella's affections for her son posed a threat. These conflicting emotions are difficult to deal with in any divorced family where young boys grow to adolescence in the presence of a mother who is dating men not their fathers. Therapy often helps, the adolescents' emerging awareness of their own identities is a necessity, and the intervention of a community and school forms a support structure. This is how our stock, standard, off-the-shelf community infrastructure is supposed to work. But it did not work for Bobby Joe Long, who had no community, no emerging sense of self, no siblings, no friends, no real schoolmates or chums, and no adolescent pride in his own masculinity. Instead he thought he was turning into a girl. In this way, what might have been a turning point in his life was more than a missed opportunity, it was an absolute wrong turn down a path that led to self-hatred, shame, guilt, and rage. It was another component of a human time bomb, an eventual prostitute killer.

When his mother had nights off, Long remembers, he would ask her to spend time at home with him. "But she would never stay home. She would always go out. I used to ask her why she couldn't spend her nights off with me. Take me out once in a while. But she always had her dates. Her boyfriends. And I'd have to stay with one of the neighbors." Even worse that the loneliness, as Long reached adolescence, was the bed he and his mother shared. For him it was shameful, embarrassing, and humiliating. For Louella it was a matter of economic necessity.

Many serial killers are so dominated by the presence of

their mothers, they perceive their father only through their mother's eyes. Accordingly most, if not all, male serial killers have complained that their fathers were rendered weak and ineffective by the mother. This theme plays out in the lives of Arthur Shawcross, Joe Fischer, Henry Lee Lucas, and Bobby Joe Long. In actuality, Long had little or no contact with his father. Bob Long, Sr., had not spent time with his son since 1956, when Louella moved out of the house, except for a visit in 1968, when Louella divorced her second husband. "They would come back to Kenova on Christmas or some other times, and I would see them. But for the most part, I didn't see Bobby Joe at all when he was growing up," Long, Sr., remembers.

During his trial for murder, Bobby testified that on several occasions when he was younger, Bob Long, Sr., would visit his family in Florida, where he would get into violent arguments with Louella, attack her sexuality, and threaten her and their young son with a knife. Long denied in court records that he had ever actually threatened anyone but remembers having "conversations" with Louella about returning to West Virginia with him. Again, the important point about Bobby Joe Jr.'s testimony may lie more in the perception than in the actuality. If Bobby Joe believed his father was threatening his mother and him, that became the reality for him even if the truth was far less menacing.

Today, Long, Sr., who has since remarried Louella and owns a fundamentalist Christian bookstore in West Virginia, speaks about his son with sadness and misery. He laments over the missed opportunities in Bobby's life, understands what his son must have gone through during those years, and describes Bobby as a "life misused." Like Louella, however, Long, Sr., blames most of his son's misfortunes on Bobby's wife, Cindy. Louella is even more direct. "Bobby was the perfect cute little boy," she says. "He was good and made good grades in school. Then he met Cindy."

Bobby began dating Cindy Jean Guthrie, a girl who lived just a few blocks away from him, when he was thirteen years old. He would marry her seven years later and turn her into the "other woman" who would become the next dominant person in his life. Observers at the Long trial were awestruck by the physical resemblance between Cindy and Louella Long and the similarities of their demeanors. Both women are petite, thin, and fair-skinned, and they have voices that sound almost identical with one another. Each blames the other for the problems in Bobby's life. "Cindy and I were inseparable at first," Bobby recalls. "She would be over at our house, or I would be at hers. We were always together." From time to time, they would break up, date other people, but drift back together again. Eventually they married and stayed together for five years and two children. But even after they divorced, Cindy remained the most important person in his life and will be one of the two women in mourning if he is executed.

Bobby said that Cindy became his second mother. She took over where Louella left off. Friends of the two of them have described her as forceful, insistent, aggressive, and domineering. She appeared in Bobby Joe's life at precisely the time when his mother was getting married to her second husband. Louella would later divorce him and remarry Bobby Joe Long, Sr. For thirteen-year-old Bobby, Jr., who was bursting through puberty to emerge with surgically altered breasts, meeting Cindy came at exactly the right moment. With his own mother—now remarrying and effectively, in his mind at least, leaving him for another man, Bobby found his mother's "body double" in the adolescent Cindy. Louella had established herself a new partner, and so did her son.

Bobby's and Cindy's romance endured throughout the stormy times in Louella's second marriage, her trips back to West Virginia to visit her first husband, and the constant fights Bobby Joe and Cindy were to have throughout their teenage years. Their romance and subsequent marriage persevered despite an angry and rebellious Bobby Joe's first brush with the juvenile authorities on a breaking-and-entering charge—which was eventually dropped—throughout high school and his abuse of drugs, and through his enlistment in the army.

Strictly from Louella's point of view, everything that happened in Bobby's life after they met was Cindy's fault. Bobby Joe Long, Jr., has said that his mother was jealous of the attention he paid his girlfriend from the very start. Even today, Cindy blames Louella and Louella blames Cindy for the missed opportunities and escalating violence in Bobby Jr.'s life. "She was manipulative," Louella Long says of Cindy. "She was one of the cruelest people I ever knew. She never really had a mother or a family for that matter and was jealous of the family that Bobby Joe had. I tried to be a mother to her and to help her with the children, but she never liked me." She remembers that her son's performance in school, which had always been affected by his changing residences every few months, had still been above average until he met Cindy. Then his grades fell apart completely, and he never finished high school.

The Bobby Joe Long, Jr., story is one of the more interesting variations of the evolving time bomb theory that has characterized the lives of Shawcross, Fischer, and Henry Lee Lucas. Long never claimed to have been molested as these other time bombs have. He was never made the overt victim of direct physical abuse. Rather, he grew up in dysfunctional situations, where the traditional support structures, present in the lives of most children, were conspicuously absent. Long's mother was alternately absent when he needed her and overly present when it was probably not in his best interest for her to be. But she wasn't malicious. She herself was only trying to earn a living so that the two of them could keep a roof over their heads and eat regularly. It was a tragic situation, but a situation in which both of them coped.

Bobby abused alcohol and drugs—but then so did most teenagers during the 1970s—and suffered from the hormonal dysfunction that transformed his body and caused him to experience protomenstrual cycles. Although he was coping with a significant degree of shame and humiliation both from his relationship with his mother—again, perceived or real—and from the transformation of his body, he was nonetheless able to cope. His relationship to Cindy and her astounding similarities with Louella—once again, whether perceived or real, Bobby believed it, and that's all that mattered—perpetuated his reliance on the same type of female figure. That would have been a stabilizing factor more than a destabilizing factor, and Bobby still was resilient enough to cope. However, the near-fatal motorcycle accident that he endured resulted in such significant neurological damage that all of his resiliency was sapped. He gradually slipped down into a hormonal and neurophysiological maelstrom of tragedy and violence before the very eyes of his army physicians, who Long claims were incapable of intervention because of military medical regulations and their own inexperience with Long's symptoms. It was this accident that created the critical mass from all of the previous difficulties that Long had experienced, including previous head traumas that had left him extraordinarily susceptible to neurological damage.

THE ACCIDENT

Bobby Joe married Cindy after he had enlisted in the army and had begun his training as an electrician. He had worked as an apprentice electrician while he was in school and saw the army as a way to get enough experience to become a licensed professional and a subcontractor on the new building development that was springing up in Florida. However, all that changed six months into his enlistment when he was almost killed in a motorcycle accident on his way to cash a check. "I must have been doing at least sixty-five or seventy when I broadsided a car. My Bell motorcycle helmet was shattered. That's what kind of force my head hit the car with. I don't remember a thing until I woke up in the hospital."

Bobby Joe severely fractured his skull in the accident and remained in a semiconscious state for weeks. He had severe headaches, which continue to this day, and was unable to focus his vision. He reports that his pupils remained dilated for a short period after the accident, and that his right pupil continued to be larger than his left for many months. His medical records indicate that he had sustained a serious head trauma, but neither his EEG nor his X rays were evaluated by a skilled neurologist at the time. During his trial for the Tampa murders, more than ten years after the accident, one of his defense psychologists reevaluated Long and found that the brain damage he sustained was serious enough to have warranted a thorough neurological examination after the accident. That examination was never performed. It has yet to be performed even though doctors have requested it.

The injuries to Long's brain from the motorcycle accident were almost critical, his doctors told him while he was recovering. However, the accident also compounded brain damage Long had received from four previous severe head traumas he experienced before he was ten. It was as if old wounds had been reopened, wounds that his army doctors couldn't know about because his medical records were unavailable until after he was arrested for murder in Tampa.

When he was five years old, Bobby Joe fell from a swing, lost consciousness, and awoke to find that a stick had punctured his eye and was embedded beneath his eyelid. A year later he went into shock after he was thrown from a bike and landed on his head, and a year after that he was hit by a car and knocked unconscious for a prolonged period of time. He was diagnosed as having received a severe concussion. The following year, he was thrown from the back of a horse and was dizzy and nauseated for several weeks. "That was the sickest I had ever been in my entire life," Long said about the event. "I couldn't even stand up without getting dizzy."

Dr. Lewis reported to Long's defense team that the aggregate result of all of these injuries was a significant level of damage to the left temporal lobe of Long's brain, with damage to the surrounding areas of the central nervous system, as well, and a loss of those neurological functions generally commensurate with that type of damage. She also noted that Long had a lesion on his left temporal lobe, indicated by the results of an EEG, and irregularities in the muscular ability on his right knee and ankle. To this day, the left side of Long's face is numb as a result of his accident and he still walks with a limp.

The motorcycle accident, more than any other single event, transformed Long's life. "Anybody who knew me before the accident and knows me now would say that it's like I was two different people," Long explains. "I knew there was something wrong with my head when I was in the hospital after the accident. I was just out of it for months and then, while still in hospital, I started thinking about sex. That's all I could think about day and night. I thought about it with my wife, with her friends, with people I knew from before. It started driving me crazy."

But his doctors weren't experienced neurologists and only followed what their radiological reports told them about the extent of his bone fractures. They were army doctors who had to follow prescribed government treatment procedures, which did not required them to order CAT scans or any other type of diagnostic test—which would have been the normal procedure for individuals seeking help from neurologists in private practice. They also thought he was malingering and trying to escape from the requirements of his enlistment contract.

The Longs' first child was born just a few months after Bobby was released from the hospital, and everything seemed to be improving. However, Bobby's troubles were only just beginning. First, there were the physical and emotional repercussions from the accident. "I tried to tell the doctors at the hospital that there was something still wrong with me. I couldn't get these thoughts of sex out of my mind, and Cindy and I had gone from having sex two or three times a week to at least two times a day. And I was still masturbating to get relief. I thought about having sex with just about every girl I met or got to know. Then there were the headaches that wouldn't go away and the feelings that the side of my face was dead. And there were the noises. The slightest sound seemed like an explosion. I would scream at my son to be quiet when he really wasn't making that much noise at all. It only sounded like a lot of noise to me. To this day, I can't take loud noises. They make me get mad and crazy."

Besides his insatiable appetite for sex, the most disturbing change to Long's personality was his violent reaction to anything that didn't go his way. "Before the accident, I was pretty much laid back. I would get mad at things, but I never really got crazy even when I was pushed. After the accident, though—and I noticed this as soon as I got home— the least little thing would make me furious. I mean, I really got so violent that I couldn't control myself sometimes, and that made me worried. I was never like that before."

Often violence would come over him like a thunderstorm with little or no provocation and leave him as suddenly. When a violent outburst of temper had passed, Long would have no memory of it whatsoever. His mother remembers one such incident when she had borrowed his car to go shopping. When she passed by where he was sitting to pick up the keys, he reached out and grabbed her, put her over his knees, and spanked her very hard on the buttocks for several minutes, raising several painful bruises. He then stormed out of the house. When he returned, he could not remember the incident. Even today, Long claims not to remember spanking his mother, and she has never confronted him directly about it since it happened. She also remembers a visit during which she uncovered a box of two hundred photographs of vaginas while she was looking on the shelf for one of her grandson's toys. The photographs had obviously been cut out of a pornography magazine, and she was shocked. She says that at the time she was so frozen with fear at the change in her son's personality that she thought he had been possessed.

The basic character disorders emerging in Bobby Joe Long's personality became even more severe. He knew—knew as much as any person can know what is wrong inside—that his condition was deteriorating, because his occasional violent headaches became constant violent headaches, often accompanied by extreme nausea, loss of muscular control, and extreme dizziness. This persisted for two years while he was in the army, at which point his career in the service came to an end when he claimed the army violated his enlistment contract by not providing complete medical diagnoses of his injuries. He worked sporadically as an X-ray technician after he returned to civilian life, but was fired from job after job for making advances toward the female patients and, in one instance, for showing obscene material to a young girl. He served two days in jail on criminal charges stemming from that incident. Long returned to West Virginia to work at a hospital there, but lost his job because he made the female patients undress before taking their X rays. Long was never hostile or overtly threatening, but there was something menacing about him even then. The neurological damage he had sustained from the accident had so impaired his ability to temper the anger that had been building in him for years that, by 1980, he was actively on the prowl looking for sexual victims. This was anger that resulted from the perceived shame of his childhood, anger over what he claimed was the army's denial of his medical treatment, and natural anger that stemmed from frustration and his inability to mediate the powerful sexual feelings that had taken control of him. He had, in effect, become an active, violent, walking time bomb trolling for victims.

THE CLASSIFIED AD RAPIST

From 1980 to 1983, Long committed more than fifty rapes in Florida as the Classified Ad Rapist and terrorized the communities around Fort Lauderdale, Ocala, Miami, and Dade County. He called phone numbers listed in classified ads in different papers offering furniture and other household articles for sale and made appointments to meet those housewives who answered while their husbands were at work during the day. Once inside the house to look at the items for sale, he would pull out his knife, tie the victim up, rape her, and rob the house. His descriptions of these crimes is almost apologetic, as if he should be excused from blame because he never committed any murders and was rarely violent beyond the actual rape itself. "I never beat anyone. I felt sorry for them. I told them that I didn't want to hurt anybody. I didn't even like tying them up. I think they knew that I wasn't violent, because many of them talked to me not like I was a criminal but like I was a person. They were pretty sad, too, because of the lives they had. If conditions had been different, we might have had a relationship."

As difficult as it is to imagine, Long says he actually believed that at least some of his victims were expressing admiration for him. While part of his description of his crimes is typical of what many serial rapists confess to—"they enjoyed it secretly and told me so"—part also reveals a side of a person actively looking for intervention in his life. It is one of the signals of a walking time bomb that he will commit a type of crime while looking for a way to call attention to something he knows is wrong but can't stop himself from committing. Were it not for the years of built- up shame and humiliation that most time bombs experienced when they were younger, they would simply ask for help from a medical professional. But serial killers, walking time bombs, and serial rapists believe they have no right to live and thus no right to medical attention. As a result, they keep committing crimes as a way to stop themselves from committing more crimes. It sounds paradoxical, but it is a violently dysfunctional condition.

The classified ad rapes continued for more than two years despite the fact that the local police had assembled task forces to catch the rapist and had brought in the FBI. During this time, Long was trying to lead as normal a life as possible: coping with a divorce and his ex-wife's remarriage, changing jobs, communicating with his parents (who had since gotten back together and were planning to remarry), and trying to carry on an active social life. Perhaps the fact that both his mother and his ex-wife had decided to remarry at the same time was more than Long in his condition could handle, and had tripped him over the edge. Other time bombs often start killing soon after "losing" a significant other. Long hadn't reached the homicidal stage yet, but he was obviously getting closer.

During the entire period, however, he was trying to appear as normal as possible, even when, ironically enough, he was being falsely charged with rape by a former girlfriend. The entire incident involved changing relationships in a love triangle from which Long had tried consistently to extricate himself. He admits that the woman was able to manipulate him because he wanted and needed to have frequent sex. However, out of jealousy over her former boyfriend's new relationship and anger at his intervention in her life when she got too drunk to drive herself home, a former girlfriend charged Bobby with raping her after she had asked him to help her from his car to her apartment. "This showed me what a real bitch could do when she didn't get her way," Long explains. "I've committed real rapes and I've murdered women. I know what happens inside of me when I get sexually violent. I know how I feel. I can tell you that I did not rape that girl. We had sex, but she was drunk, she invited me back to her place, and she announced in front of my friends before I drove her home that she wanted to have sex. Then, the next day, she told police that I raped her."

Long was formally charged with rape in November 1981,

and was convicted after a trial. After his conviction, Long wrote a letter to the court asking for a new trial, and the judge granted it. "The judge took it as a motion," Long says. "And the charges were later dropped because I had witnesses who told the police that the woman had asked me to take her back home and had come over in the first place looking for sex. She was a whore, anyway, and once that came out, the whole charge was thrown out of court."

Ironically, this took place during the time that Long was actually committing rapes and robberies as the Classified Ad Rapist—who the police had a good composite description of from victims. Apparently neither the police nor the county prosecutor made the connection between Long and the Classified Ad Rapist. Long says that he would have confessed if charged, only to get help, and it is likely that he would have received at least minor treatment. Had that occurred, the subsequent murders might never have taken place. This was another missed opportunity in his life that might have prevented him becoming a homicidal time bomb.

Long claims that he tried to stop his skein of rapes himself on more than one occasion, but that he didn't know how. "I was dating a nurse during this period, and I explained my problem to her. I didn't tell her that I was the Classified Ad Rapist, but I told her about my sexual drive and how I couldn't control it. She told me that I had a medical problem, and I came very close to seeing a doctor about it. I walked out of the doctor's waiting room, though, because I knew that once I told him what I was doing he would have told the police. If I had any idea then that my behavior might have been neurological, I would have gone to a neurologist, but I didn't know. It might have spared a lot of lives including my own."

Long's admission that he was at the point of seeking help but backed away is another important element of the time bomb syndrome. Most offenders want help. Most of them feel real pain. They claim that they are suffering as much as if *they* were victims of their own crimes. Long claims that he would have sought help had it not been for his fear of punishment and his overriding shame at having committed sex crimes. Shame is the operative word here, because it shuts down the ability of the individual to come to grips with his responsibility. People like Bobby Joe Long camouflage the shame they feel with denial, as if by denying the crimes they will go away. Shame and the consequent denial are critical aspects of a human time bomb's personality because they impede his efforts to short-circuit the continuing violence. Shame causes opportunities to be missed. Unfortunately, most people—especially human time bombs—don't realize that shame can be dealt with in therapy and can be turned off so that the individual experiencing it can be helped.

THE NORTH TAMPA SPREE

By November 1983, Bobby Joe Long was in the throes of the most violent period of his life. After each murder, in the solitude of his apartment in North Tampa, he would sleep deeply for up to fourteen hours at a stretch and awaken wondering whether he had only dreamed of the murder or had actually performed it. He would walk across the street to the Magic Market and pick up a newspaper to read whether the murder on the front page was his work. He read about the growing panic in Tampa with the discovery of each new body. He read about each girl's background, the mysterious victims who had worked the street and bars in Tampa, and their grieving families. If he could have any emotions about his victims, he would have hated them, he told himself years later.

Ngyuen Thi Long, a dancer in a bar on North Nebraska Avenue, was the first. He claimed he knew she was a prostitute by the way she moved and the way she came on to him when he walked into the lounge. Long says he detested prostitutes, women, he claimed, who were too aggressive sexually and had no allegiance to any man. In reality, he claims years later, he was sympathetic toward women. But one couldn't tell that by looking at his victims in North Tampa, where he terrorized an entire community.

Long's murder spree continued unabated as he cruised among the strip bars for victims. He had already committed eight vicious murders, strangling his victims as he raped them, and was feeling suicidal amidst his own rage. Then he saw the girl on the bike, her ponytail bobbing up and down as she rode forward over the handlebars. She had gotten off her late shift at the doughnut shop after midnight and was heading home as quickly as she could. Long's reaction was primal. To Long, any pretty girl out this late had to be trouble. She seemed too aggressive, focused as she was on pedaling her bike along the dark road. Long hid in the bushes and waited until she passed. Then he sprang out from hiding and knocked her off her bike. He easily overpowered her and tied her up.

But this victim wasn't aggressive. She didn't display a false veneer of toughness or kick and scratch out at her attacker like most of his prostitute victims did. Long blindfolded her, put her in his car, and then began a twenty-six-hour odyssey with her that eventually led to her release. She was a true victim, a girl who could be hurt. Her family had no money, she told him, and her stepfather was out of work and confined to a wheelchair. She told Bobby that she had been abused before. Her stepfather raped her when she was younger. Now she had to work the late shift in the doughnut shop to support the entire family. She couldn't even afford a car and had to bike back and forth. She was also a student.

Long knew in his heart that she wasn't like the others; she wasn't the type of women who used her body to manipulate men. She didn't deserve to die. He'd stepped over the line and actually attacked an innocent victim. Somewhere deep inside him, the fantasy broke and he felt remorse. He drove her around blindfolded for many hours and tried to talk to her the way he'd spoken to his first rape victims eight years before. He told her he didn't want to hurt her. He drove to a bank machine for cash, and she was able to peek at the dashboard and around the car from underneath her blindfold. Then he took her back to his apartment, where she was again able to sneak looks at the interior and eventually give police an exact description of where she had been and what the place looked like. Long eventually raped her, but it wasn't the same for him as it had been before. Finally he drove her back to where he first picked her up and set her free.

He knew that she would lead the police to him as soon as she was released. He had also known it was near the end when the first police task force was assembled. There was still a living part of his brain that couldn't continue the violence any longer, and it closed him down. He had tripped his own circuit breakers and set in motion the chain of events that would bring his skein of rapes and murders to an end.

Two days after he released his youngest victim, his compulsion came over him again. As he was driving along the outskirts of North Tampa late in the evening, he spotted a car swerving back and forth in front of him. He thought it was being driven by a woman and that she was drunk. He followed her. She almost swerved off the road, but then she noticed that she was being followed. She pulled over to the side. Bobby Long stopped his car directly behind hers, got out, walked over to her car, and the two of them began a conversation. In a few moments, she agreed to ride around with him, believing that she would drive him back to her car in the morning. Bobby noticed how big she was. He described her later as a hard-looking girl in cowboy boots. Not fat, but she had a large frame. She could stand up for herself, he could see, and he disliked her the minute he laid eyes on her. He almost thought he would enjoy killing her. Her name was Kim Swan and she would become Bobby Joe Long's final victim.

As soon as she got in beside him in the front seat of the car, he attacked her. She screamed and fought back with a strength he hadn't expected, kicking him in the shins, forcing elbows and forearms into his face, and putting her boots right through his dashboard. The two struggled until Long finally overpowered her and tied her hands. She kept on screaming, however, every time she caught sight of headlights approaching in the sideview mirror. Finally Long squeezed her windpipe until she gasped for air and stopped fighting. Then he began cruising with her, promising her she wouldn't be hurt if she'd only cooperate. But she started to scream again until he forced her to stop by viciously tearing at her windpipe. Finally, he strangled her until she lost consciousness and slumped forward across the seat. He drove with her until she came to and started screaming again. Then he strangled her again until she passed out.

While she was still unconscious, he undressed her. But he found, as he looked at the stirring figure on the floor of his car, that what had been a raging desire for sex had simply dried up. Now there was only hatred at what he'd become and hatred at the woman who, he believed, had enticed him into becoming a monster. When she came to for the last time, Long crushed the throat with such force that she died almost at once.

He rode through North Tampa with the naked body of the dead Kim Swan beside him for hours. Nobody stopped him or noticed anything strange, even when he pulled into a secluded area outside the city and pushed her body out of the car. He had never even bothered to rape her. Four days later he was arrested for the rape and kidnapping of the seventeen-year-old student, and the violent career of the thirty-one-year-old Bobby Joe Long was now in the courts.

After the accident and during the period of the two series of serial rapes, Long was fully aware of the moral implications of what he was feeling and doing. The psychological evaluation of Long in February 1985 found him to be competent to stand trial and to be punished for what he did, despite evidence of psychomotor dysfunction, impaired cerebral function, and lesions of the left and right hemispheres of his brain. The EEG evaluations that the court-appointed doctors performed were superficial, because they did not cover the full thirty-six-hour period necessary to document a deep brain dysfunction, and the neurological reflex test was compromised because Long was bound in prisoner's shackles at the time. The clinical experts made no mention of the hormonal imbalance that had caused Long to grow breasts, experience a protomenstrual cycle, and had resulted in gender confusion, behavior alterations, serious impairments to socialization, and physiological deformities. The prosecution's experts did not see the significance of Long's reported hypersexuality, nor did they relate it to the motorcycle accident. Relying on the medical reports written in 1974, the state's witnesses, like the army doctors years earlier, determined that Long had recovered from the accident sufficiently so that there was no permanent cerebral impairment. One doctor, however, noted that Long's hypersexuality and hair-trigger violence conformed to a pattern of behavior disorders associated with neurological damage to the limbic region of the brain.

LONG'S LAST DAYS

Long recalls feeling an escalating sense of revulsion with each rape-murder. He had no feeling of remorse for the victims at first, because in his own mind he had categorized them as whores, women who, he said, used, manipulated, exploited, and tricked men. They aroused a visceral hate in him that he claims he was never able to control after the accident. "I know what I did. I raped and murdered them. But they were the ones who offered the invitation." He remembers that the first murder began when Nguen Long, the victim, picked him up in a bar on Nebraska Avenue. "She picked me up, really, I didn't go after her. She was a whore. She cruised over to me selling everything she had for anything I had. She knew how to seduce anything that walked. She manipulated men and was after me. Once I had her in the car, I tied her up and raped her. Then I strangled her and dumped her body alongside the highway. I knew what I was doing, but I just couldn't stop myself. It was like there was a dream me doing what I really wanted to do even though I knew I shouldn't be doing it. I hated her. I hated her from the time she picked me up, but I didn't plan to murder her. I don't even think I planned to rape her either. She was just sitting there in the front seat of the car staring at me, waiting for me to show that I needed to have her, and I grabbed her, covered her mouth, and tied her up. I couldn't believe what I'd done the next morning. I was sick. I threw up. I knew I was in real trouble. Then a few days later I met the Simms girl, and it was the same thing all over again. She was just a barfly. She really picked me up, and I just turned on her on the car."

In a procession, the next six victims had invited themselves into Long's presence and unknowingly placed their lives in jeopardy. This is the tragedy of prostitute murders. Because prostitutes are already outside the law, they have even less protection than other high-risk groups. Bobby Joe has said that he had "easy pickings" because his victims sought him rather than his seeking them. Even after the third rape in only two months and formation of an interagency police task force that began warning local prostitutes, the girls along Nebraska Avenue continued to be attracted to Bobby Long. He was the cute stranger that always hung around bars. No one could place him with any of the previous victims, but all the girls wanted to make his acquaintance. Not even the local sheriff knew that he had become a regular fixture along the strip. His killing spree took place so rapidly and the bodies turned up so quickly that there was not enough time for the police to establish a missing-person alert. Bobby was just one of the strangers who cruised the strip. His only reported rape had been expunged when the charges against him were thrown out. Long said that had he not set up his own arrest, he would never have been caught.

"I knew when the police task force was announced that I was running out of time. I should have gotten out of the area, but I wanted to get caught. I was sick, heaving my guts up every morning. I wanted to be stopped. I could have gone anywhere in Florida, kept on raping and murdering, and the police would have never found me. They didn't even know where to look. I could have gone back to California and done the same thing. Then, right after I had let [the student] go and right before I was caught, the cops stopped me just to check on some report of a robbery in the area. But they took my license and looked over the car and they let me go. I knew they were following me then. I'm not completely stupid not to know what the cops were doing. It was just a matter of days. So I made myself visible and gave them all the time they needed to arrest me. Even Cindy called me and asked me if I'd heard about all the rapes in my area. As if she wasn't giving me a clue that the cops were on to me and that they'd already called her. But I wanted to be stopped because I couldn't stop myself."

Then, like most serial killers, Long, upon his arrest, confessed almost spontaneously like a dam that has burst. This is typical of homicidal time bombs who are actually looking for help even while they're killing. "Once they had me in custody," Long explained, "I couldn't stop talking. Then I realized that I could be fried for what I was saying, so I asked for a lawyer. But they wouldn't let me see a lawyer until I finished what I was saying because they said that I already knew my rights. I know now that they had to let me see a lawyer when I asked for one."

It was after he was put on trial, however, that he realized that his case had become a political issue. Serial killers tend to become political issues of the community because their crimes are acts of terror that paralyze law-enforcement agencies until they are caught. Prostitute murderers fall into an even more specific category because they are killing victims who have placed themselves beyond the help of the law. Long maintains, with an increasing degree of self-interest as his date of execution approaches, that the people he killed were outlaws and that he was doing society something of a favor. He is the victim, he still claims, despite the brutal nature of his crimes. What is obvious is that the self-hating nature of a time bomb is still at work. Long believes that even though he has no right to be alive, his death will be an affliction on the society that executed him.

"What kills me the most," he has claimed, "is that the girls that I raped [and killed] were all dope addicts and whores. Not that anybody really deserves to be killed, but they weren't saints. I'm sick, I know there's something wrong with my brain. I knew it from the first times in the hospital when I felt what I felt. I told doctor after doctor what I felt, but it made no difference. I'm no killer, not like the other guys here on the row. But it made no difference to the court or to the governor."

"THE MISUSED LIFE OF BOBBY JOE LONG"

Bobby Joe Long has said that he was headed for trouble well before he was even born. Long suffers from the same hormonal dysfunction that has plagued other male members of his family. However, had Bobby Joe been seen early on by experts in endocrinology who might have known about the chromosomal aspects of the disorder and the hormonal mood changes that Long was experiencing, he might have been red-flagged for further medical testing. But Bobby Joe was an impoverished child in a migrant family. Much like an entire generation of homeless children growing up in cities today, he did not receive medical care that he ideally should have received. Medical intervention is one of the most critical components in preventing those children who are potential time bombs from evolving into career killers.

Bobby Long's major head traumas resulting in loss of consciousness and subsequent periods of disorientation were also clear indicators that he was at risk even before he was a teenager. Children who receive severe concussions need to be thoroughly examined, because neurological damage is insidious and may take years to manifest itself symptomatically. Bobby Long's near-critical head trauma from the motorcycle accident he had as an adult was the coup de grace. However, the army doctors were not authorized to examine him completely, nor could they determine the full extent of his neurological impairment. Long has said that he knew he was badly injured and that something was wrong inside his brain. But he didn't know what to do about it except complain to the army doctors in charge of his case. It was an exercise in futility. Had he realized that his escalating fantasies of sexual violence could have been controlled, he might have sought help before he committed his first rapes. But after he had become a sex offender, he could only react to the shame and tried to hide from the crimes.

His case shows that children and adults who receive even moderate head injuries need medical attention. And the attention they receive should not be limited to immediate consequential damage but should assess the long-term aspects of what really happens after a head trauma. Various types of epilepsies can result; neurological damage can impair vital circuitry that mediates emotions of violence and rage, and resultant clotting can cause minor strokes that impair sensory and motor circuits. Had Bobby Long received more specialized medical attention at the time, he might have been helped to deal with his anger and his sexual urgings. Because damage to vital neural tissue was discovered during his trial in 1984 after CAT scans and other tests, it stands to reason this damage might have been discovered years earlier had he only received the kind of specialized medical treatment he needed. It was another missed opportunity.

The years of emotional upsets that Long claims he experienced as a child—whether perceived or real—set the stage for his subsequent attacks on women. Long was predisposed to hostility. What happened to him in later years eventually turned that hostility into actual violence. It might have been prevented, but thorough medical and psychological help was inaccessible to him until it was too late. It doesn't mean that Long should be excused from blame or from his ultimate punishment, but it does mean that the child-care system in most states must look at ways to intervene in the lives of children at risk. Had any agency intervened in Bobby's life, the time bomb might have been defused.

SUBSTANCE ABUSE

While not a specific cause of violence, prolonged substance or alcohol abuse is usually one of the ingredients that is a catalyst to violence. In Long's case, his excessive use of drugs since his adolescence markedly reduced his ability to mediate his violent reactions and wore away what little was left of his resiliency. We can only guess at the amount of drugs or alcohol Long was using during the period he was committing his rapes and murders. He had not described his use of drugs as having an effect on his crimes or on the events preceding the crimes. Nevertheless, he described himself as a heavy drug user. Even if he was not using drugs immediately prior to committing murders, the continual use of drugs, especially the hallucinogenics that Long revealed that he used, tends to blur the borderline between fantasy and reality. Individuals who are already close to the edge of their fantasies may well wander over the line and act out those fantasies after prolonged use of hallucinogenic drugs. When, as with Long, those fantasies are already tied into emotions associated with damaged areas of the brain, the effects of consciousness-altering substances are exponentially increased. In Long's case, this seems to have been what happened.

Bobby Joe Long, Jr., illustrates one of the most frustrating examples of an individual who was in the care of the largest extended medical institution in the country, the United States Army, and was discharged from it while a time bomb was ticking away deep inside his brain. Combined with whatever else took place in his life to predispose him to violence, he is a prime example of missed opportunities and critical opportunities that were not taken.

6

THE BALLAD OF HENRY LEE LUCAS

Henry Lee Lucas was behind bars again, looking out at the world from Sheriff Bill Conway's Montague County jail cell down in Texas. Henry had been in and out of state penitentiaries, reform schools, and county lockups for most of his life. Now he was being held by Sheriff "Hound Dog" Conway on suspicion of murdering his common-law wife, Becky Powell. Henry Lee Lucas was a loser, "the devil's own child who'd come to no good someday," his mother had once said. He'd killed her, too. He sliced a wound open in her neck as they fought in her motel room in Michigan, fled from the site in terror and left her to bleed to death on the carpet. But he'd served his time in Michigan and had even warned the authorities: "If you let me out, I'll kill again." They paroled him, he said he killed again within the hour, dumped the body on the road leading to the prison, and then left the state. But now in the chill damp of a Texas jail Henry was of a mind to confess.

Before the year was out, Henry Lee Lucas would become one of the most infamous serial killers in the United States, having confessed to over three hundred murders, mutilations, rapes, and dismemberments in a nationwide homicide spree. In fact, Henry confessed to murders so brutal that newspapers described him as a mad dog who should have been shot. But in the following three years he would recant all but three of those confessions and become known as one of the most notorious liars in America. Then he would recant his recantation. Eventually, Lucas was sentenced to death for a murder that someone else had confessed to committing.

How did Henry get into a position where he faced death from the executioner's needle for a crime his partner, Ottis Toole, confessed to and, based on lie detector tests, Henry Lee Lucas could not have committed? Most people who knew him said that his life, brutal from the day he was born, had turned him into this country's worst time bomb. But at least in the case of "Orange Socks," the young woman found dead in a ditch along Texas Route 35, Henry Lee Lucas would eventually be spared the death penalty by Texas's then-governor George W. Bush. Governor Bush commuted Lucas's sentence because of the very flimsy evidence that had convicted him and the results of new evidence that said Lucas was in Florida at the time he said he committed the murder.

LUCAS'S CHILDHOOD

"I hated all my life. I hated everybody. When I first grew up and can remember, I was dressed as a girl by my mother. And I stayed that way for two or three years. And after that I was treated like what I call the dog of the family. I was beaten; I was made to do things that no human bein' would want to do. I've had to steal, make bootleg liquor; I've had to eat out of a garbage can. I grew up and watched prostitution like that with my mother till I was fourteen years old." Such are Lucas's memories of his childhood in Blacksburg, Virginia. He was the last of eleven children by his mother, Viola, a snuff-chewing, alcoholic full-blooded Chippewa and her husband, Anderson, a double amputee nicknamed

"No Legs." Anderson lost both legs when, in a drunken stupor and miserable that his wife was having sex with a customer right in front of their young son Henry, he staggered out into the snow of a harsh Appalachian winter and fell under the wheels of a slowly moving freight train. "He hopped around on his ass all his life and sold pencils after that until one night he got so sick of what she was doing he laid out in the snow for a whole night, caught pneumonia, and died," Henry said. Their home was a three-room, dirt-floor log cabin up in the hills of rural Virginia that had no plumbing or electricity. The boys did all the chores and made and sold moonshine. One of Henry's specific chores was to "mind the still," and as a result he suffered from alcohol-induced toxic poisoning from the fumes of the distilling mash. Anderson owned the still and sold moonshine liquor, skinned minks, and sold pencils out of a cup for pocket money. Viola was a prostitute who often forced Henry and their father to watch during her sessions with steady johns. She beat all of them constantly, and Henry grew to hate her.

"She made us just stand and watch," he says. "Stand in the house, or she would beat my brains out if I didn't. Some people say they gonna give a whippin' with a switch or somethin'; she'd use sticks! She didn't know what a switch was. When she went and got a switch, she went and got a handbroom stick. She'd wear them out."

He remembers his father as a pathetic but kind human being who would sneak him money from his moonshine operation to go to the movies. Anderson was one of the handful of people who was actually kind to Henry. He taught his son how to work the makeshift distillery and in the process encouraged his son's taste for liquor. Henry began drinking regularly at the age of ten and is a diagnosed alcoholic today. But after Anderson died and his older brother left to join the Navy, Henry was left alone to face his mother's brutality and the violence of her johns, who often turned their anger on Henry.

Lucas's childhood was a mixture of horror and pathos, a

breeding ground for the violence that turned Texas I–35 into a mass burial ground for Lucas's future victims. Viola beat her son mercilessly with any weapons she could find. Her cruelty was such that she wouldn't even let him cry. After beating him and telling him that what she had done was for his own good, she would prophesy that he had been born evil and was, like Manson would be told years later, the devil's own child. She even went on to predict that he would some-day die in prison. Her continuing violence began to infect every level of his existence. Henry Lucas's earliest memory, he claims, is of his mother finishing up with a customer, then pulling out a shotgun and shooting the man in the leg. The blood spattered all over him in the process.

Viola Lucas also liked to outfit her son in girls' clothing. Lucas can remember that on his first day of school his mother curled his long blond hair and made him go to school in a dress. The teacher, one of the few people in official po-sitions of authority who came in contact with Henry Lee Lucas during his youth, was shocked. She took the responsi-bility for cutting his curls and dressing him in pants. As the term progressed, the teacher began feeding the malnourished youth sandwiches during school lunchtimes and took him home to her house, where he would receive the only hot meals he ever ate as a child.

"I think she was responsible for my first pair of shoes," Lucas remembers. Years later, in a rare interview, his teacher described Lucas as one of the many impoverished and des-perate Virginia hill children in her classes. But, she revealed, he was especially dirty, smelled very bad, and was con-stantly tormented as an outcast by the other children.

As Lucas grew older, the injuries he sustained from his mother grew more and more serious. Eventually, the re-peated traumas caused a progressive degree of brain dam-age. Years later, Lucas described the first serious head injury he received whose effects have lasted throughout his life. "I wouldn't go out and pick up a stock of wood," he recalls. "She went outside, got a two-by-four, and knocked my brains out. She tore off the skin and made the bone all wide open. I stayed out for about thirty-eight hours before I came to, the doctors told me. Bernie, my mom's boyfriend, got scared when I wouldn't wake up, so he took me to the hospital. He told the doctors I fell off a ladder and they accepted it. But later I proved to them what did happen."

This serious injury impaired Lucas's ability to mediate his moods and his temper for the rest of his life. This type of trauma is one of the basic similarities between almost all serial killers and episodically violent individuals. Shawcross, Fischer, Long, and Lucas all experienced serious head injuries on repeated occasions.

Lucas recalls having recurring seizures and periods of physical dissociation after the assault. "What I remember was that it was like somebody layin' down and stompin' you, and you keep on fightin' to get away from 'em. I didn't know anything happening around me. I couldn't hear, really. It was like being in a different world. I used to float through the air when I was a kid, too. I used to be layin' in bed, just feel like you're floatin' right off the bed up in the air. Just feel like I could fly. It's not a nice feeling. It's a weird feeling."

Lucas also has recurring auditory hallucinations that intrude into his very shaky sense of reality. He recalls hearing voices and animal sounds ever since his severe concussion and coma when he was eight. "Sometimes I hear stuff when there's nothing around me. I've heard my name called and there ain't been nobody with me. I've heard all kinds of noises and stuff and there been nobody around—people, animals. I've gotten up and gone outside in the daytime to go and look, but I can't see anything. I can't find it." Neurological examinations and X rays conducted many years later confirmed that Lucas had sustained serious head traumas resulting in damage to those areas of the brain that control violent behavior and the ability to manage primal emotions.

Lucas claims that when he was a child, his mother destroyed anything he liked or played with. "Everything I had was destroyed. My mother, if I had a pony, she'd a killed it. If

I had a goat or anything like that, she killed it. She wouldn't allow me to love nothin'. She wanted me to do what she said, and that's it."

He remembers a pet mule that he kept. His mother, seeing him take pleasure in the animal, asked him whether he liked it or not. When he replied that he did, she went into the house, reappeared with a shotgun, and killed the mule. Then she beat him because of the expense she incurred in needing to have the mule's carcass carted away. Incidents like these were responsible for Lucas's fear of loving and for his life-long inability to feel empathy for other living creatures. Whatever he loved as a child was destroyed. Therefore, he learned to not love. In fact, he learned that there was no value to life and that people were no different from any of thousands of inanimate objects that populated his world.

Lucas received additional head traumas during his child-hood which only served to exacerbate the damage he'd received from his mother. A year after being taken to the hospital in a coma, his elder brother accidentally sliced into his left eye with a knife, injuring the optical nerves so severely that for months, Lucas could only see shadows and phantom images. His peripheral vision was seriously impaired as well, causing him to walk sideways so that he could see what was on his left. He was eventually returned to school, where the teacher who had shown him so much kindness when he was younger purchased a special reader with large type so that Lucas could keep up with the rest of the class. Even this level of progress was interrupted when another teacher at the school, while striking out at another student, missed, and accidentally hit Henry instead, reopening his wound, and causing him to lose the injured eye completely. It was replaced with a glass eye that he still wears.

As a teenager, Lucas claims that he had sex with his half brother and with animals whose throats he and his half brother split open in a private ritual designed to arouse them sexually. Lucas often trapped small animals and skinned them alive for pleasure. He began stealing for food and money. "I stole almost as soon as I could run," Lucas says. " 'Cause I didn't want to stay at home. I figured if I could steal, I could get away from home and stuff."

Lucas claims to have committed his first murder at fifteen. He cornered a seventeen-year-old girl at a bus stop, bludgeoned her until she could no longer resist, carried her up an embankment, and attempted to rape her. When she awoke struggling and screaming, Lucas began strangling her. "I had no intention of killing her," he said thirty-three years later in an interview about his life. "I don't know whether I was just being afraid somebody was going to catch me or what. That killing was my first, my worst, and the hardest to get over . . . I would go out sometimes for days, and just every time I turned around I'd see police behind me. Then I'd be always watching for police and be afraid they were going to stop me and pick me up. But they never did bother with me."

Lucas didn't kill for the thrill of killing, he explains; he did it because it was the only way he could have sex. "Sex is one of my downfalls. I get sex any way I can get it. If I have to force somebody to get it, I do. If I don't, I don't. I rape them. I've done that. I've killed animals to have sex with them. Dogs, I've killed them to have sex; while they're still alive only sometimes. Then killing became the same thing as having sex."

When he was fifteen Lucas was convicted for breaking and entering and committed to Beaumont Training School for Boys as a delinquent. This began a pattern for the remainder of his life that stretched from state prison to federal prison to death row and to the executioner's needle at Huntsville, Texas. He was discharged from Beaumont a year after having made what the prison report calls "a good adjustment." A year after his release, he was again convicted of breaking and entering and sentenced to the Virginia State Penitentiary for four years. He escaped in 1956 and with a male companion stole a series of cars from Virginia to Michigan. Later in 1956 he was arrested on a federal charge of transporting stolen property across state lines and sentenced to a federal reformatory in Ohio. He was transferred back to Virginia to serve out his original sentence with time added for the escape. He was finally discharged in September 1959, and made his way back to Michigan to join his sister. It was there that he met his wife. And it was there that he committed the first homicide for which he would be convicted and serve prison time. "My mother came up to Michigan and we got into an argument in a beer tavern . . . that's when I killed her."

MATRICIDE

Lucas and his sister were in a bar in Tecumseh when his mother joined them and immediately began arguing with her son over his wife. Henry remembers very little of the actual killing. Both he and his mother had been drinking heavily that night. He remembers that the argument became more violent and more personal until Viola accused him of having had sex with his sister and ridiculing him in the presence of his new wife. He drove back to his sister's motel room apartment. She followed him, and their argument continued. She then hit him with a broom handle. He claims that something deep inside him snapped when he felt the slap across his face. It was as if his mother had tripped a hidden wire. He exploded, he told prison psychiatrists years later. He turned on her and began slapping her until she fell to the floor. When he reached down to drag her back to her feet, he was holding a knife in his hand. He didn't remember when he picked it up. Then he looked down at her body and saw that she was bleeding from her neck. Her breathing was very shallow. Lucas fled from the apartment, leaving her alone and hemorrhaging on the bedroom floor. By the time Viola's daughter returned to the apartment fourteen hours later, she found her mother barely alive, and called an ambulance to take the old woman to the hospital where she died the next day. Henry Lee Lucas stole a car from a nearby gas station and fled to Blacksburg, Virginia. He was arrested in Ohio and returned to Michigan, where he was tried for murder, convicted, and sentenced to forty years in the Michigan State Penitentiary.

That murder was the culmination of only one part of the twenty-three-year nightmare that Lucas experienced growing up with his mother. The rest of that nightmare—the hundreds of murders, the serial rapes, the cross-country crime sprees with Ottis Toole and his family, and the murder of Becky Powell—was yet to come.

JAIL TIME IN MICHIGAN

If Lucas thought that murdering his mother would rid him of her for the rest of his life, he was wrong. Once behind bars, Lucas attacked other prisoners and refused to perform any of his prison duties. He claims he was suffering from hallucinations during the entire period before he was eventually sent to the Iona State Mental Hospital. He says his mother was ordering him to kill himself. "I kept hearing her talking to me and telling me to do things. And I couldn't do it. Had one voice that was tryin' to make me commit suicide, and I wouldn't do it. Had one tell me not to do anything they told me to do, and that's what got me in the hospital, was not doing what they told me to do."

The schizophrenic Henry Lee Lucas, who had been so brutalized by his mother that "he eventually could achieve sexual potency only by fantasizing he had killed his victim," attempted suicide several times in the Michigan State Penitentiary. No matter how many times the prison psychologists interviewed him to find out why he wanted to die, he remained uncooperative. First, he cut open his stomach with a razor blade. That proved unsuccessful, so he tried slashing his wrists. Eventually, he was transferred to the Iona State Hospital for five years, where he went through a long-term therapy program. This might have been an opportunity for intervention, but the therapy proved to be unsuccessful. Prison doctors simply did not understand the nature of Lucas's violence or the seeds of his hatred. They processed him through normal diagnostic channels for their medical report on his condition to prison authorities.

Lucas was diagnosed as a psychopath, a sadist, and a sex deviate. At first he was cooperative, though, telling his doctors that he heard voices urging him to do "bad things." He told the psychiatrists at Iona that at night in his bunk he often felt as if he were floating in the air and that he heard voices from the dead. The Iona reports describing the inmate Henry Lee Lucas document a personality completely turned in upon itself. Incapacitated by an inferiority complex, Lucas was "grossly lacking in self-confidence, self-reliance, will power, and general stamina." There was also evidence of a "general preoccupation with sexual impotence, the same which is believed to exist as only another reflection of his deflated impression of personal qualities in general."

Lucas says he received very little treatment at Iona. Mostly, he explains, they administered drugs, forced him to conform to a rigorous routine, and disciplined the prisoners when they stepped out of line. "They made you walk around on the floor and shine the floor with your feet. They put these cloths over your shoes on your feet and you'd have to walk the floor, shine the floor. Had to. I'm not kiddin'." Other violent psychopaths, such as Charles Manson, who was treated by prison psychologists reported similar incidents involving those who didn't follow the rules.

Lucas was eventually returned to the general inmate population at the penitentiary, where his hallucinations returned. Instead of fighting them, this time, he obeyed the voices he heard, he claims, and began an intensive study into the crimes of the other inmates. Lucas explains that he immersed himself in the records of their crimes, learning the details of the cases and applying their situations to his own.

He studied the techniques the police employed in pursuing their investigations and developing leads. He says he learned how they used their suspects' mistakes to track them down and trick confessions out of them. These were mistakes, he vowed, he would never make once he was set free. In fact, he studied police procedures so thoroughly and aggressively that upon his release, he was able to commit crimes and escape the authorities with much greater ease. His new knowledge enabled him the predict the authorities' next moves. According to his own later statements, he had learned how to be a career criminal. "I learned every way there is in law enforcement. I learned every way there is in different crimes; I studied it. After I got out of that hospital, they put me in the records room. And every record that jumped through there, I would read it, study it, and see how they got caught."

Lucas was recommended for parole in 1970 even though he warned the prison officials and the staff psychologist that if he was released, he would kill again. He told them he was sick, that he was hearing voices from the dead, and that the forces that had compelled him to attempt suicide years earlier would now compel him to kill strangers if he was let loose. The state of Michigan, however, was facing a severe overcrowding problem in 1970 and feared that the court would order them to put prisoners in early release if they didn't release those who had served their minimum time. Thus, despite Lucas's complaints that he had not been rehabilitated and didn't want to be released, the parole board set him free.

"I was planning. I knew I was going to kill!" he proclaimed years later in his Texas jail cell. "I even told 'em I was going to do it. I told the warden, the psychologist, everybody. When they come in and put me out on parole, I said, 'I'm not ready to go; I'm not going.' They said, 'You're going to go if we have to throw you out.' They threw me out of the prison because it was too crowded, all right, so I said,

'I'll leave you a present on the doorstep on the way out.' And I did it the same day, down the road a bit."

Lucas stuck to his word. "I killed a woman down in Jackson, Michigan. I took her and killed her within walking distance of the prison. I gave them something they gonna remember." The case wasn't cleared up until he confessed to the murder while in jail in Texas. "When I cleared it up, they said, 'Well, I didn't think that you were going to do that.' They know now that I meant what I said."

THE LUCAS CRIME SPREE

Once out of prison, Lucas remained in Michigan, where he was arrested again for the attempted kidnap of a fifteen-year-old girl waiting for a school bus. He was sentenced to prison and released in 1975. This time he didn't stay in Michigan, but traveled east to Maryland, where he met his half-sister Almeda Kiser. He later moved in with Almeda's daughter, Aomia Pierce, and her husband in nearby Chatham, Pennsylvania. By the end of 1975, Lucas had met and married Betty Crawford. He drifted from job to job and in and out of his marriage for the next four years.

In 1979 Lucas had drifted to Jacksonville, Florida, where he frequented a storefront mission that served vagrants and "down and outs" in the community. Lucas described it as the only place in the area where he could get a free meal and a cup of coffee. Within a few weeks he met and fell into a homosexual relationship with the tall, soft-spoken Ottis Toole and moved in with his family. "I was down in Jacksonville and met Ottis Toole in a soup kitchen there. He was queer and he asked me to go home with him and meet his family, which I did, and I became part of that family. We got talking about our crimes and Ottis told me about a cult that he was a member of. This reminded me of what my friends had told me in jail, and I told Ottis I was interested in joining. This pleased Ottis very much and he grinned when I told him. He knew we could be together more and more and could become partners in crime."

It was in Toole's household in the Springfield section of Jacksonville that he also met Toole's nephew and niece, Frank and Frieda Powell, also called Becky, and, according to Lucas, took an immediate liking to them. From the first, Lucas began treating the eleven-year-old Becky like a daughter. He made her go to school, made sure she did her homework and finished her meals, and even—in a paradox of parenting—taught her burglars' skills such as breaking-and-entering and pickpocketing. Finally Toole's aunt, the nominal head of the household, objected to Henry's involvement with the family and demanded that he leave. Toole left with Henry, and Frank and Becky decided to go along as well.

The ragtag family became drifters themselves, and Lucas and Toole drove across the state in a spree of residential burglaries, gas-station and convenience-store holdups, bank robberies, and occasional felony murders—all committed by Lucas and Toole while the two children waited in the car. They spilled out of Florida into Georgia and Mississippi, and from there into Louisiana, Texas, and Oklahoma. Along the way, Ottis broke off and took Frank back to Florida, leaving Lucas and Becky to continue back into Texas. By this time, Lucas and Becky were no longer surrogate parent and child but common-law husband and wife and partners in petty crimes. Finally, in December 1981, the now-thirteen-year-old Becky was arrested and sent to a juvenile home in Florida. Henry followed her, teamed up with Toole again, and helped her escape.

Lucas, Toole, and Becky Powell quickly fled across the country, robbing and murdering over one hundred victims between them along the way, until they finally settled in southern California where Henry was able to use his prison-acquired construction skills to support the three of them. Toole eventually tired of the arrangement and went back to Florida to pursue his own separate criminal career while Henry and Becky set up their household.

THE FINAL ODYSSEY

Lucas's quiet demeanor and his ability to repair old pieces of furniture for resale attracted the attention of Jack Smart and his wife, the owners of a small antique and refining shop. Smart had picked up Becky and Henry when they were hitchhiking in January, 1982, outside Hemet, California, and he claimed to have been moved by the one-eyed man's tale of being out of work and hungry. And he took pity on the shivering teenager that the man introduced as his wife. It was the middle of California rainy season, and this pair of stragglers had no place to live. He gave them jobs in his store and put them up in an adjacent apartment. Lucas was trustworthy, it seemed, and worked hard. He was able to do many odd jobs and could repair just about anything. He and his wife, Smart thought, were probably just right for taking care of Kate Rich, Mrs. Smart's eighty year-old mother, back in Ringgold, Texas.

Henry and Becky could recognize a good situation when they saw one. Granny Rich, as the old woman was called, could hardly see and was almost an invalid. All she wanted was companionship. She was kind, especially to Becky, and tolerant of Henry. She was so trusting of Lucas that she gave him money so Lucas could buy supplies. But he never spent the money on household supplies, and that's what alerted her neighbors that something was wrong.

"He was buying cartons of cigarettes and cases of beer," a store clerk had told Montague County sheriff's officers. "And the checks had been made out by him and signed 'Katy Rich.' She never signed her checks that way." The storekeeper had notified Rich's relatives in Oklahoma that she had a strange drifter and his teenage wife living with her and spending her money on items she would never buy herself.

The Rich family swooped down on the old woman's household early in the morning a few weeks after they'd been notified. They knew from the list of charged items and deliveries that Mrs. Rich herself couldn't have ordered the supplies, and wondered whether anything had happened to her. When they arrived at her small house, they found the old woman sitting at the kitchen table amidst weeks of accumulated filth and debris. Lucas and his wife were asleep on living room couches, burns from their cigarettes in evidence all over the cushions and the rug. The house was a firetrap waiting to go up.

Without even bothering to call the sheriff, the family evicted Lucas and Becky on the spot, driving them to the center of Ringgold and offering them money for bus fare. Anywhere, they told Lucas and Becky, they would send them anywhere just so long as it was far away from Granny Rich and Montague County. But Lucas and Becky simply hitched a ride along the road, eventually getting a ride from a charismatic man who introduced himself as Ruben Moore, a local roofing contractor who also led a religious group known as the House of Prayer in an old converted chicken farm in Stoneburg, Texas. Moore heard Lucas and Becky repeat their story of hard luck and offered them food and lodging in return for Lucas's help in maintaining the shacks on the ranch. Lucas agreed, and within the space of weeks, he was also helping Moore as a day laborer and roofer.

Becky Powell quickly made friends among the members of the fundamentalist group; Lucas, however, alienated people. He was always guarded, quick to anger, and kept whispering threats under his breath. "When I'm around people, I feel tense, nervous," he said about his experience with Ruben Moore. "I guess it's because I haven't been around people. Most of the life I've lived had been alone. I have trouble talkin' to them; I always have." But the group members said that his threatening behavior turned toward Becky as she became more and more deeply involved with the group's worship services.

In fact, Becky quickly found meaning in the group's religious practices. She attended services and other meetings, made friends in the community to whom she confided her complaints about Lucas, enjoyed the communal atmosphere of the encampment, and even visited Kate Rich, who lived only ten miles away. Becky had become friends with Granny Rich during her stay at her house, and Kate Rich had come to look upon the orphaned Becky as one of her own. Between the brutality she was experiencing at the hands of Henry Lee, the encouragement from Kate Rich, and the strength she was deriving from the worship services at the House of Prayer, Becky came to a decision. She would return to Florida to serve out the rest of her sentence at the juvenile institution and take charge of the rest of her life.

She told Lucas she wanted to leave him. They fought. "Nobody would have put up with what I have," she complained to him during one of their arguments. Even neighbors at the House of Prayer heard their fights during the week. "She wants to go back to her family," Lucas told him. "I'll be going back, too."

And that was the last Ruben Moore ever expected to see of Henry Lee Lucas and Becky Powell, he told Montague County Sheriff Bill Conway. It was August 1982, and the two drifters began their trek east, hitchhiking, looking for rides along the interstates that would eventually take them back to Florida.

A day or so later, they had reached Denton County and found it impossible to get a ride. Nor could they find any room in the local motel. Though it was a hot and muggy night, there was no rain, and Becky suggested they simply lay out their bedrolls and sleep in an open field. Henry started drinking heavily and complaining. What was the point of going back? She'd only have to serve time in a reformatory, maybe even be shoved into a foster home where Henry couldn't find her. Henry would probably face jail time also. He believed there was a warrant out for him in Florida because of Becky's disappearance, and likely as not there were murder and burglary warrants out for him as well. Did Becky really want to see him back in jail, quite possibly for the rest of his life? Did Becky want him to get sent to the electric chair? What if they charged her with being an accomplice? She might spend the better part of her life behind bars as well. Too risky, Henry said. They were better off staying at the House of Prayer, where people liked them and he could make some money.

Lucas was also angry because he actually liked the House of Prayer. It was one of the first times in his life that he was ever happy, he had told the sheriff. He also liked Ruben Moore and claimed that he had friends and a legitimate job in the small religious congregation. He was actually thinking about going straight, he told her, and didn't feel the constant, nagging compulsion to kill that had eaten away at his brain like a cancer for the past twenty-five years. He was free of his demons, he lied. But now, in the oppressively damp heat of the midsummer Texas night, Lucas could feel those demons surrounding him and inciting him to violence again. Becky wouldn't stop complaining. The field mosquitos were swarming all around, feeding off his body sweat, biting him even through his clothes. Maybe he'd just drink till he fell asleep and the night's hell would pass away.

For some reason, he told the sheriff, he and Becky didn't stop fighting even though they were so tired neither of them could think straight. Their arguing grew louder, more accusatory, and more violent. Each pushed the other closer to the edge until Becky suddenly slapped Henry hard across the face. That was his trigger, still very much in place after his years at the Michigan penitentiary and Iona State and still just as fragile as that night in Tecumseh when his mother slapped him. Even before thinking about it, he confessed later, he reached for his knife in his bedroll and plunged it deep in her chest. The blade pierced a lung before penetrating her heart. She gasped for air as blood filled her chest cavity. She convulsed, went into cardiac arrest, and died within a minute and a half.

"Becky had been saved by a Christian," Lucas said years later. "She was encouraged by old Kate Rich to leave me and go back home to Florida. We were in the field drinking and fighting. Becky hit me in the side of the head and before I knew what was happening, she lay dead at my feet. She was like an angel." Henry Lucas said that he just looked at the little thirteen-year-old girl twisted on the ground before his feet and wept.

Later, he remembers, he thought he should try to hide the body, so he removed her ring from her finger and then hacked Becky into pieces. He stuffed all but the legs into two pillowcases and buried her remains in a shallow grave. Then he tied a belt around Becky's legs and dragged them into the brush where he buried them under the desert scrub. For the rest of that night and on several subsequent trips to the gravesite he talked to Becky's remains. "I wanted her spirit to forgive me," he said. He told her that he was sorry for having killed her and promised her that someday he would join her. His remorse over a reflex murder seemed to throw a switch somewhere in his psyche. He was no longer interested in covering up his tracks with the same cunning as before.

"It broke for me," he said later. "Nothin' was the same after that. It was like I was walkin' through shadows." From that moment on, his criminal career began to unravel. It was another nine months before he would be finally apprehended, but it was nine months of *pro forma* flight. His primal hatred of others no longer spurred him on. Now Becky's voice, he claimed, was among the voices searing through his brain. Only her voice was telling him to confess, he said, to find an end to misery now that he had killed the only person he had ever loved. Thus, after his capture, in the cold and darkness of his jail cell, he would confess to the murders of Becky Powell and hundreds of other victims.

Lucas returned to Ruben Moore's House of Prayer the next day after he'd killed Becky and broke down in tears. However, he was still not about to confess to the murder. "She drove away with another man," he told Moore. "She left me standing by the side of the road." He told Moore that he and Becky had been picked up by a truck driver in Denton County who drove them to the interstate and enticed

Killer George Jo Hennard, Jr., one of America's worst mass murderers. *(Killeen Daily Herald)*

Luby's Cafeteria in Killeen, Texas, the scene of one of America's worst mass shooting incidents. *(Killeen Daily Herald)*

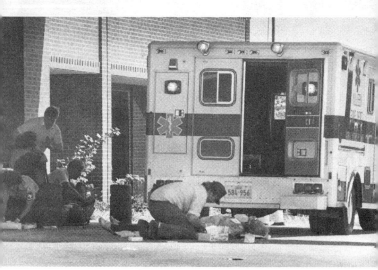

Paramedics tend to shooting victims at the Luby's crime scene *(Killeen Daily Herald)*

Police investigate the Luby's crime scene after the shooting.
(Killeen Daily Herald)

Luby's dining room in the aftermath of the shooting.
(Killeen Daily Herald)

Victim Nancy Stansbury. *(Killeen Daily Herald)*

Victim Dr. Michael Griffith. *(Killeen Daily Herald)*

Victim Debra Ann Gray. *(Killeen Daily Herald)*

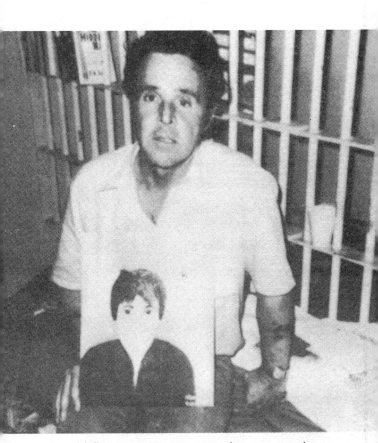

Serial killer Henry Lee Lucas in the county jail in Georgetown, Texas. He is posing here for a picture taken for *Life* magazine with a portrait he drew of "sister" Clemmie. *(Nan Cuba)*

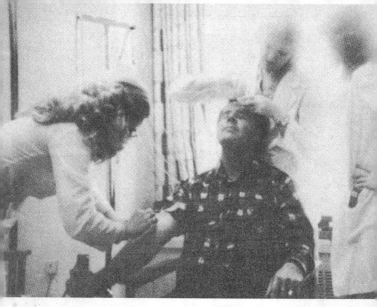

Lucas undergoing EEG testing. *(Nan Cuba)*

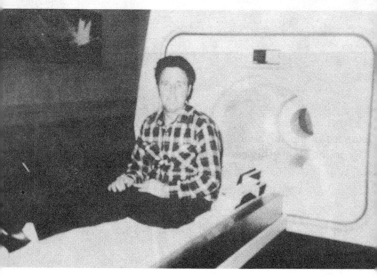

Henry Lee Lucas prior to a CAT scan at Baylor University Hospital in Dallas, Texas. *(Nan Cuba)*

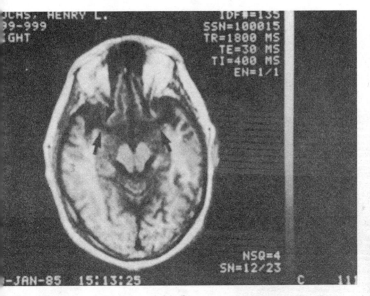

This photograph is the result of a magnetic resonance scan of Henry Lee Lucas's brain. The arrows, which are in the temporal lobe, point to a black area of spinal fluid accumulations. Some accumulation in this area is normally present, but the spinal fluid channels are widened at the expense of the surrounding brain, more on the left side than on the right. This may be the result of a past injury.

(Nan Cuba)

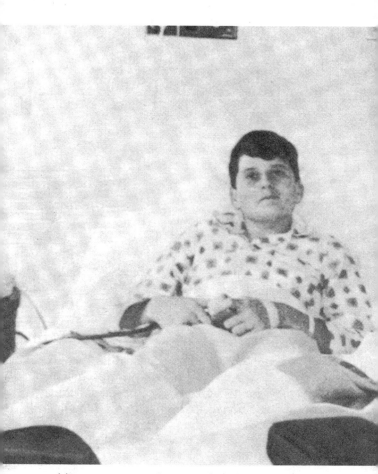

Bobby Joe Long at the age of twelve, recuperating in the
hospital after having six pounds of breast tissue removed.
Long remembers being terrified that he was
becoming a woman. *(Long)*

Louella Long; Bobby Joe Long's mother; Bobby Joe Long; his wife, Cindy. These are the two women that Long blames for his untempered hatred of women. *(Long)*

Bobby Joe Long pictured with his wife, Cindy, and their two children during the time that Long was raping women. *(Long*

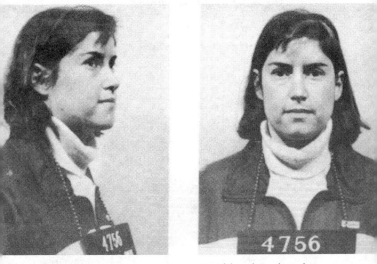

Laurie Wasserman Dann in a Highland Park Police Department arraignment photo before her final shooting spree at a suburban Chicago elementary school, during which she killed one student and critically wounded five others. After her shooting spree, she barricaded herself in a nearby house and finally shot herself to death. *(Meinhardt/Sipa Press)*

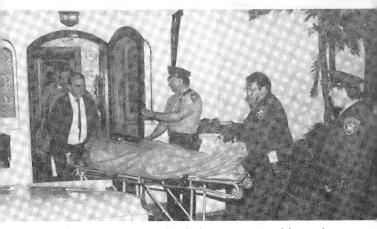

Laurie Wasserman Dann's body being removed by police from the house where she shot herself to death. *(Meinhardt/Sipa Press)*

Charles Andrew Williams being led away by a San Diego Sheriff's Deputy, after he surrenders inside the boys' restroom. *(© San Diego Union Tribune / ZUMA)*

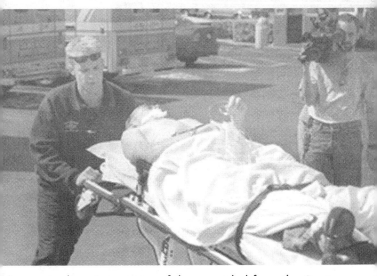

San Diego Sheriff's deputies and SWAT team officers assemble before they sweep the school yard at Santana High School to search for Charles Andrew Williams. *(© San Diego Union Tribune / ZUMA)*

A paramedic removes one of the wounded from the Santana High School crime scene. *(© San Diego Union Tribune / ZUMA)*

One of the Santana High School shooting fatalities: seventeen-year-old Randy Gordon.
(© San Diego Union Tribune / ZUMA)

Becky away from him. The two of them pushed Lucas out of the truck. The truck driver simply took her away. Now, he cried, he was truly alone and had nowhere to go. Moore and the others in the community took pity on him at first. Even Kate Rich said she believed his story, and invited him to take her to church one Sunday evening weeks later in early September.

It was a warm night and they were early. Kate agreed to drive into Oklahoma with Lucas so he could get some beer before going to church. Lucas began drinking heavily again, started to drive erratically, and Katy Rich got scared. Something was wrong. Lucas started complaining about Becky, how she deceived him, how she had led him on, how she had slapped him—and that was more than any man was going to take from a spoiled thirteen-year-old. Mrs. Rich became more suspicious, Lucas confessed months later to Sheriff Conway about that night, and started asking him where Becky was. By now it was already too late for church, and Lucas, now clearly angry, told Mrs. Rich he would drive her home. But, Lucas said, Kate Rich persisted in her questioning. She wouldn't let up. On the way back into Ringgold, Lucas suddenly turned the car off the highway and onto a dirt road leading to a remote old pumped-out oil patch where he stopped the car.

Had Kate Rich asked one too many questions about Becky? Had she challenged Henry's story in ways he couldn't answer? Had she threatened him? Not even Lucas is sure about what triggered him to kill her, but he did. He turned on her with his knife as she sat next to him in the car. It was sudden, violent, and bloody. After she was dead, he cut an upside-down cross between the old woman's breasts, had sex with her corpse, and dragged her into a culvert where he lodged her inside with a two-by-four. The he drove back to the House of Prayer, where he told Ruben Moore that he had left her at home because she was too sick to go to church. A week later, Moore told Lucas that Granny Rich's relatives in Oklahoma were concerned that she hadn't been answering her phone. Could Lucas check up on her? Lucas told Ruben Moore he would check in on her after he came back from a shopping trip to Ringgold. He needed to buy some work clothes, he said. But he never came back that afternoon.

Instead, Lucas fled to New Mexico while Granny Rich's relatives drove to Ringgold to search for the old woman. When they realized she had disappeared, they filed a report with Sheriff Bill Conway, who immediately put out a material witness warrant for Lucas, allegedly the last person to have seen Kate Rich alive. The more Conway searched for information about Lucas, the more suspicious he became. He received records of Lucas's earlier homicide conviction in Michigan, records about the disappearance of Becky Powell, and information about outstanding warrants against Lucas. But without Lucas, Conway had no direct link to the missing Kate Rich.

Conway's break came in a phone call from the Smarts in California. Lucas had turned up looking for work. There were bloodstains all over the front seat of his car. The Smarts were worried. Conway asked the California Highway Patrol to impound Lucas's car in order to take blood samples and to hold Lucas for questioning. However, the bloodstains were too old, Lucas didn't reveal any useful information, and he was later released. He fled to Illinois where he soon ran out of money and any opportunity to find a job. He was broke and had nowhere to turn. He applied for welfare assistance and food stamps, but still had to wait for approval. Finally, out of desperation and also because he believed he was not a suspect in Kate Rich's disappearance, he called Moore for money, who, at Sheriff Conway's urging, sent him transportation money and invited him back to the House of Prayer where he could stay until he found a job.

Lucas was taken into custody shortly after he arrived. He was a material witness, if not a prime suspect, because not only was he the last person to have seen Kate Rich alive, he was a convicted murderer and the car that he had driven to Kate Rich's house had bloodstains all over the seat. Conway jumped all over Lucas once he brought him to the jailhouse. He questioned him about Kate Rich, arrested him on a stolen-car warrant from the state of Maryland, and interrogated him in jail about the disappearance of Becky Powell. But Lucas refused to give up anything. He claimed to know nothing about either Kate Rich or Becky Powell's whereabouts. Soon after Lucas's arrest, the state of Maryland wired Conway that the car theft case had gone stale for lack of witnesses and that the state would not file for the extradition of Lucas. Conway had no choice but to release him.

However, once back at the House of God, Moore noticed that Lucas had a small-caliber revolver in his possession. Clearly worried, he contacted Sheriff Conway, who, now that he had a charge he could make stick, immediately rearrested Lucas on a weapons charge and began questioning him again about Kate Rich's and Becky Powell's disappearance. It was in Conway's jailhouse that Lucas finally broke down and claimed that the voice of God was in his head and was forcing him to confess.

LUCAS AND SATANIC CULTS

Part of Henry Lee Lucas's professed jailhouse conversion had to do with his previous involvement in ritualistic slayings and ritualistic cults. At one time he claimed that he joined outlaw cult groups as a reaction against his being paroled from the Michigan penitentiary. "I killed from the day I left Iona Prison," he says. "And some of the inmates there told me about cults. What I learned in prison, I asked some of the inmates there about a group that I could join that would help out on this outside. I was given several choices. The one I was told about that I liked the sound of the most was in Florida. After I eventually joined the cult, and especially after I left the cult, the killing got worse and worse and I began to hate more and more."

Cults can be a major influence in the life of an episodic

killer because the cult mind-set: obsessive adherence to ritual, unmediated violence, abuse of drugs, hallucinogens, and alcohol, and deviant sexual fantasies are almost commonplace in both types of crime. Many of the same warnings that red-flag a potential homicidal time bomb also red-flag potentially violent cult practitioners. Lucas says that he lived in both worlds. Lucas talked about violent rituals and ceremonies in which cult leaders practiced their rites, particularly in one Florida cult called "The Hand of Death." "Everyone would be high on drugs. Sometimes a member would only bring a head or another part of the victim's body and each of us would testify about the destruction we had been part of since the last meeting. Sometimes we would use our own cult members—say, if someone was about to leave the cult, then they were as good as dead. If it were a girl, they would take the horn of a bull and ram it up into her. The high priest would come in with a hooded-type cloak and could get some people so worked up that they could walk through fire around the altar and not even feel it. We would get higher and higher on drugs. We would rub each other's bodies with the blood of the victim or of the animal and some members would drink each other's urine. During all of this, someone would be chanting and praying to the devil. Towards the end, the victim would be killed and each of us would drink blood and eat part of the body. Ottis liked to eat part of the bodies, but I never could do that."

THE LUCAS SYMPTOMS

Of all the serial killers I have ever encountered, Lucas best typifies what can be called a "serial killer syndrome." He was a time bomb whose fuse had been lit very early in his childhood by a mother who told him repeatedly that he was no good and would someday die at the hand of the state executioner.

Described as a sociopath with a debilitating character disorder, Lucas's real actions have defied traditional labels. Outside prison, he has behaved as if he were a depraved animal, killing and maiming anyone unlucky enough to fall into his clutches. Inside prison, however, he has functioned at close to normal levels because of the highly structured community rules and direct forms of punishment for rule infractions. Under the care of doctors or therapists, he has been able to look upon his own crimes with such a convincing sense of remorse that even the most experienced police officers have been unable to explain it. Many have felt that Lucas was simply lying all the time to save his own skin from the executioner's needle. Others have believed that Lucas remembered specific facts that only the real killer could have known. It is likely that his secrets will go to the grave with him.

Many times during the course of his confessions and recantations in jail, prosecutors have felt that they were being manipulated by a master. In reality, psychologists have pointed out, Lucas's remorse was the result of his being confined to a stabilized environment. Completely institutionalized, Lucas is now on a regular diet, he is no longer consuming alcohol, he has undergone psychotherapy in which his hallucinations and confessions of crimes have been taken seriously for the first time, and he has claimed to have experienced several religious conversions.

The paradox of Lucas's behavior and the layering of his different medical and psychological problems are the results of years of abuse suffered as a child. Because it is so easy to dismiss him as a psychopathic killer, a deranged criminal, or a satanic fiend, it is also easy to disregard the very real factors that helped created a Henry Lee Lucas. His medical and psychological symptoms result from severe brain damage and prolonged alcoholism and nutritional deficiency. CAT scans and nuclear magnetic resonance tests performed on him reveal that the repeated head traumas he received during childhood damaged the sectors of his brain that control primal emotions such as love, hate, and fear. Lucas's chronic drug and alcohol abuse also contributed to his criminal behavior by diminishing his voluntary control over his emotions and increasing the length and depth of his mental-blackout periods.

Lucas claims that he always drank heavily immediately preceding every murder. Furthermore, the high levels of lead and cadmium content in his blood indicate a nonresilient personality, one that is unable to cope with any negative stimulus. All of these factors—the brain damage, his savagely violent childhood, his substance abuse, and his nonresiliency—fused and depressed his abilities to control his most primal of emotions. Each aspect of his life would have contributed independently to a psychologically crippled adult existence were it not for the negative parenting that taught Lucas that life was without value and that he was a person of no worth in a hostile world. It was as if his mother's negative parenting, the constant reinforcement that Lucas was the child who would come to no good, was indeed a self-fulfilling prophecy. It was the single factor that acted as a catalyst, combining all the other negative factors in his deviant childhood into the violent individual who could only relate to creatures after he had killed them.

Lucas was ghoulish in the true sense of the word. He came alive only upon the death of another being. He gained sexual potency after he had bludgeoned and strangled his sex partner into a coma or to death, and he would then have intercourse with the victim's remains. He existed in the world of the living by subterfuge and camouflage and by trusting no one. He even turned on those who had been his companions, killing Becky Powell because she confronted him as his mother had. He killed Kate Rich for probably the same type of confrontation. He failed at everything positive in life, succeeding wildly only at murder and creating misery and pain.

Clinical evaluations conducted on Henry Lee Lucas after his murder conviction revealed extensive neurological damage to vital areas of his brain. There were significant contusions to the frontal poles that indicated a frontal lobe injury—severely impairing cognition and logical thought. There was severe damage to his temporal lobe, and pools of spinal fluid were discovered at the base of his brain. He must have been in severe pain most of the time. There was an enlargement of the right and left sylvian fissure, at the expense of the surrounding brain tissue, which indicated significant loss of judgmental functions and was the result of head traumas received after birth. Neurologists, commenting on the results of both CAT scans and NMRs, confirmed that the extent of brain abnormality indicated an individual who was not able to control violence with the same degree of success that people with more normally developed brains are able to do.

The neurological diagnoses were also supported by symptoms of hypergraphia, the inability to control one's self-expression through writing, painting, and speaking, and by periods of either blackout or grayout, in which the person experiences long periods of floating sensations and the inability to perceive different objects around him. The experience of floating sensations also indicates a form of deep sensory-motor epilepsy that requires constant EEG monitoring for periods of thirty-six to forty-eight hours to diagnose. The length of the test is necessary for the machine to pick up the telltale deep spikes of the seizures. In addition, Lucas's hypergrandiosity and hyperreligiosity are traits common to people who have incurred damage to their temporal lobes. The loss of judgmental ability, the loss of the ability to balance feelings against logic and sensory input, leads to a form of internal feedback in which the brain acts directly upon its own delusions. In other words, what the brain thinks it sees becomes reality. Lucas's extreme dealings with satanic cults in Florida and his sudden—almost too sudden—conversion to born-again Christianity in jail only a few years later are examples of this symptom. Even after his conversion to

Christianity, Lucas continues to manipulate those around him with an almost uncanny ability to sense what he thinks they want him to say.

Toxicological tests also reveal that the high level of lead and cadmium found in his nerve tissue, combined with the years of chronic alcohol and drug poisoning, destroyed a significant amount of cerebral capacity and left him with no physical or psychological resiliency. The three indicators of active cadmium poisoning—loss of dream recall, excessively strong body odor, and loss of sense of smell—are all well documented in Lucas's medical tests. In fact, the killer still does not remember most of his dreams, and allegedly drove around in a car for three days with the decapitated head of one of his victims on the seat beside him without noticing the acrid and foul smell of decomposing flesh.

Like all serial killers and most multiple murderers, Lucas demonstrated bizarre and violent sexual activity combined with a confusion regarding his sexual identity even before he committed his first serious crime. He claimed that he had sex with relatives, committed bestiality, and engaged in forms of necrophilia with parts of his victims' corpses. He has killed, he says, in order to gain sexual potency, because he was unable to have sex or achieve orgasm with a living person, who, just by being alive, challenged Lucas's superiority and posed a life threat to him. Any ability to rely on his own sense of being was so completely destroyed by Lucas's mother that even today he realizes that in order to have any relationship with a person he must kill that person. And after he has killed his sex partner, if the relationship had been positive in his own mind, he mourns for the victim and for himself. If the relationship was only sexual, he had coitus with the remains and left them in a shallow grave or in a roadside culvert.

Forced to watch his mother have sex with her clients and forced to wear girl's clothing to school and to wear his hair in curls, Lucas developed a hatred of women that has contaminated his entire life. Even Becky Powell had only to argue with her up-to-then protector, and in the next moment she lay dead from a knife wound through her chest. And with the memory of Becky's murder still playing back in his mind, Lucas turned his attention to Katherine Rich and killed her only a short time later. Thus, he put to death the only two women with whom he had had any close relationship, because he did not have the personal resiliency to sustain those relations in moments of confrontation.

Throughout his life Lucas has demonstrated an escalating propensity toward violence, another important trait that most time bomb personality types demonstrate. As a very young child, he was a firestarter and was maliciously cruel to animals. As an older child, he practiced bestiality, rape as an adolescent, and single murder as a young adult. As a fully emerged serial killer, Lucas committed multiple murders, spree murders, necrophilia, torture, mutilation, dismemberment, and totemic preservation of the remains of his victims. He had even admitted that despite his conversion, he recognizes that he can exercise no control over himself, and was grateful for the intervention of the criminal-justice system for that control. He admitted on more than one occasion that if he were released through some quirk of justice, he would probably kill again. He recognizes society's laws but maintains that punishment has no meaning for him because he has been through what no human being should ever have to endure. Even though he had been diagnosed as sane, Lucas knows that within him there is a darkness that nothing can reach.

Thus, Lucas has lived his years in a kind of phantom world, in part because his brain was never able to process information in the same ways that healthy brains do, and in part because the normal conditioning was twisted by his mother into an aberration of morality in which evil became her version of good. The successive malnutrition, and the poisoning of the cerebral tissue from alcohol and drugs, all combined to cause a progressive degeneration of Lucas's neurological system. The physical connections between the different areas of the brain, the hundreds of thousands of electrochemical switches that balance primal feelings of violence with logical, socially ordered behavior, simply don't fire. As a result, when pushed to a certain point, Lucas becomes incapable of controlling his own actions. When asked how he perceived his victim at the times he had murdered, he explains, "It's more of a shadow than anything else. You know it's a human being, but yet you can't accept it. The killin' itself, it's like, say, you're walkin' down the road. Half of me will go this way and the other half goes that way. The right-hand side don't know what the left-hand side was goin' to do." But even more important,, the combination of the physiological, chemical, and psychological events resulted in a type of nonperson, an individual who was so far beyond the bounds of normalcy that the traditional categories used to described deviant behavior no longer apply. Henry Lee Lucas, like the other killers here, belongs to the walking dead, creatures who prey on the life force of others. He is a man who died emotionally and socially before the age of ten and for whom existence had become only a hunt to satisfy his primal urges from each moment to the next.

Lucas lived in a world of shadows while outside prison. Inside the walls of a penitentiary, deep within the rules of prison life, he is as docile as he is manipulative, conforming to the needs of others so as to make them conform to him. He is in an almost symbiotic relationship with his jailers and counselors. He was miserable before his professed conversion to Christianity and even attempted suicide on many occasions to stop the hallucinations that were thundering across the hemispheres of his shorted-out brain circuitry. Finally, in death row, Lucas has adapted the structure of the institution as an external skeleton.

Lucas's entire story, whether his confessions are true, his recantations are true, or the recantations of his recantations are true, points up the gaping flaws in our health-care and justice systems. Lucas says that he practically begged his psychologists and parole officers in Michigan not to let him out of jail. He says over and over again that even though he had served the time allotted to him before he was to be paroled, he knew how much hatred had welled up inside him. "Don't let me out. I know I'll kill again," he claims he wrote to the doctors. But he was released despite his threats and claims.

One way to have stopped somebody like Lucas was to have listened to him at the time. As crazy as he might have sounded, raving to doctors that he was hearing voices telling him to kill, he was nonetheless making threats that were ultimately borne out. It only stands to reason that, looking back on the number of felons like Lucas who have said to doctors that they needed help, an inmate's assertion that he has not been rehabilitated should be one of the factors cited in remanding him to a prison health facility to serve out the remainder of his sentence after he had served enough jail time to qualify him for parole consideration. Part of the irony and tragedy of walking time bombs is that all of them have been in custody at one or more points in their lives at which times they made threats against their "enemies" or against society. Understanding the medical nature of these violent individuals means that doctors have to take these threats seriously enough to investigate the components of their fantasies. Unfortunately, there are far more people on the edge of committing violent acts than most professionals are willing to admit. In Lucas's, Shawcross's, and Fischer's cases, they were so far over the edge that the missed opportunities in their lives stand out like blinking red lights on a traffic board. Time bombs will be stopped only when the professionals in charge of correctional systems realize what they are dealing with.

After all the murders he said he had committed and all the confessions he recanted, Henry Lee Lucas wound up cheating the executioner, after all, when he died of a heart attack in prison in March 2001. Expressing his admiration for serial killer Rafael Resendez-Ramirez, the "Texas Railway Killer," Lucas told reporters that if he had been on the loose when those murders were committed, he would have confessed to them as well. He was out to make law enforcement "look stupid," he said. And that's just what he did when he confessed to over three hundred murders around the country. After Lucas's body was found in his cell, it was taken to the Huntsville Funeral Home. It was the final chapter in the mysterious life of a person who had claimed to be America's most prolific serial killer but who, in reality, was probably America's most prolific confabulator.

7

THE APOCALYPTIC VISION OF DANIEL RAKOWITZ: "DIE, YUPPIE SCUM"

A dull, pale, sullen hostility hangs over Tompkins Square Park in New York City's Lower East Side like a damp rag during the dog days of summer. The permanent homeless population residing in the park cluster around the clamshell where West Indian musicians bang out folk rhythms on their metal drums, competing with the electronic megawatt sounds of a skinhead death rock band. Occasionally one group or another will torch a garbage can to the delight of whoever is watching. The fire burns whitehot and furious, spitting off sparks in a thousand directions, and eventually dies. The fire trucks do not come.

The homeless are gesticulating vigorously into the air, fighting with themselves in an angry staccato like priests of some exotic religion. Some of them simply bark at imaginary demons, or nod off in narcotic stupors on the concrete benches. They fight their private wars with invisible armies, long-dead parents or children who abandoned them to the city's welfare system, spouses who might have disappeared years before, or the ghosts of their tormented childhoods. New York's homeless are the new armies of the night, trapped in their endless schizophrenic nightmares, out of contact with time and place.

Occasionally on summer evenings, when the air is especially hot and muggy and the patrol officers from the Nine—the local precinct house on the Lower East Side—seem to disappear, one of the park residents—a babbling psychotic, a too-aggressive beggar, or an angry drunk—will lunge at one of the Yuppie joggers who've recently invaded the neighborhood. She might be one of the area's newest residents, urban pioneers investing in one of the new co-ops in the renovated buildings that line the park. She has a stake in the community, an investment, that she believes none of the homeless people, the crazies, the drunks, or the cokeheads squatting with their huge collection of recyclable cans on the little patches of grass can possibly match. The jogger is practiced at running this course. She dodges and squirms away, still glaring at the blotched, toxin-spotted hand as it recedes into the distance, and focuses on the next obstacle ahead of her. Her evening's run would be more like a video game if the homeless didn't actually touch her.

Tompkins Square was known as Needle Park in the 1960s when Timothy Leary first appeared there to proselytize among the teenagers and head shops dutifully sprung up all along St. Marks Place and First Avenue. In the 1980s, the influx of investment-banking wealth transformed the undervalued area. And by the end of the decade, gentrification was well on its way to creating another "growth area," as the real estate agents called it, in Manhattan. But nobody told the homeless people about it. They just assumed the park belonged to them as it always had. That was what the street people who hustled through the East Village living off handouts, street assaults, and drug deals told them. And that was how the trouble started.

DANIEL RAKOWITZ AND THE
TOMPKINS SQUARE RIOT

On the surface, the ghoulish murder and dismemberment of dancer Monika Beerle in 1989 and the ugly 1988 riot that broke across Tompkins Square Park like the explosion of a summer-afternoon thunderstorm were completely unrelated. After all, the street people said for months after the murder that everyone who knew Daniel Rakowitz—the individual who called himself Jesus—also knew that he was headed for trouble. Rakowitz had himself predicted it, announcing to anyone who would listen to him that he was going to kill police officers from the Ninth Precinct: he'd "tear their heads off," he told a Channel 2 news team headed by correspondent Mike Taibbi. "The cops aren't prepared for someone crazy like me," Rakowitz said almost a full year before he was arrested for murdering Beerle, boiling her skin off, decapitating her, cutting her body into small parts, flushing them down the toilet, and stashing her bleached bones in a locker at the Port Authority Bus Terminal.

As one of the park's human fixtures, Rakowitz saw himself as a leader of the homeless and the crazies, a facilitator of the coming revolution, the provider of food and dope, and a street philosopher for anybody who would listen to him. He had migrated to the "Alphabets" by skateboard earlier from Washington Square Park, where he had sold dope to NYU students sopping up local color and hobnobbing with the local freaks. Now, by the summer of 1988 in Tompkins Square, Rakowitz saw himself as the center of the coming revolution, keeping the network alive. He would beg for food outside the local supermarket and distribute it among the homeless people who couldn't fend for themselves. But Rakowitz was seething with rage, and began following any streams that would lead him toward the apocalyptic event he believed he was destined to experience.

In the late spring of 1988, after Rakowitz had arrived in

the neighborhood, he became loosely involved with a "combat rock" band called Missing Foundation, whose performances were punctuated by staged confrontations with members of their audience. Missing Foundation concerts were often marked by extreme violence. Band members set fire to themselves, set fire to garbage cans and piles of trash, destroyed the stages on which they performed, and launched physical attacks on individuals in the audience. Their performances were alive with soaring flames, flying furniture, and other articles. The Missing Foundation claimed to have a political validity: they represented the underclass who were being displaced by the Yuppies of the 1980s. The rock group's logo was an upside-down champagne glass, a symbol that represented the message "the party's over." Lyrics to their songs were punctuated with death threats and chants such as "Die, Yuppie scum." People in contact with the group claimed that band members also participated in satanic rituals, performed cultlike sacrifices of small animals, and observed the rites of the black mass, although band members have denied participating in satanic practices. Rakowitz fell under the influence of this group and, some of his acquaintances from the Lower East Side said, adhered to their beliefs. Missing Foundation was just not another band, he claimed; it was part of a class struggle.

In July 1988, according to a CBS investigative news team's reports, Missing Foundation was one of the groups fomenting against the gentrification of Tompkins Square Park. When the New York City Parks Department attempted to impose a curfew on the park to control the homeless population in permanent residence there, the disparate groups came together to protest. It was as if tinder had been struck in dry underbrush. Suddenly, the anger and resentment at the area's new residents that had been building ever since the city's downtown real-estate push of the middle eighties welled up and became focused upon the young urban pioneers seeking to reclaim the Lower East Side. In his own words, Rakowitz became politicized. He told friends that he saw the anger as a lever, an instrument for his personal apocalypse. For the first time since he had arrived in New York from his native Texas, he saw a purpose for all of the rage that had been building up in him. He understood that he was an outsider fighting against the insider. He saw himself as a new Hitler and promised that when he came to power, people who had abused him were going to pay. Thus, it was in the context of a personal fantasy of social revolution that he quickly became one of the people involved in planning the protest. However, according to Rakowitz himself, his aims went beyond purely political motives.

Armed with the message of political violence channeled into a throbbing, incessant, electronic beat, Rakowitz began organizing. He absorbed the meaning of the group's confrontational violence, saw in the human bonfires that marked the group's concerts the bonfire that he himself would create when the police came to enforce the new curfew. In his mind, he revealed in background interviews, the coming violence at the park would be his personal statement of violence as well. "They're gonna get more than they bargained for," he promised. He threatened to kill the police officers assigned to enforce the curfew even as he mobilized the forces of the homeless and the psychotic. This would be his war.

One month later, Rakowitz's private war had gone sour. The mass civil disobedience that had been planned for Tompkins Square Park in August 1988 turned into more of a police riot than a riot of the homeless. At first, as the police refused to take the protest seriously, Rakowitz and other park dwellers cavorted grotesquely before the television cameras in a kind of street theater. Suddenly it wasn't New York, 1988, it was Berkley, 1965, and the freaks and crazies abounded. But the drama turned into real life when the police, outnumbered by the gathering crowds, called for reinforcements.

The personnel deployed from the Ninth Precinct, mostly young officers who had not spent much time in the force, seemed on camera to have been grossly inexperienced in crowd control. They arrived in buses and vans and set up barricades before they realized they were in sudden danger of being overwhelmed, but then they struck out with considerable force. Orderly lines of crowd control deteriorated into individual fights between helmeted cops and small knots of demonstrators. As the mobs overturned garbage cans and began hurling glass and bricks at the police, the young officers formed into separate lines and attacked. The police units charged ferociously into the protesters, dispersing them with clubs and truncheons. Within minutes, the street people were overwhelmed. Before Rakowitz had a chance to put his private strategy into effect, he was routed along with the other demonstrators, and he disappeared into the surrounding neighborhood.

In a few hours it was all over and the park had returned to its muggy sullenness. Nothing had changed. The homeless still hovered around the outskirts of the park, rotting garbage was still piled up around the bandshell, Yuppie joggers returned later that night to weave their paths through the obstacle course of beggars and vagrants, and advocates for the homeless returned to pull individual psychotics off the streets and bus them to the shelters. There were more cops around the park, glaring at the residents, sightseers, and reporters. Local TV news crews returned to take their final establishing shots for the eleven P.M. broadcasts before packing their vans and heading back to their studios. There were a few foreign correspondents wandering around the park, a writer for *Stern* and a reporter for Tass, trying to interview one of the psychotics dragging his bag of cans along the sidewalk. Nothing at all had changed except perhaps for the thwarted Daniel Rakowitz, who lurked on the edge of the darkness, still angry, still at war with society, still plotting his revenge.

"I AM THE LORD OF LORDS"

Rakowitz was born in Texas on Christmas Eve, 1960, and claimed that from the time he was a young child he knew that he was the reincarnation of Jesus Christ. He told reporters after the riot that he had had hallucinations when he was very young in which he was visited by the "Wise Men." "They floated above me," he said. "In and out of walls." In addition, Rakowitz said in interviews that he had been diagnosed as a hyperactive child. He claimed that even from the time that he was in early elementary grades, he had been taken to psychologists, some of whom recommended aggressive drug therapy for the child. He was institutionalized on more than one occasion, he claimed, and complained to friends in Tompkins Square Park years later that he had received shock therapy when he was fourteen. (When journalists called Rakowitz's father, Tony Rakowitz, to ask him about these claims, he declined to answer any questions about his son.) By the time he was in his late elementary grades, Rakowitz recalled with bitterness to his friends, he had been mercilessly picked on by the other students in his small Texas school district.

Even worse than the shock treatments, Rakowitz claims, and the constant trips to psychiatric hospitals for evaluation, was his two-year dosage of the drug Ritalin. Ritalin was the drug of choice for controlling difficult children in the 1960s and early 1970s before its routine use was discouraged. Ritalin was routinely prescribed by overzealous doctors who simply wanted overactive children to "behave," it was recommended by school psychologists who responded to teachers' complaints that certain children couldn't "sit still in class," and it was routinely administered by school nurses to control "problem" children during the school day. The use of Ritalin was recommended to parents, who actually believed that it was a wonder drug that could turn their hopelessly hostile children into socially adjusted and successful achievers. Parents believed it was like taking an aspirin for anti-social behavior.

But psychologists, school administrators, and parents didn't realize then that when incorrectly prescribed, Ritalin could also mask a variety of childhood symptoms that might have ranged from schizophrenia to reactions to abuse in the home; for many children, there was simply no way of knowing. In Rakowitz's case, according to his own fragmented recollections, there were a variety of problems, not the least of which was the death of his mother at a young age and strict disciplinarian attitudes of his father, the town deputy sheriff. Whatever Rakowitz's childhood problems were, the Ritalin not only seemed to mask the symptoms, it also so sedated Rakowitz that he walked in a physical and emotional fog through much of his preadolescent years.

It was as if he was sleepwalking, Rakowitz told his friends at Tompkins Square. Or like he was wearing chains or weights. He told a newspaper reporter that he was the slowest runner in the school and the joke of the class. Rakowitz describes his fights with other children in his school. Because he always seemed dazed or crazy, the clown or the fool, the other kids picked on him relentlessly. Like other children who in later life exploded into violence, he was physically intimidated and beaten by other children. Yet, when he tried to defend himself, he was punished with a paddle because he was supposed to be crazy. In this way, he became an enemy of the system at a very early age, was taught to internalize his rage, and was taught to see himself as a victim. By age eleven, he was already well on the road to a violent adolescence in which he was seeking revenge and retribution against anything he perceived as an injustice. This need for blood vengeance would fuel him throughout his years in New York, right up through the Tompkins Square Park riot, and through his dealings with Monika Beerle, the woman for whose murder a New York County jury found him not guilty by reason of insanity. Rakowitz was remanded to the Kirby

Forensic Psychiatric Center on Wards Island and has petitioned the court for his release.

Rakowitz was also hampered by the routines he forced himself to repeat on a daily, even hourly basis. He had an obsessive need to keep himself clean, constantly washing his hands and bathing, and he feared coming in contact with other people and articles he referred to as alien. He shunned schoolyard games and didn't want to play contact sports. In fact, even touching people repulsed him. None of these reactions helped him adjust. In fact, the more his teachers saw him withdrawing from people around him, the more they branded him as antisocial and punished him.

Rakowitz's childhood rage at the injustices of the world and the hopelessness of his own life was further exacerbated by the death of his mother. While he was still a child and causing no end of trouble for his family, his mother collapsed of a heart attack right in front of him. She went into cardiac arrest and all attempts to resuscitate her failed.

Daniel apparently didn't knuckle under to his father's demands for discipline. He complained to his friends that things only got worse after he became a teenager. Rakowitz claimed to his friends that at age fourteen he was in a mental hospital getting shock treatments. But after he was released, Rakowitz fell back into old behaviors and began experimenting with drugs, which caused more tension between him and his father during his teenage years. Tony Rakowitz was described by his boss as a "straight-laced fellow, a real disciplinarian." Daniel Rakowitz would have been a direct challenge to all that his father stood for. Tony had always been a conservative police officer who believed in discipline and law and order. To a deputy sheriff in a rural Texas community, kids like Daniel Rakowitz were seen as troublemakers and real threats. Now his own son—a boy who was always a misfit, a square peg—was turning out to be as bad as other kids his department was busting. The escalating tension and hostility between Tony and Daniel culminated in

Tony's discovery of marijuana in his son's bedroom. He ran him down to the Rockport station, where he was booked on a misdemeanor possession charge. And that was the end of any relationship between Tony Rakowitz and his son. Shortly thereafter, after Daniel turned eighteen, he enlisted in the army and left home.

After earning his marksmanship certification, Rakowitz went on a fourteen-week training program in the army's law-enforcement school. Normally, this training program qualifies graduates for the MP program in the service and for jobs in law enforcement once they've left the military. This was Daniel Rakowitz's hope. Shortly after his discharge from the service, he applied for the position of deputy sheriff in his father's office. Rakowitz was rejected, he learned, partly on the basis of the prior-possession-of-marijuana charges filed against him by his father.

Daniel Rakowitz's rejection by the sheriff's department only increased the bitterness and resentment he already felt toward his home and family. He had tried to make amends, but there was no future for him in Texas and he realized it. He told friends in Tompkins Square Park years later that he still harbored big plans for his return to Texas. He would become a sheriff there, he told them. He could carve several counties out of the rural Texas scrub brush where people could smoke dope and turn on whenever they wanted. He would be the lord of this community, he told friends, and would create a haven where all pot smokers could live in peace. Rakowitz also got married, he told friends, to a very young girl. Their marriage quickly foundered and Rakowitz, after trying to reconcile with his teenage wife, packed up what he owned and headed for New York.

SKID ROW

Rakowitz began dealing dope almost as soon as he arrived in New York in the early 1980s, friends said after his arrest. His first residence was a hotel/flophouse just off the Bowery near New York City's Chinatown. It was there he made quarter-pound scores of marijuana from hard-core dealers which he would later resell to students and street users. He also sold to Yuppie "Wall Street types," as he called them, who were moving into ToHo, the Tompkins Square area, and the East Village as the money began flowing in huge bonuses out of the investment houses. College graduates not any older than Rakowitz himself were finding themselves looking at the potential of six-figure salaries with no end in sight on the corporate ladder. Rakowitz was as bitter and resentful over the appearance of these individuals as he was grateful for them as customers.

Rakowitz was always fearful of being caught up in police undercover buy-and-bust operations, and he sometimes took elaborate precautions. His friends said he trusted no one at the hotel.

His paranoia didn't prevent him from being taken in what he described as a swindle a few years after he had set up shop on the Bowery. Rakowitz claimed that he always wanted to move back west and wanted to rule over a band of his followers on his own land. A friend of his recalled that Dan jumped on a deal to buy some land in Colorado where he was going to build a church and grow marijuana. His friend told him he'd been taken, but Rakowitz kept making payments on the land. "Danny, it's a sham," his friends said. Rakowitz said that the land would be there when he'd made his score.

Rakowitz finally left the Bowery and headed north of Houston Street to Washington Square Park. There, in a new police precinct, he sold pot to the NYU students until he headed east to Tompkins Square. There, in the relatively free atmosphere of the park, Rakowitz set up shop again, panhandling for money to buy dope, and selling the drugs to buy food. It was here that he finally landed an apartment again, and it was the loss of this apartment in a city lunging toward a crisis of homelessness that finally pushed Rakowitz over the edge.

TOMPKINS SQUARE

Daniel Rakowitz quickly established himself in the Lower East Side community around the park. The local residents later described the Rakowitz vision of the world that Daniel inflicted on anyone who would listen to him. He promised a new master civilization, which he would create by having several children with different women. He also told everyone that he wanted to kill cops and then donate their money to the homeless.

The police at the Ninth Precinct also knew about Daniel and his constant refrain about attacking the police. On more than one occasion in 1988, officers at the stationhouse remember, Daniel told them that there would be a riot, the entire neighborhood would burn, and he would kill the police who were putting down the riot. Other officers told newspapers after Rakowitz was arrested for the Beerle murder that they had recognized him as a Tompkins Square Park character who was cavorting through police lines on the night of the riot. Others remembered his ravings, his constant complaint that he wanted to control women. Another police officer remembered that Rakowitz was always talking about raping women and killing them.

Months before the riot, Rakowitz walked into the precinct station on E. Fifth Street and asked for a job. Rakowitz boasted to friends later that he had been discussing employment with the police, but the precinct commander, Deputy Inspector Mike Julian, said afterward that nobody ever offered him a job. Julian was quoted after the murder as saying that Rakowitz had threatened the police, threatened to cut Julian's head off and tear his heart out, but Julian never took it seriously. Nobody took Rakowitz seriously, the commanding officer said, because he was always babbling, always muttering about violence and murder, and always threatened everybody around him. The police just thought he was crazy, like the hundreds of other crazies who lived in the park. Rakowitz was no different from any of them, other officers remembered, he just blended right in. Not only had no one ever suspected any violence, they explained, even after rumors of the murder had begun to circulate, when they centered around "Danny," they were dismissed as part of his ego trip.

Residents remembered the pets he killed or tortured. One man claimed that Daniel had killed cats and dogs. Another described an incident that took place when Rakowitz was smoking marijuana and the rooster started dispersing the marijuana leaves. Rakowitz began pummeling the rooster until people pulled him off in an attempt to save the rooster.

In fact, Rakowitz was desperately in need of his animals. They were his only means of exercising any control over his own life. Squatting in Tompkins Square Park, homeless, living off drug sales and panhandling, Rakowitz had very few measures of self-determination. His animals were his victims, and by killing them, by demonstrating to his friends how he could control his rooster by putting a sock over its head, he was executing the last means of control still left to him. It was a precursor to his final explosion when a woman threatened to exercise another form of ultimate control over him by throwing him out of his own apartment.

By the time he'd met his first two roommates in the Tompkins Square area, Rakowitz had developed a reputation as a harmless psychopath. The area was littered with them and had developed a very distinctive atmosphere. Their constant ravings and mutterings about conspiracies and their threats to kill friends and enemies alike were almost like a choral refrain among the area residents. Even the police took the threats lightly, not finding it necessary to check up on the hundreds of murder confessions they received every week. Daniel Rakowitz easily fell into this category. He was known as a local drug dealer, but in that section of the city drug dealing was the least of the police's problems. Rakowitz had also told many of the local cops that he was planning mass murders, but they'd heard that before, as well. In fact, when rumors of Rakowitz's murder of Monika Beerle first began to circulate, the cops didn't even believe it. They didn't believe Rakowitz even after they'd visited the apartment and were unable to locate Monika herself. Rakowitz was just too much of a "psycho" to be taken seriously, most people thought.

Rakowitz also seemed to have developed a fullblown set of obsessive-compulsive disorders by the time he found his first apartment at Tompkins Square. He was repelled by dirt, frightened and attracted by sex at the same time, and locked into discrete routines of repetitive behaviors that enslaved him at the same time they defined his reality. Friends described the ways Rakowitz would seem almost fascinated with objects he picked up on the street. They watched the show as he would take a filthy bandanna out of his pocket, gently wrap it around the object, fold it neatly into a precise package, and tuck it into his back pocket. What he did with what he found no one knows. But the ceremonies that surrounded his forays into the world outside the boundaries of the park clearly delighted his spectator friends. Rakowitz, the tall, thin, blondhaired young man from Texas, was the best show folks had seen in a long, long time. But for all the grandiosity of his rap and the eccentricity of his behavior, Daniel Rakowitz was just another homeless person shuffling along from one end of the park to another. In the community of the Lower East Side, he blended into the montage of homelessness, the growing, spreading dry rot eating away at the underpinnings of the city. He was just a part of the greater human tragedy, but he was terribly, terribly angry.

Daniel's life began to change the day he was invited to share a third-floor walk-up at 700 East Ninth Street just off the park. He could more than scuffle up the couple of hundred of dollars in rent necessary to keep a roof over his head, by dealing drugs and panhandling. He didn't even need a job. But shortly after he moved in, the young couple who had been living together and were his roommates decided to split up. Now he was alone, with no claim on the apartment, and no means of meeting the $500-per-month rent. He was staring into the deep chasm of homelessness again and decided that anything was better than that. He decided to take a roommate himself and invited a young dancer from Switzerland to share the apartment. She seemed all too anxious to move in, but friends told him he was making a mistake.

His former roommate told him she was using him and that after she moved in she would move Daniel right back on the street. But Daniel didn't listen. He would make her over into his girlfriend, he told his ex-roommate. She would take care of him and he would care for her. At last he would have a mate. But it wasn't to be. Like the Colorado land deal, Rakowitz was only believing what he wanted to believe, not seeing the reality staring at him.

MONIKA BEERLE

Billy's Topless, the bar over on West Twenty-fourth Street and Sixth Avenue in the no-man's-land between the trendy Flatiron District and Chelsea, is almost a New York City landmark. "You Must Be 21 Years Old," the neon sign flashes in the otherwise darkened window, and that is all passersby can see from the street. Monika Beerle, the young modern dance student and choreographer from Saint Gallen, Switzerland, who'd studied at the Martha Graham School, had applied for a job there. She needed the money and, friends told her, the tips were good.

"She liked to walk on the wild side," childhood friends from her hometown in Switzerland said about her. "She was smart, but she always took chances."

"It's not that she was crazy," one of her boyfriends said. "She didn't follow the crowd. She always wanted to be different. It wasn't artistic, more emotional."

A girlfriend from her school days in Saint Gallen described her as a loner, always the first to challenge authority and convention. "That was one reason she left," the young woman explained to television reporters who'd come to Saint Gallen after Monika's murder. "She couldn't take the convention and wouldn't follow the rules."

By the time she had left Switzerland, Beerle had already earned a teaching certificate in choreography from the Sigurd Leeder School and was establishing a reputation as something of a new-wave artist. Friends at the school said that Beerle was fascinated with performance art as an expression of dance more than she was with traditional dance forms. "She wanted something different and would go anywhere to find it," a former classmate explained.

Although her friends tried to dissuade her from coming to America, it only seemed to stiffen her resolve. And once in New York, Monika Beerle seemed to gravitate toward the most dangerous situations. "She was pretty wild," one of her former roommates said. "But she wasn't what you'd call crazy and she knew when something was dangerous."

"Some people thought she was stupid," a friend of hers from the Lower East Side said, "but that was only her stubbornness. She wasn't stupid and she knew how to play percentages."

"She didn't talk much," friends remember. "That was why some people thought she was stupid. But she knew how to use her body and that was how she spoke."

Besides looking for work at Billy's Topless, Monika also worked as a topless dancer at a longshoreman's bar at the edge of a commercial pier in the Red Hook section of Brooklyn. There, in the tough, hardheaded old Italian neighborhood, she learned to fend off menacing physical advances from dockworkers and cargo handlers and tugboat crewmen. Regulars at the bar say they remember that Monika almost seemed impervious to danger, as if she knew her time had not yet come.

Monika was always on the move, changing roommates

and changing apartments with blinding speed. Her friends said she knew where she wanted to go and was single-minded in getting there fast. "She kept light in her feet and mobile," one of her friends said. "When she saw a place she wanted, she went there fast." Daniel's friends said that what Monika wanted was the second bedroom in the Rakowitz apartment at 700 East Ninth. She was already cramped and felt crowded out in her present apartment on Avenue B and wanted more privacy. The second bedroom meant she wouldn't have to share a room with anyone else, and it was as good as being in a hotel. The rent was cheap and Daniel seemed more benign than weird. There was nothing else to think about.

For Daniel, Monika Beerle was a dream come true, the turning point in his life, he said. He gave a friend the impression they had sex the first night after she decided to move in with him. He kept telling friends that she cared about him and wanted to live with him.

Monika moved into the apartment at the beginning of August, almost a year after the Tompkins Square Riot. During the entire first week, Monika was at the center of Daniel's constant rap. Instead of muttering on about taking over the world and killing the women who wouldn't follow him to Colorado, Rakowitz kept talking about Monika. But Daniel's former roommates thought she had a different agenda. It didn't seem right to them that Daniel was able to go from loner to spouse in only one week. This girl was doing a number on Rakowitz, they believed, and he was just sucker enough to believe it. Both of his former roommates warned him that Monika Beerle, whom Daniel began introducing around as his new girlfriend, wanted no part of him and wouldn't put up with his fantasies.

"She's gonna have the lease in her name, and once it's in her name she's gonna throw you out," one of them told him shortly after he bragged about Monika's moving in. "So if she throws you out, you're out—you're homeless again."

IS IT SOUP YET?

Within the same week that Monika moved in, there were signs of trouble in the apartment. For the first time in his life, friends told the newspapers, Rakowitz believed he had someone he could take care of. He cleaned the apartment for Monika, panhandled food for Monika so she wouldn't have to shop, and cooked for the both of them. Always an obsessive television watcher, he constantly monitored the dials and wooed Monika to the television to share fantasies. But she wanted none of it.

Because Rakowitz had no job and no verifiable income, he could not qualify for a lease. Monika, however, had an income, wasn't homeless, and could lease the apartment in her own name. The lease was transferred from Danny's former roommates to Monika within one week, and Daniel Rakowitz became obsessed with fear. Within the space of a few days, he had gone from an apartment renter to a squatter, living in his apartment at the pleasure of a woman who had become decidedly colder and more hostile once she had the lease in her name.

"Monika knew how to play the game," one of the park residents said. "And when Danny saw that, he went crazy."

For a sexual control freak like Daniel Rakowitz, whose masculinity had been challenged from the time he was the victim of schoolyard brutality, Monika threw the gauntlet right into his face when she started bringing men home to the apartment. Rakowitz was in shock. He'd boasted that Monika had moved in to be with him. His friends had told him that Monika was only interested in herself. Danny was important because he had the apartment. Once she had it, Danny would mean nothing to her. But Rakowitz didn't listen. His own fantasies had become reality. Now, looking at Monika and the parade of men she was bringing back night after night, his fantasies collapsed before his eyes.

One evening she brought back a black man. According to one of his friends, Daniel really hated gays and blacks, so

Monika's actions were the ultimate insult to him. Daniel was so beside himself and so consumed by his anger that Monika's friends urged her to kick Daniel out of the apartment.

In the end her dancing friends prevailed, and Monika confronted Rakowitz with the news his friends had predicted all along. "Be out in two weeks," she told him.

At first Rakowitz pleaded with her. But Monika was stubborn. Once she had made up her mind, friends told police and television reporters after the murder, no one was able to change it. Then he threatened her. She told friends that Rakowitz said he was going to kill her, that she'd never get him out of the apartment, that he's strangle her and cut her up into little pieces like the animals he killed. But Monika apparently laughed in his face. "I'll kill you first," she was reported to have said to him.

Another acquaintance said that Monika was foolish to have gotten involved with Daniel in the first place, adding that she knew he was crazy and suggested that Daniel's direct threats should have been enough of a warning.

Finally Monika herself began telling her friends in the community and Danny's friends in the street that he had threatened to kill her. They were both talking about it. It was common knowledge in the area that Rakowitz was threatening his roommate. Rumors of Rakowitz's fury and his wild ravings once again reached the police who patrolled the park. But the police laughed off the rumors. They'd heard them before, and Rakowitz never caused them any trouble.

On Thursday, August 17, Daniel told his former roommate that he was going to kill Monika the next day. He just couldn't take it anymore, he complained. She was going to throw him out and no amount of pleading or threatening was going to do any good. Either he was going to be homeless or she was going to be dead. There was no other way.

The young woman who had lived with Daniel in the apartment on Ninth Street was frightened, but still in a state of disbelief. She tried not to think about his killing Monika

Beerle, but finally curiosity got the best of her over the weekend and she returned to Tompkins Square to see for herself that everything was okay. She could see from the street on Saturday evening that the apartment was dark. Under the pretext of wanting to recover some of her belongings from her old room—the room that Monika was living in—she knocked on the door. There was no answer.

She went into the kitchen where the television was playing very loudly. There on the stove in a large soup pot was Monika's head. Its eyes were closed and the head all scorched.

In a state of shock and revulsion, she crept her way toward the bathroom, dreading what she would find there. It was worse than she could imagine; worse than anything out of a slasher movie. There in the porcelain tub, swimming in a sea of blood and entrails, was a ribcage all sawed off from the rest of the body. It was only the bones. The skin and muscle had been taken off, and blood was halfway up to the brim of the tub.

Reeling with revulsion and horror, Daniel's exroommate staggered toward the door. She wanted to get out as quickly as possible, but she also didn't want to be seen. There was no escaping it. Daniel had not only killed Monika, he had chopped her up, cut her head clean off, hacked the skin from her body, and left her in the bathroom.

Daniel told the story to other people in the park. He bragged that he had paid Monika back and deprived her of the pleasure of throwing him out into the street. He told anyone who would listen that when Monika had ordered him to be out of the apartment by the next day, he killed her and chopped her up into many little pieces. According to one of his former roommates, he had choked her first, then stomped on her head several times, and finally he stabbed her repeatedly, using her chest "as a carving board." The other roommate recounted to newspaper reporters and to police that Rakowitz had claimed that he had eaten parts of Monika's brain. Daniel also claimed to this former roommate that he was going to serve Monika to the homeless people in the park as well. In Rakowitz's videotaped confession to the police, he said that he killed Beerle accidentally by punching her in the throat. He disposed of the body, he told the cops, because he didn't want to go to prison.

According to one of Daniel's former roommates, Rakowitz had said that a friend of his from a satanic church in Brooklyn was with him when he killed Monika. In fact, the roommate recalled that Daniel had said that it was his friend who had encouraged him to kill Monika on the night of the murder. It took place, she says, after Monika confronted Daniel and his friend in the apartment and told Daniel that if he and his stuff were not out of the apartment by the following morning, her friend and his pit bull would force Daniel out of the apartment. With that, she turned and stomped back into her room, prompting Daniel's friend to urge him to kill Monika.

Daniel Rakowitz lived in the apartment for several more days after he told his friends about killing Monika Beerle. During that time, he continued disposing of her body, flushing her organs and skin down the toilet, boiling down the remaining flesh from her bones. He also cleaned the apartment, scouring away the blood that had hardened in the tile grouting and between the floorboards. Finally, Daniel told friends, he decided to dispose of the bones by packing them into a bucket and ultimately checking it at a baggage storage locker in the Port Authority Bus Terminal. And that became the mausoleum of Monika Beerle.

During the entire period from the middle of August to the beginning of September, Daniel kept bragging about the murder to people in the park and to his former roommates. Other members of the park community were so fascinated with this new twist to Daniel's rap that they began making songs about the murder, and one person even wrote about it on the walls of the apartment building.

Meanwhile, Daniel's friends could see that Rakowitz was growing increasingly scared. After he moved the bones out to the Port Authority and there was no more meat to flush, cook, or distribute, he lived in the apartment alone. It was then, amidst the wildly circulating rumors around the park whenever he walked through, that his former roommate convinced him to leave the apartment. And Daniel fled uptown, where he stayed in an apartment with a girl he had met.

After Daniel left, one of his former roommates told the story of the murder to the building's superintendent, who reported it to the police. Ninth Precinct detectives visited the apartment, found Monika Beerle's belongings strewn all over, but found no evidence of murder. Daniel had gone and nobody knew where he was. Nobody believed the story of the murder, either. It all seemed too bizarre: a harmless, homeless crazy like Daniel who'd been rapping about murder and mayhem for over a year, a topless dancer from Switzerland with a reputation for cutting out on boyfriends, a murder scene where there was no blood, no signs of a struggle, and no body. This was just another Rakowitz goof, the detectives said, but realized they had to interview Rakowitz himself just to play by the numbers. They dialed his beeper number and convinced him to go down to the station for a talk about Monika Beerle.

It was during the interview that Daniel reportedly told them that if he had killed Monika, he would have disposed of the remains down the toilet. According to reports, the police then pulled the toilet and searched the pipes for remains of the missing person. But they found nothing. They were tempted to drop the whole matter, but Daniel's inability to deny that he had killed Monika had them troubled. They decided to pursue the investigation by interviewing any witnesses and looking for more clues. When they returned to the apartment the next time, they found Daniel's other former roommate.

The Ninth Precinct detectives were convinced that if one of the roommates knew about the homicide, the other roommate knew about it as well. They told her that they had written statements from a neighbor and Daniel's other roommate, her former companion. She broke down and told the police everything she knew, including seeing Monika's head on the stove the day after the murder and seeing her remains floating in the bathtub.

The police took Rakowitz into custody as a material witness, confronted him with the statements made by his roommates, and asked for his cooperation. "I need help," Rakowitz reportedly told the police, and then confessed to the murder and the dissection. He led detectives to the Port Authority, where they recovered the bucket of bones and positively identified the skull as that of Monika Beerle.

The police sealed the apartment up as a crime scene, leaving the graffiti still scrawled on the walls. For the Lower East Side residents who knew Daniel and Monika and who received almost daily reports from Daniel on the progress of his descent into murder, the most gruesome aspect of the crime is a piece of graffiti inscribed on the hall outside the apartment. "Is it soup yet?" someone wrote, referring to the head of Monika Beerle, which Daniel claimed he would serve to the park homeless for at least a week after the murder.

THE WARNING SIGNS OF DANGEROUSNESS

Almost everyone who knew Daniel Rakowitz knew that he displayed signs of abnormally bizarre behavior. Even in the environment of Tompkins Square Park and the Lower East Side, where most people display bizarre behavior, Rakowitz stood out. "He was crazier than most," observers said about him. "And that's what made him seem harmless." In an area where people routinely threaten others, where violence and homicide occur everyday on the street corners, and where people are constantly nodding off into catatonic-like states, the appearance of another wildly gesticulating crazy should certainly stir up no new concern.

Daniel Rakowitz was different, however. His behavior stood out from the rest in three major areas. The first was his almost spiritual adherence to the combat-rock group Missing Foundation. It was the group's ability to focus Rakowitz's critical mass of rage and direct his pent-up violence that indicated Rakowitz was not merely a harmless psychotic who should have been institutionalized. It was, in fact, borne out by the murder of Monika Beerle and the jury's findings that he was criminally insane. Rakowitz's stated intention to attack police officers and others was an example of his homicidal rage looking for an outlet.

Was it simply Missing Foundation's political message that stirred Daniel Rakowitz up? Had he become so motivated by the plight of New York City's homeless population that he was striking out at the invading Yuppies? Monika Beerle was not a Yuppie. If anything, she belonged to the same group of combative rockers that Rakowitz was aspiring to. Perhaps that was why she was able to stand up to him and to threaten him to the point of homicidal behavior.

It is likely that Rakowitz responded to Missing Foundation's use of fire and self-immolation as part of its act. One of the clearest indicators of a potentially dangerous personality is an individual's fascination with fire, his need to become involved with the consuming and violent nature of flames, and his consistent attempts to start damaging fires. Most serial killers at some time in their youths have been fire starters, and most have taken some delight in scorching or incinerating their victims. Rakowitz falls into that category.

The second clear indicator was his treatment of animals. To a person, almost all serial killers display great cruelty toward animals. Some routinely kill and dismember animals. Henry Lee Lucas tortured animals; Arthur Shawcross talks about having sex with dead animals, and Daniel Rakowitz killed cats and dogs. People who have animals around them for the purpose of torturing and killing them need to exercise control and show themselves that there are at least some creatures they can dominate. Most, if not all, serial killers and mass murderers are individuals who cannot exercise control over their lives. They are losers; people who've been dominated and abused by others. Their abuse of animals, and their public display of cruelty to animals, is a clear early indicator of impending violence. It is one of the surest signs of potential dangerousness.

The final clear indicator of Rakowitz's growing dangerous inclinations was his focusing of violence on Monika Beerle. As long as Daniel's violence was free-floating, it was diffuse. He was dangerous from the time he had moved into the park, but by announcing specifically that his victim had a name, an identity, and a place where he could find her, Rakowitz had started the process of convincing himself that he was going to kill her. He was too afraid to confront her until she had pushed his last trigger: she challenged him in front of a friend. In his own mind, she crossed the last barrier.

The levels of violence Rakowitz must have lapsed into as he first punched her, then carved her, cut off her limbs, dismembered the rest of her, and then boiled off all her flesh might have been cathartic. By the time he had completed the acts of violence, Rakowitz was also depleted as well. He was then able to walk away from the apartment and experience the posttraumatic-pattern stress associated with what he did. In Daniel's case, had he not been arrested, he would have probably killed again, despite what his former roommate said to reporters about him.

The pressures were building inside Rakowitz from the time he was a child. His conflicts with an authoritarian father are reminiscent of the infamous John Wayne Gacy's conflicts with his father and California serial killer Leonard Lake's conflicts with his stern grandfather and uncle. Both Gacy and Lake reacted to these parent figures by, first, doubting their own masculinity and then attacking those victims who reminded them of what they believed their disciplinarian parent figures represented. What Gacy saw in the gays he picked up in bus stations were the types of drifters and failures that his father said he was. Lake's uncle condemned women, called them weak, and said they undermined what men stood for. At Lake's military school, much of what his uncle represented was inculcated into the cadets. Thus, Lake reserved for women he considered "loose" and corrupt his most vicious types of torture.

Rakowitz also reacted to his father. His mother's death left him without an anchor or linchpin in the world. When his father—at least in his own mind—turned against him, Rakowitz became an enemy, an outsider. Rakowitz saw himself as a perpetual victim. Most serial killers see themselves as victims rather than as abusers.

The murder of Monika Beerle that Rakowitz bragged about to his friends in Tompkins Square Park may have shocked a city, but it was a long time in coming. Sadly enough, the murder of Monika Beerle and the extraordinary levels of violence associated with the disposal of her body might be only harbingers of the levels of violence our society will experience when the current generation of crack children comes of age. Rakowitz might have only been the beginning. It would be at least some consolation if out of the Rakowitz case, his doctors and therapists come to a greater understanding of the medical nature of violence. Wherever Rakowitz is confined, he will provide his doctors with an insight into the visions and violent fantasies of a tortured individual never able to come to terms with his own humility. If his doctors understand the biological and psychotic forces that compelled Rakowitz, perhaps they will be able to help someone else avoid the fate that Daniel Rakowitz did not.

8

LAURIE WASSERMAN DANN: THE MAKING OF A KILLER

Her life ended with a gunshot. She closed her lips around her revolver and put a single .32 round through the roof of her mouth. The bullet shattered the bones of her hard palate, burrowed right through her brain, and splashed the top of her head against the closet wall. Laurie Dann was dead. When the police announced that the heavily armed young woman named Laurie Wasserman Dann had shot and killed herself, no one who knew her was surprised in the least. They had all predicted that something like this would happen. The police announcement said she entered a Winnetka, Illinois, elementary school, where at gunpoint she lined the children against the wall of a second-grade classroom. She opened fire, killing one child and wounding five others, and then ran from the building to a nearby home where she sought refuge from police units sealing off the area. Once inside the home, she took the family hostage and wounded the young man who tried to disarm her. When he fled, she quietly crawled into an upstairs bedroom closet and ended her life.

Her ex-husband, Russell, who had once charged that she had stabbed him with an ice pick after their separation, Russell's brother and sister-in-law, Laurie's former boyfriends, and even the people she'd known at the colleges she'd attended all understood the inevitability of what the police had announced over the radio. They were all victims of her crazed obsession to seek vengeance. Their lives had all been damaged by the unhappy woman who had been slipping into madness for most of her young adult life. The only people who were surprised at what she had done were her psychiatrists and the police. They said later that based on the information they had at the time, they thought she was not capable of such violence.

All the people whose lives she had touched who were listening to the local radio that afternoon had complained to the police on scores of occasions that Laurie Dann was a runaway train on her way to disaster. She had made harassing and threatening telephone calls, savaged the insides of their houses, sent them threatening letters, physically accosted them in parking lots and on the street, and had even stabbed and wounded her ex-husband with an ice pick. Almost all of her victims had filed formal charges against her in their different municipalities but all the separate complaints ran into administrative roadblocks. The cops in three or four cities and in three different states knew about her activities, some police units had formed task forces to track her movements, but all attempts to apprehend her had been put on back burners because the police did not consider her an imminent threat. Finally, the FBI had even investigated her for telephone harassment, had prepared an indictment against her, and had prepared an arrest warrant against her on federal charges involving her making death threats over a telephone. But the FBI's case moved too slowly and the warrant was served too late. She had fled Wisconsin the day before the FBI agent arrived at her dorm, and disappeared until the day of the shooting.

Laurie Dann was left relatively free to create havoc in the lives of the people she perceived to be her enemies while police investigators, local prosecutors, her doctors, and even her parents failed to recognize the web of denial around her that no one could penetrate. But as the police announcement continued to describe the scene of devastation and the final shot that took Laurie's life, no one, absolutely no one she'd ever touched, was surprised. And that's the saddest commentary on the life of Laurie Dann that anyone could have made.

AN UNHAPPY GIRL

Laurie Wasserman was a child for whom nothing seemed to go right. From the time she was a little girl, people recalled about her, she hardly ever smiled. She would sometimes "zone out," one of her friends remembered, sitting wherever she happened to be and staring out into space in a trancelike state. Friends remembered thinking that Laurie was always just a step slower than the other children, always the butt of her mother's criticisms, always a poor second in comparison to her bright older brother, Mark. But, people who knew Laurie Wasserman as a child recalled, she was almost always morose. They can only remember the somber, beetlebrowed unfocused stare of the unhappy child who would ultimately gaze at them from the police photo on pages of the *Chicago Tribune* after she shot and killed herself.

Laurie came from a family that had a history of clinical depression on both sides. Her maternal grandmother, who died when Laurie was a young child, had been treated for severe bouts of depression. Laurie's early mood swings, her clearly somber disposition, and her glowering expressions could well have caused her parents to pay more attention to the achievements of their older son, Mark. Laurie, as a consequence, could have felt unloved, abandoned, and angry. And this pattern of anger might have easily established in Laurie a reflex reaction to cite as "enemies" and worthy of her vengeance anyone whom she perceived as having rejected her. This list included her former husband, Russell Dann, his family, her former boyfriends, and even acquaintances from high school and college. On the final morning of her apocalyptic rampage of self-destruction, she sent packages of poisoned food to a long list of people—even people who didn't know her—whom she had elevated to her list of mortal enemies. Laurie struck out at anyone who entered her tightening circle of defense. Perhaps like the grandmother she didn't know, she might have been angry at her affliction and angry at the people who shunned her because of it.

Laurie's paternal great-grandmother also suffered from clinical depression. Her father, Norm, might not have known very much about his grandmother's condition. After all, his parents migrated from Russia shortly after World War I, and the gulf between the Old Country and the New Country was enormous, especially for a bright, first-generation American looking to make his mark in the world. Although no one can say whether Laurie had inherited some genetic predisposition to depression, by the time she had turned thirty, she had gradually turned into a killing machine that unloosed itself on a classroom of elementary-school children on a warm sunny Friday in late May of 1988.

But Laurie's future was only a dim outline on the horizon by the time she was in junior high school, discernible, perhaps, only to a prescient school counselor, teacher, or psychologist. Whoever it may have been, that person was far, far away and certainly not a part of Laurie Wasserman's life as she painfully lurched toward preadolescence. Someone who had come in contact with the stone-faced little girl with the big, hollow eyes and the large flappy ears had recommended that she be placed in a supplementary special-education class for troubled and learning-disabled children. It was in this unhappy situation that Laurie found herself—in a class populated with chronic underachievers, hyperactive children with severe behavior disorders, socially dysfunctional children who could or would not make friends, slightly retarded children who were too close to the norm to be institutionalized but too far out of the norm to be mainstreamed, and children who were already plagued by teenage addictions to drugs and alcohol. It was into this mix of dysfunctional children, sorely in need of intervention or other therapies, that Laurie Wasserman, "the spaced-out misfit," as other children called her, was placed for remediation purposes.

People who knew her then remember that it was one of the only times in her life, prior to her abortive adult therapy sessions, that she ever attempted to communicate with others. Laurie described to her fellow students in the special-education class how she felt ostracized within her own family, shunted away by her mother and neglected by her father, forced to stand in the shadow of her brother, and feeling that she couldn't succeed at anything. Like most teenage girls with progressive emotional problems, Laurie Wasserman was angry. She walked through her days with a storm cloud of anger raging over her head. And her anger compounded almost all of her problems. It colored the way she perceived others, distorted the ways she related to the outside world, and certainly affected her abilities to see herself.

Her anger made her lash out at anyone w ho tried to enter her inner circle of fear. When her teachers or the counselors in the special-education program tried to get her to talk about her problems, she would begin to open up, but then would quickly shut down. They commented on her severe mood swings—from a "zoned-out" teenager seemingly out of touch with reality to an extraordinary enraged adolescent, who at the instant before she could control it, seemed capable of just about any level of violence. And then when the anger would pass, Laurie would sit there, glowering with hostility at anyone who had tried to help her, or tried to communicate with her, or tried to offer the least bit of advice about her situation. It was clear to teachers and counselors that Laurie was unreachable by normal means.

Professionals who encountered Laurie during her years in junior high and high school were struck only by the mood swings and persistent sullenness of the teenager. They were unaware of her earlier troubles with what, years later, would be diagnosed as an obsessive-compulsive disorder, As a preschooler and even in the early elementary grades, Laurie would become fixated in the need to touch certain objects repeatedly. It was as if she were testing to see whether she were real, the objects in her world were real, and, indeed, whether the world itself was real. What psychologists now know is that these touching rituals are a means of self-orientation for certain types of emotionally or neurologically impaired people who suffer from secondary psychological dysfunctions. As a young child in later elementary grades, Laurie also became fixated with what she would later call "good" and "bad" numbers. This fixation would also crop up, along with her need to touch objects, years later when she entered therapy, but in the early 1960s the problem was probably dismissed as a childhood phase that she would eventually grow out of. Laurie never grew out of it. Her behavior simply became sublimed into a simmering hostility that was never adequately addressed by her parents, her teachers, or other professionals. But it was the loneliness that seemed to torment Laurie Wasserman the most, the isolation that she felt because of her perceived worthlessness and insufficiencies as a person. These feelings would rise up to haunt her every day of her life until the very moment she shot herself.

THE LONELY ADULT

What was a lonely childhood became a pitifully lonely young adulthood. As Laurie Wasserman passed through the stages of adolescence, she bounced off a number of friends and boyfriends, dating fitfully throughout her teens and failing miserably in the dance of the sexes. It was not as though Laurie wasn't attractive. Photos of her as a teenager show that she had moments when she could flash a bright vivaciousness. Boys would become interested in her, casually at first, and then they would try to get to know her better. However, the natural self-interest that motivated the lives of most teenagers was absent in Laurie. Not only did she not like herself in the least bit, she couldn't figure out for the life of her why anybody else would like her.

Her relationships took on an all-too-familiar pattern. At first, boys were attracted to her because she was bright-eyed and pretty. Laurie, when she took the trouble to wear makeup and look happy, could be a very attractive girl—her ears had been surgically corrected years earlier. Often, boys were attracted to her because she seemed needy. Unfortunately for them, Laurie's neediness was no act—it was the real thing, and nobody would be able to fill up the gaping pit of need at the center of her personality. But most boys in high school were unaware of the types of problems a girl like Laurie could have, and so willingly fluttered over to investigate the girl with the lost expression.

If the boys themselves were attractive or socially important, Laurie would allow herself to flirt with the concept of intimacy, the threat of bringing someone close enough into her orbit to be able to inflict pain. Perhaps they would date a few times. Perhaps they would date only once. But inevitably there was an invisible line in Laurie's psychological territory that each boy would cross that would trigger a response. For Rob Heidelberger, who took her to one of her proms, it was showing up late after having had an automobile accident. Laurie, who was used to being hurt and feeling abandoned, could not get beyond her own feelings when Rob arrived and announced that he'd smashed up his father's car. Rob had jerked one of her strings. In her mind, he had provided her with evidence that she wasn't worthwhile enough to be picked up on time for her prom. It was irrelevant that Rob himself had been in an accident, Laurie felt. Laurie's own psychological reactions, her own waves of emotional pain, completely blotted out all other reality. Her hostility that night, her barely disguised fury at the mere possibility of being stood up for a date, made the event intolerable for all who came in contact with her. She cut the evening short, and the next week, Rob broke up with her. For

Laurie, it was an inevitable routine: a boy— any boy—hurts her and then blames her for being hurt. Laurie was becoming used to playing the game.

In college, Laurie had similar experiences with boys, and also found out that she could not integrate with groups of women, as well. Her experiences in trying to "go Greek" failed dismally after she was asked to depledge by one of the socially important Jewish sororities in campus. Shortly after that experience, she met a boy and actually told herself she had fallen in love. That, too, ended in disaster and would be one of the threads that carried through her disintegrating personality as she spun into self-destruction.

David Schwartz, her first real romance, was a premed who became attracted to Laurie after they had turned up in the same psychology section. They were tentative at first, but eventually Laurie, possibly realizing that she could actually have a relationship with this boy, became overly possessive. She clung to him for dear life, taking care of his every need even before he expressed it. Laurie smothered him, isolated him from his friends, and made it impossible for him to lead an independent life. In reality, Laurie was holding on to dear life and she probably knew it. Of course she would only stifle him and eventually drive him away, but something forced her to hang on. Maybe, she might have thought, she could get him to need her as much as she needed him.

In reality, Laurie Wasserman didn't need David Schwartz romantically as much as she needed David to help her not to be alone. Laurie tended to define herself in terms of others. The mere thought that she needed another person made her pathologically afraid at the same time it forced her to grab on the way a drowning person grabs at the first person who swims to the rescue. Maybe Schwartz realized that, or maybe his own survival mechanisms had begun to kick in, because he told Laurie in no-uncertain terms that she had cut him off from all his friends.

When the time came for David to leave for dental school on the west coast, he told Laurie he did not want her to come along. "Get a life," he suggested as nicely as he could. Find a job and start a career. Perhaps, he hoped—because he still liked her—if Laurie could establish some independence, the two of them might have a relationship after his own life was in order. Eventually, David decided after he had struck out on his own, he did not want Laurie in his life at all, and he suggested to her father that he let her down as gently but as firmly as possible. Laurie understood that David had truly abandoned her and years later pursued him, harassed him and his family over the phone, spread malicious false rumors about him in an attempt to ruin his medical practice, drove him out of New York City where he was in residency, and even threatened to kill him and his family.

What Laurie could never grasp, but what was obviously the case, was that her deepest fears of being alone caused her to be alone. The more she struggled against the current, the more the current captured her. The more she fought against David Schwartz's natural needs to lead an independent existence, the more David Schwartz fought to get away. But Laurie didn't realize it when she and David Schwartz broke up. It would take her failed marriage to Russell Dann to present her with the awful truth about her own needs and her inability to satisfy them.

RUSSELL DANN

Laurie's relationship with Russell Dann began while she was still on the rebound from David Schwartz. She caught the glances of Russell Dann one day while she was working at the Green Acres Golf Club restaurant in 1981. His interest blossomed into his asking her out, and soon the two of them were dating. Russell had gotten to know Norm Wasserman, Laurie's father, and had judged him wealthy enough and respectable enough to satisfy his curiosity about Laurie's pedigree. Laurie had started off their relationship by telling Russell a pack of lies but it is likely that Laurie believed that she could patch through the web of lies if she ever let their relationship get serious enough. For the time being, it was enough to tell Russell only those things she wanted him to know about her and to make up whatever was necessary to spark his interest. Laurie was a consummate liar about herself because she believed she wasn't interesting or desirable enough to attract men without the need of a fabricated past.

Laurie established her traditional pattern of relationship with Russell very quickly. She began living her life for him. As with David, Russell became the center of Laurie's universe. She hung on his words the way she physically hung on him, denying her own needs and even her own sense of self. Because Russell so dominated her attention, Laurie took no pains to include anyone else in their relationship. For two young socially active adults in their twenties, Laurie seemed strangely possessive and was threatening to isolate them from everyone else. Russell's friends could see what was happening. They saw that Laurie was dampening his natural enthusiasms and natural fires. One by one they tried to alert him to the changes that were taking place in his life, but Russell would hear none of it. Then gradually, his friends started dropping out of his life. They commented to each other, however, that Laurie Wasserman was a strange girl. "Odd," they called her. "Bizarre," and downright "weird."

Eventually, Russell and Laurie decided to marry. She had successfully kept her past hidden from him, shooing out of their relationship anyone who might have been able to challenge her stories of her successes in college and drawing the web of lies so tight around them that she could be confident of his loyalty. Whatever mistakes she had made with David Schwartz, smothering him to the point where he had to flee for his own life and sanity, she had avoided with Russell. She had moved the relationship along quickly. She was able to get him to take care of her so that her need for him seemed only natural, and she was able to endear herself to Russell's family and friends. But after the wedding, the old fears that plagued her began to resurface. Marriage, Laurie had hoped, would have provided her with a secure emotional high ground where her own glaring personality flaws would not become apparent. After all, wasn't marriage a pledge of eternal faith? Couldn't she now relax and stop worrying once and for all? But she discovered that marriage was only the beginning of a new emotional battle in which she had to work all the harder to survive. As the pressures of being married and being an emotional partner mounted, Laurie found herself too ill-equipped to cope.

Now that she was married, Laurie's ritualistic behavior cropped up again. They became her coping mechanisms. Perhaps they were harmless at first, but gradually they became all-too-consuming ends in themselves, directing her attention away from the need to establish a home and forcing her to become obsessive about adhering to them. They also made her terribly unhappy.

Some of her rituals were small and childlike, such as carefully avoiding every crack in the sidewalk when she walked down the street, touching every lamppost or power-line pole as she passed by them, or being afraid to replace the original caps on food containers and bottles. What is usually a superstition among married couples—the need of the spouses to share a kiss before one or both of them leave for work—became with Laurie a need for her to lay her hands on the couch before Russell left the apartment for the office every morning. Russell Dann later reported that Laurie said it was her way of guaranteeing that nothing bad would happen to him during the day. This, psychologists say, is not far from the truth, although the truth has little to do with superstitions about one's spouse. This routine has much to do with the obsessive person's need to control the environment physically so as to confirm its existence while at the same time confirming her ability to confirm its existence.

Obsessive-compulsives have at their core a real sense of doubt concerning their physical world and the ways the physical world relates to them. By touching the couch, Laurie wasn't just saying that Russell would be all right. She was exerting as much control as she could to guarantee that Russell would return to her at the end of the day, that she wouldn't be alone again, and that her world wouldn't spin upon its axis and attack her in the ways that she had been attacked ever since she was a child. It was a pitiful display, but it was all she had.

As her reliance on daily rituals increased, so did her inabilities to maintain any semblance of order within the house. Russell was not a traditionalist, although he was raised in a home in which his mother carried the responsibility of managing the housework and raising the children.

Laurie had limited experience in taking care of a household and was incapable of on-the-job training once she got married. On the other hand, her inabilities to organize an environment that she believed was out of her control became obvious during the early weeks of the marriage. The house was becoming sloppier and sloppier, and Laurie couldn't even manage to organize a simple linen closet. Maybe she even looked out of control to Russell, who came home after a day at the office to the misery of his domestic situation. And Laurie was clearly unhappy. At first, he tried to show her what to do. He believed that if he taught her how to manage their apartment, she would pick up the skill and all would be well. Or, he might have thought, he would gradually confront her, challenge her about how she was managing the place, and ultimately she would come around.

Russell was also concerned that his wife kept getting fired from job after job. At first she didn't even tell him that she was in trouble at work. He happened to learn that she was fired from a waitressing job only because he had stopped in at the tavern for a drink and didn't notice his wife. The boss then told him about Laurie's inability to deal with the customers and her explosive temper. When he confronted her about it, she lied. He became furious. She wept like a beaten child, and he relented. She only lied to him, she said, because she was afraid of not meeting his expectations. But Laurie kept on lying. It was their fault, she would say.

They didn't understand her; the customers were always nasty; it took a long time to get adjusted. She kept weeping about Russell's special family and their talents in the workplace. Next to them Laurie was hopelessly outclassed. Laurie never admitted that she was wrong, she only blamed her bosses or the customers; always them, never her.

"Don't worry," Russell would say to her. "You'll get another job. You'll show them all you can do it." And that would make her feel better until the next time.

Laurie's performance in the workplace didn't improve. In fact, as she moved from job to job, from office to office, it actually deteriorated. People who remembered her during this period shortly after her marriage remember a young woman who would seem to fall apart within a few weeks after landing a job. She would get the job by falsifying her credentials and lying during the interview. After she began working, she seemed to sparkle at first, really taking to the demands of the office. Then she would start displaying odd behaviors. She would wear the sarme outfit day after day. Her personal appearance became more and more unkempt until the people around her realized that something was really wrong.

Laurie's physical appearance was also an indicator of the level of work she was performing. At job after job, her supervisors realized that not only didn't she have the skills she claimed to have had when she was hired, she wasn't even making an attempt to keep up. At various medical offices where she worked and from where she was summarily dismissed, her bosses complained about her losing telephone messages, her inability to handle patient records and files, and her constant misfiling of information, including cash receipts and financial records, which impeded the work of the entire operation.

At job after job, people also complained that Laurie didn't know how to deal with patients or clients. She simply mistreated people by either snapping at them or dismissing them. She couldn't listen to other people and didn't know how to talk to them. When people challenged her or demanded to know why she wasn't able to take down their information correctly, Laurie lashed out and sometimes even threw ugly temper tantrums. She was simply impossible, most of her bosses concluded, either hopelessly incompetent and short-tempered or downright crazy. Either way, no one wanted her around. And by the time she and Russell had a second heart-to-heart talk about her employment prospects, she had been hired at and fired from over ten jobs.

Had Russell Dann known about or had even a hint of the critical nature of his new wife's problems, it is likely he would have forced an intervention that would have gotten her into intense therapy. But how could he have known? Laurie came from a good Jewish suburban Chicago family just like his. Sure, she was weird, and her parents, as he had told her right to her face, were too standoffish for his tastes, but these were just the habits of different families. Laurie wasn't crazy like the people he'd read about in his abnormal-psych textbook. She wasn't "crazy." Like most people, Russell had no reason to know what truly "crazy" was, and he had had no experience with emotionally disturbed people, and he had no idea that Laurie was reaching a critical stage of psychological distress. Neither Russell nor anybody else realized that under the pressure of trying to maintain normalcy in a marriage, under the tremendous burden of playing a role that she had no experience for, Laurie Wasserman Dann was drowning in despair.

To Dr. Robert Greendale at Highland Park Hospital outside Chicago, Laurie Dann's behavior was more than simply a neurotic reaction to getting married and starting a family. There was something much deeper there. Greendale was aware that Laurie was having difficulty adjusting to reality. She was afraid of reality, and attempted to control it by physically touching objects in her vicinity. She reported to him that she had dark thoughts concerning her husband—"bad feelings," she called them, foreboding—and was only able to control them by touching objects, such as the sofa, so that the bad feelings would go away.

One of Greendale's first approaches was to control Laurie's symptoms, her wild mood swings and deep depressions. But rather than merely tranquilize her with Valium to control the anxiety reactions associated with her obsessive behavior, Greendale prescribed thioridazine, a drug usually prescribed for depressed and psychotic patients. Thioridazine is a much-heavier-duty tranquilizer, sometimes used under institutional controls, that also evens out mood swings often associated with violent behavior. Greendale apparently believed that his first step was to alleviate Laurie's fear and anxiety over her own violently somber thoughts before approaching her deeper problems. But he also must have known that at some point, Laurie needed to address those deeper problems before she would feel any measurable relief from her brooding pessimism.

Unfortunately, Laurie quickly withdrew from therapy, as she would withdraw on at least two subsequent occasions, before Greendale had the opportunity to work his way to some of her root disorders. He was probably aware that Russell was in no position to help Laurie through any crises even though Russell was supportive. He warned Laurie that she was in no position to help herself, her problems were too deep-rooted. No one knows whether he ever learned that Laurie's maternal grandmother and paternal great-grandmother also suffered from the condition. Greendale's strongest protest over Laurie's withdrawal from therapy was a warning letter he sent her, in which he advised her that the medication he was administering only relieved her symptoms, but did not solve any of her emotional problems. He implored her to return to therapy.

Russell tried to enlist Norm Wasserman's support in returning Laurie to therapy, but his father in-law seemed strangely withdrawn and distanced from Laurie's problems. He said that he saw no possible benefits from therapy. The next time he saw his daughter and her husband in Florida, Laurie's condition had grown so serious that she refused to step on one of the carpets and kept walking around it. Her obsession about riding a bike with only one hand on the bars almost resulted in a serious accident. But Norm and Edith were apparently unable to comprehend the seriousness of Laurie's problems. They denied that anything was wrong with their daughter and insisted that they had seen nothing to alarm them. Russell Dann realized that he was all alone in dealing with his wife, and he knew that he didn't have the ability to help her solve her problems.

In the following months, Laurie's behavior deteriorated even further. She couldn't adjust to a new house that Russell bought for them and simply sat while the movers piled the Danns' belongings around them. She continued to find every excuse she could to avoid dealing with Russell's family and her nieces and nephews, and finally began to display downright psychotic behavior under the most innocuous of circumstances. To Russell, who was trying to deny the obvious about Laurie for as long as possible, the pressure became too great and he couldn't bear the strain alone anymore.

He told his sister everything. The weird behavior, the strange reactions to the smallest provocation, and her obsessive rituals, which were becoming more and more deranging to their homelife. He told Susan about how Laurie could not keep jobs, about how the manager of a restaurant where she had worked described her sudden emotional outbursts at his patrons, and he described her constant lying. He even told his friends about Laurie's need to be taken care of as a child instead of being a partner in marriage. He revealed that it had become hopeless for him and hopeless for their relationship.

Laurie's deepest nightmares were coming true, and the pattern that she had established long before had again risen to destroy another relationship. As Russell spoke to his friends and his family, it was becoming obvious to all that he had only one option: divorce. He and Laurie would have to split up for her own good as well as his. His mother tried to explain that this might force Laurie to seek help and to force others to intervene in Laurie's life. Understandably, Elaine Dann was concerned about her son and his entrapment in a destructive and unhappy marriage. Laurie had been right again. Russell's family and friends—people she'd always believed would plot against her—had indeed begun "plotting" against her. They were counseling Russell to divorce her. As deep and dark as Laurie's foreboding had been, they had been correct. Her behavior in reaction to them had been a self-fulfilling prophecy.

Months later, after Laurie had begun to leave rotting food around the house that he had to clean up when he came home from work, Russell finally confronted her about her behavior. He was miserable, he told her. All of his friends could see it. Their marriage wasn't a marriage at all, but a father/daughter relationship—and he hadn't signed on for that. He pointed to the spoiling food all over the kitchen, the cabinets and drawers that were left open because Laurie refused to close them after she'd touched them, and her inability to get out of bed during the day. He complained to her about what seemed like her fixation on wearing the same exact clothing day after day until it became filthy. Why couldn't she just change her clothes once in a while? But Russell was going head-to-head with Laurie and had lost his objectivity. It was only natural, because of his intimate relationship with her. Had Russell been able to step back and see Laurie through an objective but all-knowing pair of eyes, he might have realized that she was experiencing panic reactions. But no one understood the nature of Laurie's fear.

Russell's challenge brought those fears right up to the surface. Laurie panicked and withdrew to a corner. She acknowledged her problems, promised to work them out, but begged him not to leave her. Anything was better than being abandoned. She would try Dr. Greendale again, put herself back into therapy if Russell thought that would help, but she couldn't face the thought of his leaving. Her outbursts helped to hold Russell in place for the time being, but the damage had already been done. Laurie's worst fears about what was going on in her marriage and about Russell's feelings had been confirmed. She needed to pull the wagons around her even though she was in therapy, and, subsequently, her symptoms became dramatically worse. She became even more morose and more violent, more antisocial and unable to deal with friends and family, and at times she seemed to slip into a catatoniclike state that resembled the trancelike states of her earlier childhood. Laurie was deteriorating fast and there was nothing Dr. Greendale or Russell were able to do about it. Russell finally had had enough.

ALONE AND ANGRY

The break finally came during one of Laurie's therapy sessions with Dr. Greendale, when it became obvious that Laurie hadn't even told her therapist about the deteriorated state of her personality and their lives. All Greendale could do was to patiently urge Laurie to return to the problems she had refused to discuss, and Russell stormed out of the session. It was all over for him. It was also obvious to Laurie that she would have to prepare for the worst. All she could hope for, she told her husband, was for him to help her adjust to living alone. At least, Russell could probably console himself, this was better than an endless marriage with no hope of happiness in sight. He agreed, and tried to bring her in for as soft a landing as possible. It didn't work.

It was the nature of Laurie's affliction that she was able to draw people in close to her by the best of their intentions. That was how she had attracted the few friends she had had when she was younger, how she was able to keep her relationship with David Schwartz alive as long as she did, and, of course, how she was able to maintain her relationship with Russell even after the formal separation. Russell admitted that it would be too cruel to simply walk away from her or force her to leave the house. He wanted to provide her with a transition period during which she would wean herself away from dependence on the marriage and toward greater independence. He looked for help from Laurie's parents, but that was too little, too late. He looked for help from Laurie's therapist, but the therapy sessions were not proving helpful.

The truth was that Laurie was very, very sick and had no intentions of letting Russell go. As long as Russell was making it easy for her to deny reality and rely on his presence, the more she was inclined to perpetuate a difficult situation. Russell's inability to walk away from Laurie—he never was able to force the issue with her—only made matters worse. He allowed her to share the house with him from time to time. Sometimes Laurie stayed at her parents' house, sometimes she stayed in the house she nominally owned with Russell. The two occupied separate bedrooms, but Russell actually had sexual relations with Laurie during the separation. He might have told himself that it was all for the better, that it would make the separation easier, but, in fact, it was a terrible mistake. Laurie was not forced to confront the separation, and kept on hoping for some sort of reconciliation. If he was still making love to her, she must have reasoned in her distorted mind, he still loved her. Sex became another way for her to deny her problems and the state of their dissolved marriage.

To Russell's friends and family, Laurie maintained that she would never allow Russell to go through with the separation. The more hostile the two became toward one another in the same household, the more Laurie decided she would find a way to win him back. As her situation became more desperate, she became more vocal and more public. Eventually, she began calling the police to respond to domestic-violence complaints. It was during this period that the problems of Laurie and Russell Dann came to the attention of the authorities. By filing complaints against Russell, Laurie also inadvertently blunted any police investigations into her own increasingly violent behavior until it was too late, because the police, who'd been called to the Dann household night after night, suspected that any complaints against her by Russell and his family stemmed from the Danns' acrimonious divorce.

For the next months, the skirmishes between Laurie and Russell turned into a full-fledged war, with parents on both sides dragged into the battle. As respective lawyers began maneuvering for position, it seemed to Russell that Laurie was actually drawing strength from the fray. She seemed to have found a new reason for living, a way to focus the hatred and anger that had been building up in her since she was a child. She had enemies. Actual human beings who were trying to destroy her. It was wonderful; she was at war.

After a new round of complaints and countercomplaints, Laurie faked a burglary at her own house, blamed Russell for it, and then staged a raid on Russell's house. She had been hiding in his closet and listening in on his calls for months—she had even been intercepting his mail for months—but this was a direct attack on him. When he found her hiding in his closet after vandalizing his clothing, Laurie threatened him for the first time. A short time later, Russell charged that Laurie stabbed him with an ice pick. Russell told reporters that Laurie said if she couldn't have him, nobody would. This was more than Russell had bargained for. And when he received reports that Laurie had purchased a handgun, he contacted the police in Highland Park and in Glencoe to seek protection. Laurie had armed herself and the stakes had just gone up.

THE ENEMIES LIST

Russell was only one of the persons on Laurie Dann's private list of enemies. As the months wore on and Laurie thought about all the people in her life who she perceived had injured her, her list of enemies grew and grew. Now that she was alone and fighting the last great battle to keep from sinking into the morass of her own hopelessness, she began singling out individual after individual who had slighted her in some way. The list became an ingenious network of people who at some point in their lives had shared one common thread: Laurie believed that in some way, even if they were unaware of it, they had declared themselves her foes. The development of this list was one of the most intricate and careful things Laurie Wasserman Dann ever did, even though it made no sense to anyone who had not followed her trail for thirty years.

One of the first people she had called immediately after the separation was her old boyfriend David Schwartz, whom she'd tracked down to a hospital in New York City where he was in residency. At first she seemed genuinely friendly to David—so friendly, in fact, that he congratulated himself on having had the courage to walk away from a painful part of his life. By exiting the relationship with Laurie Wasserman, he had given her a chance to grow. But as Laurie kept on calling him, calling his wife, and making false accusations about his professional and personal life, David realized that she was like a monster. She just kept coming and coming for no reason at all. He finally had to contact the police just to stop the harassment.

Laurie began harassing her acquaintances from the different colleges she'd attended, she made hang-up calls to members of the sorority that had forced her to depledge, and she even targeted the owners of a house down the street from where she and Russell had bought a house. The Danns had paid thousands of dollars more for their house than their neighbors had paid for an almost identical house, and consequently, Laurie had wanted to get even with them almost from the day they closed title.

Laurie also sought revenge on families for whom she had been a babysitter, the one job she repeatedly sought after her separation from Russell. But Laurie had problems as a babysitter as well. Families usually discharged Laurie after one or two jobs, and in so doing were added to her enemies list. The usual pattern involved Laurie's babysitting once or twice, stealing items of clothing, emptying the refrigerator, trashing the interior of the house while terrorizing the children, or any combination of these. One family contacted the police about Laurie's habits and was told that Laurie was under treatment, and to seek restitution from her father. Norm, without admitting Laurie's guilt and after getting the complaining party to agree that there was no proof that Laurie was at fault, settled up with the family. Soon thereafter, Laurie began making harassing hang-up calls to others until she simply got tired. However, when a new event shook up her life, she would sometimes place fifty to sixty harassing phone calls a day, making sure not to forget the phone numbers of old established enemies while adding new enemies to her list.

Harassing phone calls were Laurie Dann's way of asserting her control over people she believed had wronged her, and control was what she was seeking. It was her small way of seeking revenge, but it was self-sustaining as well. The telephone was an easy device to use; she did not have to face her victims, she could even disguise herself. It was a guerrilla war that disrupted the lives of hundreds of people. But these were the early eruptions foreshadowing a major violent psychological event.

THERAPIES AND DRUGS

Throughout the period of her separation and divorce from Russell, Laurie was in and out of therapy. As her behavior became more erratic and abnormal, as her symptoms and fears rendered her almost completely dysfunctional, her father sought more intensive and specialized therapy for his daughter. In 1987, Laurie gravitated from Dr. Greendale to Dr. Phillip Epstein at Rush-Presbyterian in Chicago, who specialized in obsessive-compulsive disorder therapy.

At the beginning of 1987, Norm Wasserman was especially hopeful about his daughter's condition because of the research conducted on pharmaceutical treatments for obsessive-compulsive disorders and the indications that OCD might be more than a traditional emotional problem. He was reading popular reports about the way the condition was being controlled with new experimental drugs and how neurologists and psychiatrists had believed they had finally found the key to alleviating the symptoms of the disorder.

Phillip Epstein ordered a cognitive workup on Laurie from Allen Hirsch at Mercy Medical Center, which showed that she was suffering from a neurological disorder in which she confused left and right. Perhaps she was dyslexic, but she had an extraordinary problem that was impeding her on every level. Since Hirsch was only asked to conduct cognitive tests on Laurie, she was not diagnosed as suicidal or potentially violent. Accordingly, Hirsch prescribed alprazolam, commonly known as Xanax, a minor depressant.

The contraindications of alprazolam were described three years earlier in a 1984 *American Journal of Psychiatry* study entitled "Emergence of Hostility During Alprazolam Treatment." In that study, ten percent of a group of patients who were treated with alprazolam (Xanax) became angry, hostile, and committed potentially aggressive acts against other members of the group. In one case, a patient became so violent as a result of taking the drug that she attacked her mother with a steak knife and held it against her throat until she was restrained. This patient had no specific history of "overt violence" prior to taking alprazolam. In a later study, almost six out of ten patients became violent as a result of being treated with alprazolam, and some of them actually became suicidal. Finally, in the same year that Laurie Dann killed Nicky Corwin and then herself, James Watson killed a number of children in a Greenwood, South Carolina, elementary school while he was under treatment for severe anxiety. His doctors had prescribed numerous drugs to him, including alprazolam.

Thus, by the time Laurie received a subsequent diagnosis from Phillip Epstein, she was already taking a drug that has been known to cause severe violent reactions in individuals who may have been predisposed to violence even though they had showed no overt signs of violent behavior. Unbeknownst to Epstein and Hirsch, Laurie Dann was not in the nonviolent category. She was a particularly violent individual who was having homicidal and suicidal fantasies, who had suffered from transient catatonic states, and who had already attacked her former husband with an ice pick, savaged his apartment, and was beginning to arm herself with a variety of handguns. Laurie Dann was in serious trouble by the time she was medicated with alprazolam, although Dr. Hirsch was not aware of the trouble.

Phillip Epstein diagnosed Laurie as an obsessive-compulsive whose severe anxiety reactions critically impaired her ability to function. Like Greendale, Epstein was concerned about Laurie's morbid anxiety and sought to control it with medications. He prescribed a powerful psychotropic drug known as clomipramine, a tricyclic antidepressant that acts directly on the receptors in the brain that are sensitive to the neurochemical serotonin. Serotonin plays an important role in sensory perception in the brain, and the proper flow of serotonin is directly connected with healthy sleep cycles and dream states. In Laurie's case, the inability of her serotonin receptors to be satisfied by the presence of the neurochemical resulted in an abnormally high secretion that caused sensory overload, anxiety fantasies, and the need to exert control over those powerful and threatening fantasies by the performance of established rituals and routines. In prototypical obsessive-compulsive disorders, tricyclic antidepressants have become the drug of choice. Given what Dr. Epstein may have known and observed, his diagnosis may well have been within traditional medical standards.

Laurie's case, however, was not simply a case of obsessive-compulsive disorder reactions. Most OCDs are extremely passive because they want to avoid being hurt and hurting others. Laurie was actively aggressive and had displayed violent tendencies. And trancelike states, which she had experienced off and on since she was five, had begun a new cycle, suggesting other problems such as schizophrenia—for which tricyclics are contraindicated. After leaving Epstein's care, she had begun treatment with Dr. John Greist at the Anxiety Disorder Center on the University of Wisconsin campus in Madison, but students in Laurie's dorm later reported to the press that they would find her staring catatonically into space in broom closets and in the elevator. Laurie was also taking other drugs to control the physical side effects of clomipramine, and she was being tranquilized on Xanax at the same time.

In a multimillion-dollar wrongful-death suit filed by the estate of Nicholas Corwin, one of Laurie Dann's victims, against Dr. Epstein—a suit that has since been settled out of court—the plaintiffs contended that Epstein's use of the tricyclic psychotropic drug clomipramine, in its brand name Anafranil, was illegal at the time he prescribed it to Laurie, because the drug (prescribed in several other countries and now approved for general use here in the United States) was not yet approved for prescription use by the FDA. It was still in its trial experimental stages, and the only physicians allowed to prescribe the drug were "investigators." Dr. Epstein was not an investigator and did not have FDA approval to write prescriptions for clomipramine. As a result, Epstein wrote a prescription through a pharmacy in Montreal, in a country where the drug had been approved, and Norm Wasserman purchased it through the mail. Among Laurie's belongings the police searched after her suicide on May 20 was a vial of Anafranil, which had been obtained from the Lud Bock Pharmacy in Montreal with Epstein's name on it as the prescribing physician. This, the Corwins contended in their lawsuit, was an act on the part of Epstein that put him and his therapy group at the center of their wrongful-death suit. The Winnetka police report issued after the Corwin murder and the Dann suicide indicated that the police were cooperating with the Medical Disciplinary Board of the Illinois Department of Professional Regulations, which was investigating Phillip Epstein's prescription for the drug.

In his defense to the wrongful-death suit, Epstein denied the allegations, claiming that he had no legally recognizable duty to Nicholas Corwin, that his actions did not cause Corwin's injuries, and that the FDA and customs statutes were inapplicable to the negligence case.

Laurie had four visits with Phillip Epstein and then contacted Dr. John Greist at the University of Wisconsin whose name she received from a Connecticut-based OCD self-help organization. Laurie moved to the Madison campus of the University of Wisconsin to begin therapy and, ostensibly, to regain control of her life. However, even though she was scheduled for sessions three to four times a week, Laurie's situation went from bad to worse. First, Greist and his assistant tripled her clomipramine dose in an effort to control her aggressive obsessions. (Dr. Greist was one of the doctors that had been authorized to prescribe clomipramine in clinical trials in the United states.) Laurie, however, probably overdosed on the drug and went into cycles of toxic reactions that had to be controlled with Compazine. Compazine, however, is strongly contraindicated when a patient has been taking Xanax. The cross-reactions from the drugs can produce psychotic symptoms. Thus, even though Laurie's severe vomiting stopped, she began hallucinating from the drug combination. Greist, in a phone consultation with Laurie's father, pulled her off all medication. but when she went into clonic muscle spasms during the night and looked like she was in danger of going into a full-blown seizure, the emergency-room physician at the Highland Park hospital where her father took her medicated her with benztropine, a muscle relaxant that brought her out of spasm.

By this time, drugs were coursing through Laurie's system that were absolutely contraindicated in combination, and she was hallucinating on and off periodically. All of these symptoms were sitting on top of her aggressive obsessions and her deep-seated fears that she was going to perform some terrible act that she would not be able to control, and now she had been transported to an emergency room. It was at this crisis point that Laurie clearly should have been hospitalized, if only to purge her system of all medications in a controlled clinical setting. But that did not happen. Therefore another opportunity was missed, and Laurie was summarily released from Highland Park Hospital and returned to her parents' house, where she began an aggressive phoneharassment campaign against the enemies on her list. She'd expanded that list with her former babysitting clients and friends of the Danns. The following day, Greist put her back on clomipramine, and a few days later she purchased her third handgun. She was out of control now and on a collision course with destiny.

Between Christmas 1987 and New Year's Day, Laurie's phone campaign against her enemies became so intense, some of the people who were most afraid of her asked for and got a meeting with the Glencoe, Illinois, Director of Public Safety. Glencoe was one of the communities in which Laurie had lived with Russell and in which she was conducting her campaign harassment. In fact, it was Glencoe police detective Floyd Mohr who had taken the lead in investigating Laurie Dann and her domestic problems with her exhusband, Russell. At this meeting, Laurie's victims lodged a number of complaints against her. They argued that she was probably certifiably insane, she had probably attacked Russell with an ice pick, thereby attesting to her ability to commit violent acts, and that the threats she was making over the telephone were increasingly violent. "And now she has a gun," one of the victims said. "And there's nothing we can do about it."

The Glencoe Public Safety Director promised that he would increase vigilance on Laurie Dann, but explained that unless she committed an actual crime in his jurisdiction, there was little he could do. He also apologized for the inability of the police departments in surrounding jurisdictions to coordinate their efforts. The police in different towns don't always share information, he explained, illustrating how Laurie could slip through the net and commit violent acts almost at will.

"She's a ticking bomb," a member of Russell Dann's family said. "And she's going to go off and kill somebody."

Laurie returned to Madison, where her doctors tried to control her mood swings with lithium. At the same time, Laurie was also taking the Xanax prescribed for her by Dr. Epstein. None of her doctors seem to have focused their diagnoses on Laurie's schizophrenic reactions, her catatonic states, or her homicidal fantasies, because no one seemed to have the whole picture and no one seemed to communicate with anyone else involved with Laurie. The Xanax and antianxiety medications alone would have been contraindicated in the presence of the psychotic personality disorder Laurie was displaying toward Russell and her babysitting clients. The addition of the powerful tricyclic antidepressants in the presence of lithium in her system only made Laurie s behavior more and more dangerous. But since Laurie was displaying different behaviors to different groups, no one person could see the whole picture.

By early 1988, there were three separate groups—an ad hoc collection of her victims, an ad hoc group of police investigators, and a group of unrelated psychologists and psychiatrists that had formed up around Laurie Dann. Two groups, ostensibly, had the same aims: the protection of innocent people from Laurie Dann, the prevention of violence and the investigation of Laurie's activities. The third group also wanted to prevent violence, but it was more concerned with investigating Laurie's condition. The only "organized" group was composed of her victims. They were in constant communication with one another and with police agencies in their respective areas. Unfortunately, each group was acting out of self-interest, which was to be expected, and not out of any greater goals. Her former boyfriend from college, David Schwartz, for example, had the strongest case for prosecuting Laurie for phone harassment. However, he and his wife were concerned about going forward because they felt Laurie was crazy enough to show up on their doorstep with a gun ready to get revenge.

The Dann family's complaints of Laurie's activities were considered biased because of the divorce action, and Laurie's babysitting victims were not aware of each other's existence. Laurie was threatening all of their lives, but there was no way they could come together in an organized fashion to protect themselves.

The police were equally ineffective. Each agency was only able to investigate Laurie's actions within their respective jurisdictions. Typical of suburban police departments, the different investigators rarely coordinated their investigations across municipal lines, especially where crimes of violence had not been committed and there was no hot pursuit. As a result, offenses perpetrated by Laurie in Glencoe might not come to the attention of Highland Park officers. The FBI stood the best chance of prosecuting Laurie and coordinating the investigation, but they were stopped when David Schwartz declined to press his complaint, and by the time the FBI field office in Madison, Wisconsin, had been called to investigate Laurie's pre-Christmas phone harassment campaign, she had already left the campus for her parents' house in Highland Park, Illinois. The agent found only an empty room, and the investigation wasn't pursued.

Laurie Dann's psychiatrists were the least effective of all, because no one doctor had the whole picture. They were heavily dosing her on medications that had severe cross-reactions. Drs. Epstein and Greist, both of whom independently reached an OCD diagnosis, were prescribing drugs that should not, according to the *Physician's Desk Reference*, be administered at the same time. Yet, each psychiatrist was relying only on Laurie's and her father's descriptions of her obvious symptoms. Laurie did not confess to stabbing Russell, even though she admitted as much as to Russell, and her father denied her responsibility for any violence whatsoever. Laurie did not describe her violent activities in the homes where she was babysitting, and her father apparently did not reveal to her doctors that he had had to make restitution for Laurie's destructive activities. The two psychiatrists apparently did not know that Edith Wasserman's mother had been diagnosed as a clinically depressed individual, nor were they aware of Laurie's schizophrenic reactions and her catatonic states. We do not know whether either doctor had been authorized by their patient to speak to Dr. Greendale, Laurie's first psychiatrist, or to her ex-husband, Russell Dann. Had they been given a picture of Laurie's aggressively violent acts, they might have diagnosed her differently. Nonetheless, each psychiatrist pursued an independent treatment of Laurie, and each, independently, had, by not receiving complete information about her condition, missed the biggest and most critical symptoms. It was this third group that was directly responsible for the maintenance of Laurie's medical care, and the members of that group were completely unaware of one another and the medications that each had prescribed. It is this lack of internal awareness that, without our assigning any specific blame, is what we call "linkage blindness."

As impossible as it is to believe, none of these groups was able to prevent the violence that was erupting right below the surface of her personality. Only Laurie knew that she was on a collision course with extreme violence, but none of the signs she was deliberately sending out had sufficiently caught anyone's attention. She was calling for intervention, but no one took the first step. She had even gone to the extreme of personally threatening individuals over the phone and describing the levels of violence she was disposed to commit. But even those people who believed her were too afraid to act. They were all in Laurie's power, and Laurie was powerless to stop herself.

By spring 1988, Laurie was clearly out of control and heading for disaster.

THE FINAL NIGHTMARE

A Winnetka, Illinois, Police Department report issued on June 15, 1988, less than a month after the shootings at the Hubbard Woods Elementary School, graphically described the incidents of May 20 and attempted to put them into some sort of logical perspective. The report—assembled from the results of a task force of police officers from neighboring municipalities, Cook County sheriff's deputies, FBI agents out of Chicago, and agents of the Bureau of Alcohol, Tobacco, and Firearms—represented the first coordinated investigation into the events of and preceding May 20, 1988. Unfortunately, the task force, which the Dann family had begged the police to assemble six months earlier, was too late to prevent the day of violence that shocked the entire suburban Chicago community.

The cold language of the police report cannot even begin to penetrate the mind of Laurie Dann in those days prior to May 20 as she assembled her weapons and planned her rampage in the neighboring communities around Chicago. Laurie had clearly determined to raise an alarm that would punish everyone who had ever known her. She had compiled her list of enemies and had at last surrendered to the dark thoughts that had caromed through her psyche. This would be her personal apocalypse.

The last act of her life began in March 1988, when she stole arsenic and lead from laboratories on the University of Wisconsin campus. She was technically still in therapy, and was depressed that her behavior was deteriorating so rapidly. Her doctors increased her dosage of medication, but the medication did not control her antisocial and violent fantasies.

The police surmised that Laurie's theft of the arsenic and lead was part of her grand scheme to attack her enemies on a murder spree she was planning. During this period in March 1988, people observed Laurie Dann in a "near catatonic state" aimlessly riding the elevators up and down in the Madison residence hall where she lived, vandalizing offices and rooms in the residence hall, and setting numerous fires. The campus security team was assembling evidence in its own investigation when Laurie Dann left the campus, thereby forestalling their efforts to intercept her.

Laurie escalated her phone campaign against David Schwartz in March. Her phony charges against Schwartz, which Laurie had leveled against him while he was in New York, forced him to discontinue his residency there and move out to Arizona in an attempt to run away from her. When she announced to him over the phone that she had discovered his whereabouts in Tucson and that she would kill him, Schwartz decided to prosecute her. However, he and his wife later decided to withdraw his criminal complaint, and the FBI was unable to proceed against her.

On March 18, the police report continues, Laurie officially terminated her therapy with Dr. Greist, who soon thereafter contacted Norm Wasserman so that he could have her committed to a mental institution. At this point, it had even become obvious to Greist that Laurie was in no condition to care for herself. However, Norm Wasserman proved resistant to committing his daughter and was unable or unwilling to provide any information to Greist that would allow him to have her committed involuntarily. In the state of Wisconsin, the police investigative report stipulates, there has to be substantial documentation of a patient's ability to inflict harm on others and himself or herself before that person can be committed involuntarily. Without the substantiation, Greist claimed, he was powerless to act.

Norm Wasserman refused to promise Greist that he would convince Laurie to commit herself voluntarily, but he eventually wrote a letter to his daughter imploring her to hospitalize herself for her own well-being. However, Laurie disregarded his letters and escalated the level of her own violence. In March she began calling her ex-sister-in-law and Russell Dann's friends and threatening them directly over the phone. Previously, Laurie had simply called repeatedly at odd hours, waited for the phone to be answered, and hung up. Now, she began announcing that she was "a psycho" and would kill them and their children. But Floyd Mohr of the Glencoe Police Department, who had originally investigated the Laurie/Russell Dann situation, remained unconvinced that Laurie was any threat to the Danns or to anyone else. He told the complaining parties that he had spoken with psychiatrists who had treated Laurie and that they assured him she was not violent. Yet it was Mohr himself who had called Laurie years earlier to get her to give him the handgun she had purchased. Mohr knew that Laurie Dann had a gun and that she was at least accused of having attacked Russell with an ice pick even if the police didn't have the evidence to charge her with the crime.

Between March and May, Laurie stepped up her phone threats and was implicated in a number of break-ins at the dorm. Besides having been discovered riding up and down the elevators, she was also discovered in trash bins, in the basement, and hiding in stairwells. Sometimes she was naked when people found her, other times she was dressed in winter clothing, and still other times she was discovered wearing plastic bags. On one occasion, Laurie was discovered slamming a heavy fire door in the hallway, evidently transfixed by the noise of the door and the way she could control it and its echo by the rhythmic slamming. During this period Laurie had also been charged with shoplifting items of clothing from a Madison store, and police in retrospect reasoned that she might have been planning to use them as disguises.

Laurie left the Madison campus on May 16 and headed back to Illinois by bus. She stayed at her parents' house while Norm and Edith Wasserman were in Florida, and prepared a number of poison fruit juice and food packets that she intended to distribute as "free samples" to people on her list of enemies in Glencoe, Highland Park, Winnetka, and the surrounding communities. It was part of her master plan to stage a "day of rage," killing people and setting fires throughout the suburbs and then having the poison food packets create panic and confusion for days to follow. Laurie Dann succeeded in all of her plans.

Very early on the morning of May 20, Laurie began making deliveries to the persons on her enemies list in the communities of Winnetka, Evanston, Highland Park, Glencoe, and Wilmette. She drove up to the driveways of her intended victims and placed the food or poisoned juice packets, each marked Free Sample, inside the mailboxes. She'd packaged over twenty poisoned foods for delivery that day, including a poison drink that she was about to feed to the victims she was scheduled to meet in person.

Shortly before nine A.M., Laurie finished her rounds and stopped by Marian Rushe's house in Winnetka to pick up her two children, Patrick and Carl, for a kiddie carnival in the neighborhood. She'd already prepared snacks for the children, Laurie told Marian, some milk and cereal. Not to worry, Laurie said, she would feed them. She packed the two boys in the back seat of her car and drove off, leaving their mother in the doorway still wondering about Laurie's odd behavior and desultory mood.

Her first stop was the Ravinia Elementary School in Highland Park, where her former sister in-law's son was a student. She planted one of the incendiary bombs she had made that morning in a cardboard box, lit the fuse, and ran from the school. A passing student saw Laurie flee the school, noticed the licking flames through the window, and told his teacher, who managed to extinguish the fire before the noxious gases were ignited. Afterward, according to the Winnetka police, two other incendiary devices were discovered in the school but were unactivated.

Before she set the bombs, Laurie had given Patrick and Carl, whom she had left in a playground alongside the school, some of the poisoned milk to drink. The milk tasted foul from the heavy dose of arsenic and the boys spilled it out on the grass. They thought it had gone sour. By the time

Laurie returned to the car, the fire was already burning in the school and Laurie hustled them off to their next destination, the Young Men's Jewish Council Day Care Center in Highland Park. It was there that Laurie's former niece was enrolled, and Laurie was planning to set the building aflame with gasoline from the can she was carrying. She brought Carl and Patrick into the building with her, pretending that she was going to enroll them and wanted to look around. She checked her niece's room and found that she wasn't due until the afternoon. No matter, she told herself, she would still set fire to the building. But after she left the building and attempted to return with the gas can, she was met again at the door and concocted an excuse that she needed help pouring gas from the can into her own car's tank. The school director helped her fill the tank and Laurie drove off, frustrated, but intent on carrying out the rest of her plan.

Working her way back to Marian Rushe's house, Laurie dropped off more poisoned food packets and juice samples and probably waited in expectation for the news that the Ravinia Elementary School was now going up in a huge wall of flame. She didn't know, of course, that a teacher had already discovered the fire, extinguished it, and called in a report of arson to the local police. Meanwhile, people who had already sampled Laurie's poisoned concoctions were reporting sick to emergency rooms and doctors' offices in the area. A few parents who noticed the obvious evidence of tampering and the leaking liquid from the containers had called the police. The community, without realizing it, had already begun to mobilize in the wake of Laurie's final murder spree.

Laurie dropped the Rushe children at home at approximately 10:15, according to the official police report, and told Marian Rushe that she had gotten her dates for the kiddie carnival mixed up. "I took them to the park instead," Laurie told the children's mother. "I don't think they cared about not seeing the carnival." It seemed obvious to Marian that her children were happy enough, and she invited Laurie to hang around and watch them while she did the laundry.

According to the police, Laurie was able to lure the entire family into the basement rec room. There is still some speculation about whether Laurie even intended to attack the Rushe children any further, now that it had become obvious to her that her plans to poison them had fallen through. But, Marian was preoccupied with getting the laundry done before her older children came home from school, and when Laurie said she had to get something from the car, Marian assumed that Laurie's discomfiture at being invited to stay meant that Laurie wanted to surprise the children. Thus, inadvertently, Marian kept the children with her in the basement while Laurie went upstairs, locked the basement doors, set fire to the downstairs of the house, and then locked the rest of the doors as she fled. In this way, she hoped to prevent the fire department from rescuing any of the family.

Fortunately for the Rushes, Marian had the presence of mind to lift her children through the basement windows and send them for help. By the time the fire department had arrived, Marian herself had managed to climb through the basement window and was worrying that Laurie might have gotten trapped upstairs. She had no idea that Laurie Dann had set the fire herself with the gasoline she was carrying in the car. Glencoe police detective Floyd Mohr, who was responding to the fire call, likewise had no idea that Laurie had set the fire, He also had no idea that the calls that had been flooding the neighboring police departments about attempted poisonings and a fire at the Ravinia Elementary School were the work of Laurie Dann either. Mohr stayed at the Rushe house to handle some of the hoses from the truck once the fire was brought under control, while Laurie was already on her way to the Hubbard Woods Elementary School in Winnetka with three loaded handguns on the front seat and a bag of ammunition. She was going to finish off the rest of Marian Rushe's children, who were enrolled at Hubbard Woods, now that the Rushe house was probably aflame and the family incinerated. She would show them, she thought. She would show them all.

Laurie pulled up to Hubbard Woods, burst through the open door past two teachers, and headed for the bathroom. One of the teachers followed her, calling out after her in case she needed help. Hearing no answer, the teacher believed that the disheveled woman must have left, and went back to her own business. Laurie Dann was on her own in the school with three revolvers jammed into her waistband. Laurie at first set up shop in an empty boy's bathroom. She left the heavy .357 Magnum in the sink, fearing that if she had to run for it the huge bore gun would only slow her down. Instead, she took the .22 Beretta and the .32 handgun with her.

Her next stop was substitute teacher Amy Moses's classroom, where the teacher believed that Laurie was one of the many parent observers who paid unannounced visits to the school. Moses invited Laurie to sit in, handed her a copy of the day's lesson, and continued with her class on bicycle safety. Moses was nervous that the morose-looking unkempt woman kept staring at her in such a sullen and somber way, but she obviously acted like she belonged there, so Moses didn't think anything was amiss. She was relieved, however, when Laurie suddenly jumped up and left the room. Weird, she thought, how some of the parents came to school looking that untidy. She wondered what Laurie's kids must look like.

Once in the hall, Laurie spied Robert Trossman leaning over the water fountain. She didn't know who he was, but it didn't matter—he was alone, and she was quickly losing what little was left of her composure. Laurie pushed Robert Trossman into the boys room, pulled out the Beretta, fired, and missed. Then she fired again, hitting Trossman in the chest. As he fell to the floor, Laurie saw two other boys entering the bathroom. She pulled the trigger at them, but the gun didn't go off and the boys fled, running down the hall and shouting that someone was shooting a gun in the bathroom. Laurie walked back into Amy Moses's classroom, stood in front of the teacher, pulled the gun, and demanded that she line the children up in the far corner away from the door. At first, Amy Moses remembered, she thought Laurie was part of a joke or a drill. The gun looked like a toy. Maybe even this was a test for substitute teachers, Moses thought, because the .22 gun was so small. Maybe they were shooting a movie or something and nobody told her. But Laurie was insistent, and the glowering hatred in her eyes and the rising tone of her voice convinced Ms. Moses that the stranger with the revolver meant business. Laurie demanded that the teacher herd the class into a corner and Amy Moses flatly refused. Then she grabbed Laurie's arm and began wrestling her for the gun. The Winnetka police report credits Amy Moses's instinctive reaction to go for the gun as primary reason more children were not wounded or killed. Undoubtedly Ms. Moses's actions prevented Laurie Dann from collecting her intended victims in a convenient spot, thereby saving numerous lives, the police report reads.

Amy wrestled Laurie over toward the door of the classroom while the two of them struggled wildly for the gun. During the fight, Amy called out the open door for help while she also forced two live rounds out of the Beretta. Finally Laurie, who was stronger and heftier, managed to wrestle herself free from Amy's grip on her gun hand, pushed Amy away, pulled out her .32 from her waistband, and pointed at Amy while she kept the Beretta trained on the kids. With guns in both her hands she motioned the children into the corner. But now the children had been emboldened by Amy's action and challenged the stranger. Laurie didn't even argue. She walked up the first group of children, leveled the .32 at them, and fired, dropping Mark Teborek instantly. Then Laurie walked past the children while Amy tried to usher them out of the classroom, and fired directly at them. Nicky Corwin was the next child she hit, fatally wounding him. She hit Peter Munro next and then Lindsay Fischer. The classroom was a sea of carnage with blood flying all over the walls, the smoke and singed smell of spent powder hanging heavy in the air, and screaming children fighting for the exit. As Laurie fled through the rear of the classroom she spied Kathryn Miller near the door and hit her with a single round. Then she ran toward her car, which was parked across the street. The police had still not arrived.

Laurie herself was close to panic at this point. She had committed the outrage she had threatened she would, and now the bloodlust had completely taken her over. She started her car, saw a police officer near a barricade, drove in the opposite direction, and turned up a dead-end street where her car struck a tree and became lodged on a rock as she tried to make a U-turn out of trouble. Now she was in a real fix. Sirens were breaking out all over the neighborhood and her car was jammed tight on the rock, its rear drive wheel spinning futilely. She decided to run for it. But first she took off her pants and wrapped herself in a blue plastic garbage bag. tried to conceal her two guns at her side, and ran through the bushes in the dense underbrush toward the first house she could get into.

Ultimately, she crashed through the back door of Ruth Andrew's house on Kent Road, where she told the family in the kitchen that she had just been raped in her car and had shot her attacker. "I hit him," she told Ruth, "I'm afraid the police'll get me." The Andrew family didn't take her seriously at first—that is, until Phil Andrew saw a round in the barrel of her .32. She was the real thing, he said to himself, and so was the gun. Phil convinced Laurie to make a phone call to her family to calm herself down while his mother, Ruth, went upstairs to find a pair of shorts Laurie could change into. Anything to distract her, they thought; anything at all that would divert her attention would allow them to get to the police. But for some reason, Phil Andrew thought he could get the gun away from her.

Laurie called her mother, Edith, shortly before eleven and announced that she'd hurt some people and would now have to kill herself. Phil knew that she was capable of anything and that he would have to move quickly if he intended to prevent more violence. He edged toward her while she was

on the phone and heard Laurie continued to complain to her
mother that she was about to hurt people who hadn't hurt
her. But when he came toward her, she jumped away. Finally
Phil asked Laurie to hand her the phone while she kept him
covered with the .32. Phil told Edith Wasserman that her
daughter was holding his family hostage with a gun. He repeated to her the story that Laurie had told him. But Edith
seemed unimpressed and this astonished Phil, he later told
police and reporters. He asked Edith if Laurie had any history of violence or disturbances. She didn't, Edith replied,
and asked that Phil make sure that Laurie got home safely.

By this time the police had arrived at the school and had
begun setting up roadblocks in the area. They didn't know
Laurie was at the Kent Road house, but Glencoe detective
Floyd Mohr had already identified Laurie Dann as the
shooter and the person who had escaped from the fire and
Marian Rushe's house. His worst suspicions about Laurie
were unfolding horribly before his eyes as he fought his way
through the thick underbrush toward Kent Road after receiving a report that she had abandoned her car with the motor
still running. If he got to her in time, Mohr thought, he could
prevent her from killing anybody else.

Laurie finally put down the guns when Ruth Andrew
handed her a pair of yellow cutoffs to change into. She didn't
turn her back on the family, however, while she dropped the
plastic bag to put on the pants. Phil saw his chance. He
grabbed the .22 Beretta off the table before Laurie could
lunge for it. She immediately trained the .32 on him and demanded he put down the .22. However, Phil, still believing
that Laurie was a victim of a crime and too frightened to do
anything, unloaded the Beretta in front of her and put the
gun away. At that point his father walked in and described
the police roadblocks all over the area.

"Why don't you call your mother back?" Phil asked
Laurie. "Maybe she could pick you up." Laurie called Edith
back and again started explaining her situation to her, and
again Phil took the receiver from her and asked that she get

Laurie right away. But Edith was still too confused and blase for Phil to understand. She tried to explain that her husband wasn't home and that she didn't have a car.

The situation continued through another phone call, while Phil considered whether to make a move for Laurie's .32, until Laurie herself finally told her mother that it was good-bye. At that point Ruth convinced Laurie Dann to let her go outside to keep her daughters away. When Laurie agreed, Ruth escaped and notified the police that a woman was holding her husband and son at gunpoint. When Ruth Andrew's description of the assailant matched the description of the shooter at Hubbard Woods, police stationed near Kent Road contacted Floyd Mohr, who at that point was working his way toward Laurie's car.

After he got Laurie to agree to release his father, Phil was still judging the distance between him and Laurie—he was going to disarm her before this went any further—when she aimed and shot him in the chest. He fell behind a piece of furniture, and while Laurie was still in a state of shock over shooting him, he escaped by crawling out the door, leaving Laurie alone in the house. Phil staggered toward the converging police, who first challenged him and then called for an ambulance to take him away when they realized that he was a victim and not a perpetrator. The police sealed off the neighborhood, sent choppers hovering overhead, closed in around the house with SWAT teams, and began hailing Laurie from the street.

LAURIE WASSERMAN DANN VS. THE WORLD

By the afternoon of May 20, 1988, Laurie was living out the absolute worst of her nightmares. She'd already shot five children, set fire to a school and to Marian Rushe's house, tried to poison numerous victims in Winnetka and the adjoining towns, shot this person who was trying to talk her mother into picking her up, and was now surrounded by what looked like an army. It was Laurie against the world, just the way she'd imagined it would be. This was the end of her life, no doubt about it. And she didn't like it one bit. She could hear the police calling her name through their bullhorns. "Laurie Dann, Laurie Dann, we can help you. We can solve your problem." And that damned phone wouldn't stop ringing. It just kept ringing and ringing. If only she could get it to be quiet.

Reporters saw detective Floyd Mohr pacing back and forth around the perimeter of the house. Later he told Russell that if only he could have seen the truth it would have been different. All the signs were there, he kept telling himself while the police tried to convince Laurie to come out. What if it had been his kids inside that school and he'd been the one responsible for letting a ticking bomb like Laurie Dann wander around with a car full of guns. The worst part about this was that he had actually spoken with her and her father. He'd dealt with her, looked her right in the eye and believed what she told him. Her psychiatrists told him she wasn't violent, he'd accused Russell Dann of inflicting the puncture wound on himself, he hadn't even jumped into high gear when he heard that Laurie had bought a gun. And now here they all were in the middle of a hostage situation, at least two fires, and a mass shooting at a neighborhood elementary school. Then he saw Russell Dann and he went pale.

Russell had been contacted earlier by the police. His sister and friends were already fixed in front of their television sets. For them, this was the nightmare they had dreaded all along. They knew Laurie better than anyone, and they knew that she was capable of doing everything the television announcers said she had done. What could Russell do now as he watched the police emergency-response teams in their black uniforms and camouflage makeup deploy around the house, the sharpshooters poking their rifles out the windows of adjoining houses. What could Russell say? "I told you so"? He knew he had been right all along, but it was like spitting in the wind. Russell knew that had someone listened to him and moved on Laurie, this entire tragedy, this para-military action that had cost the lives of children and was now tearing apart the fabric of life in these innocent suburbs, could have all been avoided. But no one took the risk. This was no consolation at all. If only they had listened. Then he saw a clearly distraught Floyd Mohr.

Russell tried to console Floyd—odd that he should feel the need to do so—but he tried to put the best face on the situation. Floyd wasn't the only person Laurie had hood-winked. She was crazy, and only these people who knew her intimately knew how sick she was. Even the shrinks couldn't penetrate the mask. She'd lied to them as well. Hadn't she lied to Greendale during the entire course of their therapy? There was no shame attached to this. But in his heart he did-n't believe it. Russell must have believed that had they done their jobs, Laurie would have been stopped a long ago. Secretly he also must have felt that the one person whom he thought was most to blame had not yet arrived—Laurie's fa-ther, Norm. Indeed, Russell would later accuse Norm of not intervening when he should have.

As the afternoon wore on and more police units arrived at the scene, the Laurie Dann story began breaking into the headline segments of the national news broadcasts. Not only was Laurie holding off an entire police force, she was doing it on CNN: the whole world was watching. In households around Chicago, in Arizona where David Schwartz watched, in Madison where students retold the stories of the bag lady who rode the elevators, Laurie Dann was all over the place. That's how Norm Wasserman picked it up as he turned on his car radio to keep him company on the trip to Madison. Norm swung off the interstate and pulled back onto the east-bound lane for Chicago.

Norm picked up Edith and together they drove to the scene of the standoff, which was only a short hop away from their Glencoe home. At first sight of the scene on Kent Road,

Norm almost went into shock. This wasn't a police action, it was war. Scores of combat troops in flak jackets and black paint with M16s were all after one, lonely, crazy girl: his daughter. While Floyd Mohr restrained Norm from rushing into the Andrew house, Edith, in a conversation with one of the Cook County prosecutors, was reported to have said that given the seriousness of the charges against Laurie and the amount of trouble she was in, she believed it would be better for Laurie not to come out of this alive.

The standoff continued through the afternoon, with police forces manning barricades, FBI agents roaming around as if there were a terrorist group planning attacks on the community, and police dogs sniffing around under the bushes. By three P.M. it was a media circus. But no one knew what was going on inside the house. Norm Wasserman had called Laurie a number of times, but there was no answer. Laurie refused to pick up the Andrews' phone, which had been ringing constantly since the police command post was set up. Russell Dann was still meandering through the line of the police officers telling them that he believed Laurie was hiding in a closet somewhere in a pile of dirty clothes. He told them that she could stay there for days—in suspended animation, almost—so they might as well go in and get her. But, strangely enough, even at this stage, the cops refused to listen to Russell, who simply shrugged his shoulders and waited for the worst. There was even talk about bombing the Andrew house with tear gas.

Shortly after seven in the evening. as the long shadows of the afternoon had turned to dusk, the police encouraged Norm Wasserman to make another appeal to Laurie. He stood in front of the house and kept calling her name, as if she were a little girl down the street in a friend's backyard being called home for dinner. "Lauree," he called out, accenting the final vowel of her name. She might well have been a small child again on an innocent summer day at the lake years ago. But now they were all trapped in a nightmare that was no dream. "Lauree, please pick up the phone." But there was no response. As Norm kept calling, over and over again with an agonizing regularity to his voice, a police assault team entered the house through the basement windows, secured the lower floors, and prepared to storm the upstairs. There was no need for that, however, because one of the police dogs came running down the stairs exhibiting the telltale signs to his handler that he had just sniffed the stench of a corpse. And sure enough, when the police climbed the stairs, they found Laurie Dann's body slumped face-forward in one of the bedrooms, a single gunshot wound through her mouth. The bullet had exited through her brain and killed her instantly. She had been dead for over three hours.

Edith Wasserman seemed relieved that it was all over, according to the prosecutor who spoke with her on the scene, and relieved that she would never have to confront her daughter about what had happened. For her, Laurie became the past, someone to weep over, someone to mourn, but, most importantly, someone to bury. For Norm, there was a long silence of incomprehension. To his logical, numbers-oriented mind, nothing here made any sense. Hadn't the doctors told him she was not dangerous? Hadn't he pressed them over and over again for a definitive diagnosis about her prospects? Why hadn't anybody told him this could happen? Why did they just give her the damn drugs? Why did she do it? Why, at least, didn't she wait for him?

Only Russell Dann seemed to have a momentary insight into the final moments of agony his ex-wife experienced. Russell had seen her close to her worst. He had faced down her black rage when he challenged her, had seen her quivering and cowering in a linen closet with clothing piled over her head, had seen her when he had come home from work at the end of the day, lurching out of the bedroom and stinking from dirty linens and stale urine, and listened to her manic voice threaten his life on the phone. He had seen her moods change, as rapidly as clouds streaking across a summer sky, from sunshine to a thunderstorm. And he had confronted what he thought was the deepest darkest center of

Laurie's insanity, and he fled from it as if he were escaping
from the gravity of a giant swirling vortex. Russell was convinced that he had looked into her soul of madness, and, sur-
prisingly, as the cops broke the news that she had swallowed
the barrel of her own gun, he could feel no anger toward her
at all, only pity. His anger was reserved for the Wassermans
as he saw them being led away by Floyd Mohr. He felt that
perhaps it would have all been different if Edith had only
recognized the terror in her daughter's psyche and if Norm
had not thought that he could feather out her problems with
phone calls and money. Perhaps it would have all been different if just one person had listened to a word he said. But
that was all in the past, and his ex-wife Laurie was dead.

WARNING SIGNS OF DANGEROUSNESS

The descent of Laurie Wasserman into a fatal madness
has been documented with a grim thoroughness in all the
postmortem reports. Police investigators, lawyers involved
in the backwash of litigation, newspapers, and other researchers have left their footprints in records that begin with
the legacy of her family history, then document her problems as a learning-disabled child, her difficulties in high
school, her divorce, and her final year of insanity. Laurie
Dann's case has been so thoroughly researched and debated,
the only question that remains is why her problems got so
out of hand.

Clinical depression has one of the highest percentages of
genetic causalities of any emotional disturbance, because it
is linked to the transmission of specific neurochemicals that
control sensory perception and brain reaction response.
Childhood depression is a particularly acute problem, because it can affect all areas of cognitive development and social interaction. In Laurie Wasserman's case, her bouts of
depression and feelings of loss of control caused her to develop rituals through which she attempted to exercise con-

trol over the outside world. Her parents possibly never understood the depth of Laurie's problems and their own inability to deal with it. It is also possible that Norm didn't realize that by adjusting and solving immediate family problems without resolving them, by cleaning up the messes Laurie left in place after place or relationship after relationship, Laurie never was forced to confront the real-world consequences of her own actions. The Corwins argued in a wrongful-death lawsuit against the Wassermans—which, like the suit against Dr. Epstein, has since been settled out of court—Laurie was allowed to rage at the world, that she was never made responsible for her own actions, and that the Wassermans should be responsible because they continued to protect her even while she was harassing others.

In the aftermath of the tragedy, the Wassermans' attorney commented that Norm believed he was doing everything possible to address his daughter's problems. Laurie, according to the Wassermans' attorney, was an emancipated adult who was not under her parents' care. She, he says, was responsible as an adult for her own actions. Norm, the attorney said, helped Laurie seek medical attention. He took Laurie to recognized specialists in the area who were treating what he believed to be Laurie's condition. Both specialists—Dr. Epstein and Greist—diagnosed Laurie as an obsessive-compulsive and prescribed drugs to deal with her behavior. Norm Wasserman was not a psychiatrist and relied on their diagnoses. He followed the doctors' instructions and told Laurie that she should follow her doctors' instructions as well.

Laurie Wasserman was an angry child for whom it is clear that no amount of special attention in school accomplished anything positive. It may have been that she needed therapy even as an elementary-school child and probably by the time she was in junior high. By the time she entered therapy after her marriage, her symptoms had become very convoluted—and since she was not forthcoming or candid with Dr. Greendale, he could only start to unravel what was lying beneath the surface. That's what he had said to Laurie and Russell. Greendale also complained that he did not spend enough time with Russell Dann to get a true picture of what was going on in the household.

After the FBI began contacting Greist about telephone threats that Laurie was making and instances of wanton destruction of other people's property, Greist told them he felt compelled to protect the confidentiality of the patient-doctor relationship. By the time Greist recommended that Laurie be institutionalized for her own good, she was already leaving the Madison campus and planning her day of revenge.

Epstein's and Greist's drug therapies seem counterproductive in retrospect. Their prescriptions may have only exacerbated her condition while minimally controlling the OCD. Her rituals might not have been a true representation of OCD, but, rather, might have been Laurie's conscious attempts to channel her aggression and fury into systematic behavior patterns to prevent her from hurting herself and others. In retrospect, Laurie's ritualistic behavior patterns do resemble those of a serial killers rather than that of the boy who couldn't stop washing his hands.

To make matters even worse, there seems to have been linkage blindness throughout the entire case. Did Epstein, Greist, or Greendale know one another or get authorized to share any meaningful information about Laurie? Most psychiatrists know that fire-starters are only two steps away from committing homicidal violence, but it does not appear that anyone ever told Greist that Laurie was riding up and down the elevators in her University of Wisconsin dormitory and starting fires in the garbage. Nor does it appear that her doctors knew that Laurie was suspected of attacking her husband with an ice pick or that she had purchased a handgun, that the FBI and local police in five different jurisdictions were actively investigating her for making death threats over the telephone. All of these actions, had anybody known about them and recognized them as such, were clear indicators of Laurie's potential for dangerousness. The rules governing the patient doctor relationship themselves often prevent information from being shared.

The police, it is clear from their own reports and by their own admissions, also ignored clear warnings that Laurie was headed for a violent confrontation with the criminal justice system. It could reasonably be expected that the police would be suspicious of Russell Dann's complaints that he had been attacked with an ice pick, given the history of marital disputes that had come to the attention of the local police. However, after many more of Laurie's victims begged the police to intervene, the police department's hesitancy to take more steps in Laurie's case is difficult to comprehend. In the aftermath of Laurie's rampage on May 20, the Winnetka police chief, Herb Timm, acknowledged the lack of effectiveness on the part of the police and the mental health practitioners in not addressing Laurie's deteriorating mental state. "We are convinced that opportunities existed prior to May 20th for Ms. Dann's condition to have been successfully addressed," Chief Timm said in a prepared statement, adding, "Unfortunately, it is apparent these opportunities were missed because critical information was not auffitiently provided to police authorities or mental health practitioners to adequately address the deteriorating mental state which Dann exhibited. It was also apparent that many opportunities for prosecution were lost either through withdrawal of criminal complaints, insufficient evidence, or lack of cooperation from Ms. Dann or other interested parties."

Chief Timm's assessment of Laurie Dann's case is particularly distressing in light of the amount of time and the amount of energy devoted to her activities by psychiatrists, the police, the FBI, and her many victims. Had one person been able to assemble all the parts into a coherent whole—as Russell Dann attempted to do—it is likely that Laurie Dann would have been institutionalized. And it is likely that Nicky Corwin would never have been killed.

9

THE EXORCISM
OF CHARLES GERVAIS

"I'm worse than Charles Manson." Charlie Gervais tells his interviewer on a local New Orleans television station. "I done what I did, but I put my own hands in the blood. I hate," he says, leaning forward into the camera. "I hate everything. I always did." Charlie is agitated. Each of his confrontations with the police, his lawyers, his doctors, and the court that convicted him for murder are playing through his mind and flashing against the insides of his eyes as he talks. "I've spit in people's faces. I shook my dick at 'em."

The details of the actual murder are still as alive in his mind as they were the night he gave them to Captain David McKenzie of the Pearl River Police Department. He relives each bloody moment of the crime and his manic flight across rural Jefferson Parish in the truck stolen from the victim. This was a crime so violent and bloody, even veteran police officers were shocked at it. But it was the cults that created the violent fantasies that danced through his brain every night.

Gervais is a classic example of the way cults destroy an individual's capacity for independent thought. Cults inculcate shared ideas among their membership. Cults promulgate collective thought and actions and so dominate the personalities of the members—which, in most cases, are already damaged to start with—that the members have little choice but to follow what they believe the cult wants them to do. The cult leaders need not be explicit in their instructions to the membership. In many cases, members will interpret what they believe the leader or the collective membership wants them to do and will act on those thoughts.

The emotionally abandoned Charlie Gervais was accepted as he was by the cult. He was accepted as a sociopath and as a violently angry person. He was accepted because he was a thug and liked to hurt other people. Acceptance is one of the primary ingredients in cult influence over potential time bombs. Gervais enjoyed being seduced by the prostitutes in the group. The cult, in this way, provided him with pleasure. He was rewarded by the cult for petty thievery and had the means to sell his stolen goods. And, even more importantly, he was encouraged by the cult to indulge in magical thinking as a substitute for taking logical responsibility for one's actions.

The cult actively encouraged Gervais's clinical vampirism, feeding him animal blood, menstrual blood, and donated blood from other members of the cult. They whetted his appetite for human blood and told him that he would be closer to the devil by consuming the blood of the living. At the same time, the cult provided him with drugs and taught him how to mix and match the drugs of his choice. The cult, he says, made him into a poly-drug abuser and set him up as a local pusher.

On spiritual and emotional levels, the cult freed Gervais from guilt—it empowered him, he says—and reinforced his primal impulses to violence and the satiation of his lust. It took whatever impulses society wanted to control in him and taught him how to turn them toward violence. Finally, he says, the cult took him out of his hopeless situation on the streets, gave his life a sense of purpose, taught him the value of magical ritual, and turned him against the rest of society.

In Gervais's case, because he was taken in by the cult when he was young, he was already a prime candidate for being raised according to his cult's value system: rob, steal, sell drugs, sell sex, and kill. Gervais internalized the cult's values as if they were the values of his own family. Gervais illustrates that long-term membership and membership at an early age are among the danger signs of a cult time bomb. As we'll see, he also displayed other signs of a cult-influenced time bomb, including the use of drugs and abuse of alcohol, the rejection of social authorities, and the reliance on violence to enforce cult standards and practices.

Charlie murdered for money, he told the Jefferson Parish police captain after he had signed the waiver to his Miranda rights. He said he had watched the police interrogating his accomplice, Michael Phillips, and told the detectives they weren't going to pin this one on him. He'd only been out of jail forty-seven days, and he wasn't going to get set up for murder by Phillips.

The gruesome murder of Andre Daigle had brought Charlie Gervais to the culmination of everything the cult had taught him to do. The cult had preached that Gervais was above the law, that his accumulated rage was all that was necessary for him to murder in order to achieve his aims. The cult taught him that murder was a legitimate means to achieve power and that no law could punish him. By the time Charlie Gervais and his accomplice Michael had killed Andre Daigle, he believed that. The fuse set by the New Orleans cult that raised him from the time he was a teenager in the French Quarter had finally exploded into violence.

THE NIGHT OF THE MURDER

According to Gervais, their plan was to wait until Andre Daigle, the john that Charlie's girlfriend Thelma, had lured to her apartment, fell asleep. Then they would kill him and take his money. They would use the money to finance their own prostitution operation in Texas and start their own cult-like organization. But eventually the reasons behind the murder were eclipsed by the challenge of who between the two of them could actually summon the will to commit the crime. It was the idea of the murder itself that spurred them on at the end.

"He was sleeping for a while and me and Mike kept passing the hammer back and forth to each other, saying which one of us is gonna hit 'im, and then it ended up Mike had the hammer and we was both just frustrated. We had been watching this man sleep for about six hours on the sofa and then we, Mike hit 'im, I think, four times."

At first, Gervais says, Mike Phillips was in shock. They both were. The level of violence gradually escalated, however, as each of them tried to involve the other deeper in the crime.

"Phillips ran upstairs," Charlie continues. "And he was shaking and all nervous and both of us was. And he give me the hammer and told me now, now, me get mine. So I hit the man two times on the head and he kept breathing, moving. By then he made it off the sofa and was on the ground. The man didn't want to die. He just . . . he wouldn't. We just beat him, and I hit him two times and then gave Mike back the hammer and Mike hit him some more times and then he give me the hammer and I hit him two or three more times and then Mike hit him about four more times and then he still wouldn't die."

Gervais recalled that Daigle kept on fighting and gasping for air. He kept on struggling against the hammer attack; kept on trying to crawl away from Gervais and Phillips, even though he was bleeding all over the floor and would have eventually died from the shock of the blows. But his continual movement threw Gervais and Phillips into an even greater frenzy.

"We got a hanger and put it around his neck and I stood on his back, jumping on his back, trying to knock the air out of his lungs while pulling the hanger up. And Mike had his hood on his head and was pulling the hanger with me. And then we thought he was dead, so we took the hanger off 'cause it started smelling like he shit and stuff and we took it off."

Even though he was still alive, Daigle's sphincter muscles had collapsed in the death throes of his body. Then he gasped for air again and began twitching. Gervais became more crazed as he plunged the hammer deep into Daigle's brain in an attempt to deliver the death blows.

"We cut a cord off this light thing that was in the apartment and we put that around his neck and the hanger was still on his neck. And we pushed the hammer through him, kept turning it, turning it, and turning it, making it get real tight, but it broke. So we got the vacuum cleaner in the back, in back of the truck. We cut the cord off of it because it was a real heavy black cord and we did the same thing with that and we held it. I held it while Mike was trying to get his self straight because he was really going out of it. And I held the hammer and I held it and I turned it some more and tightened it. And I stick it on a side of his head where it wouldn't move or do nothing, and we just waited until he stopped moving and then we took it off. He still like gave a gasping sound of one thing of air and then he didn't do nothing no more."

According to Phillips's signed confession, Gervais did most, if not all, of the actual beating and strangulation and Phillips helped by providing the vacuum cleaner cord and then dealing with the body afterward. What had seemed like a night-long ordeal of violence had only lasted ten to fifteen minutes. But then, Gervais confessed, the second ordeal of disposing the body and cleaning the blood began.

"Mike went outside to just look around and he put this curtain in the window, this big curtain, where nobody couldn't see in. 'Cause the curtain was real thin so he put this other one on there and then me and Mike got another big, long curtain, and we laid it out on the floor on the carpet and we got the body on another smaller curtain that was just big enough for the body so that we could pick it up and drag him and put him in the bag, the big one that he's wrapped up in, big curtain. And then we folded it all up and we put that big red couch over him and left him there until the next day."

Out of sight was not out of mind, however, because, as Gervais later said in a television interview, the apartment was literally awash in blood, cranial tissue, bone fragments, urine, and feces. Moreover, the sheer trauma of the violence was already beginning to affect both Gervais and Phillips. The two of them were slipping into shock. They covered the wrapped-up body with the couch and dragged it against the side wall of the apartment where they left it during the night. Then the cleanup began.

"I cleaned up the mess," Gervais remembers. "I cleaned it up because Mike was getting sick every time he looked at all the blood. I cleaned up most of the blood and stuff that I could get. The floor in the apartment is still full of blood, all over the place now. We cleaned it up the best we could, but it's no way. The man bled and bled and bled; just puddles of it."

But the body had already begun to smell, especially since Daigle had eliminated all of his waste in the final moments of his struggle. While they planned ways to dispose of the body, Gervais and Phillips turned the air conditioner up to full power and left the apartment with Thelma. That way, they thought, the ventilation would prevent the smell rising in waves off the rotting corpse from alerting the neighbors that something was wrong in the apartment.

"We let him sit there all day with the air conditioning turned up all the way," Gervais explains. "And we stayed out the whole day 'cause it was too cold with the way we had the air conditioner to keep the man from stinking. That night we were debating where to bring him and dump the body."

But the man was too big to haul away as simply as Gervais and Phillips had wanted to do. Consequently, there were still more machinations the two were required to complete in order to dispose of their body. As Michael Phillips described it to Sergeant Jim Gallagher of the Kenner Police Department, he and Gervais fussed with Daigle quite a bit before they figured out what to do. Finally, in a cruel replay of a crucifixion, the two killers nailed Daigle's arms and legs to the underside of a couch frame in order to support the corpse. Eventually, they were able to move it by simply hoisting the couch over their heads.

"This was an old couch. It didn't have no cushions or nothing or it. All right, we turned the couch upside down. We put him in it, nailed him down, Charlie screwed them down, and we tacked down a little"—he pauses—"the sheet going across. We picked him up, put him in the back of the truck, went down Airline Highway about, I think it was about six or seven miles, away from Kenner. It was pretty far away from Kenner. Dumped him at a dump. Two days later we went back and the sofa and everything was gone."

The murder of Andre Daigle was uncovered by police in Pearl River, Louisiana, after Daigle and his pickup truck were reported missing by his brother, Chris. Chris Daigle and his wife, Virginia, had been told by a southern California psychic, Rose Marie Kerr, that their brother's killers could be found along one of the Jefferson Parish roads driving the victim's black pickup truck. The desperate family members followed Kerr's advice and began their own search, driving along the deserted roads on the Saturday night the psychic told them they would spot the killers. Charlie Gervais believes to this day that it was his own magical thinking that allowed the psychic to "home in" on him and locate him for the victims. He literally illuminated himself psychically for her.

Chris and Virginia contacted the police after he had spotted his brother's truck being driven along a deserted road shortly after midnight. Nearly hysterical with panic, Chris and his wife stopped Tom Corley's police car and told him they had just been passed by Andre's truck, which was driven by two strange men. Corley passed by Andre's truck, lights flashing, but the truck, driven by Gervais and Phillips, sped away and a high-speed chase followed along the rural back roads of Jefferson Parish outside Kenner. Corley radioed for backup and Detective Captain Dave McKenzie joined the pursuit. When they caught up with the truck, they noticed while checking the truck's inspection sticker that there were weapons inside the cab: a handgun and a semiautomatic rifle. McKenzie's search on the NCIC computer revealed that both Gervais and Phillips had been previously charged with felonies and that Gervais had a felony conviction on his record. His possession of the weapons constituted a felony. The two were immediately arrested on suspicion of driving a stolen vehicle. The truck was later identified by Chris as belonging to Andre Daigle, after which Gervais and Phillips became material witnesses into Andre's disappearance. It was only at the police station in Pearl River that McKenzie heard Gervais and Phillips confess to the murder of Andre Daigle.

POSSESSED BY DEMONS

Charles Gervais had been out of jail less than a month before he committed the brutal murder of Andre Daigle. And now it is likely that he will never get out of prison alive. Gervais explains that the act of the killing itself was more of an initiation to the life to come than an act committed in this life. He talks to his television interviewers about the life that is to come after death and about his own future as if it were a certainty.

"In hell I will command souls," he tells talk-show host Bill Elder in a local New Orleans television interview, his voice growing more and more crazed as if he sees the roaring fires and pits of burning sulfur in his own mind. "Legions of souls, ten thousand souls, all to rule over in hell. This is what he promised me if I obeyed him."

Gervais looks forward to his life after death and the punishments he says he will inflict on the souls promised to him.

"I'm going to torment them," he says with relish. "I'm going to have them fight against God in the final war."

He tells his interviewers that he still has times when he thinks about this constantly, obsessively. It is what keeps him going as he lies in his bed in the prison hospital at Angola State Prison. "I'm going to torment them physically, but I'll be immortal. I'm going to do the same things that were done to me like the people who fucked me. I mean, mess me over, I'm going to fuck them and mess them over." He becomes descriptive for his television audience, explaining the ways he was abused. "I'm going to beat and rape the children when they come here. I'm going to just do it. I'm going to treat them real bad."

In his description of his "deal" with the satanic cult that raised him, Gervais says that depending upon the amount of evil each member performs, cult members will have increasingly larger numbers of souls under their command. "It's different for each person depending upon what you are doing and how far you go into the church. Some have ten thousand souls parceled out to them, some have more. The more evil you do, the more people you hurt, the more souls you get. I'm not through with my evil. I hope to have more by the time I'm thirty."

Gervais still fantasizes about murder. "If I was out now," he had said. "I'd become a terrorist for Saddam Hussein."

LITHA AND THE SATANISTS IN
NEW ORLEANS

Gervais explains that he first aroused the interest of the satanic cult when he was still a child. He says that his father had already left the family and Charlie, the youngest of six children, was left to fend for himself. His mother had no control over the children, he says, and he believes she blamed them for her own misfortunes. "I just always felt left out. Most of the time I just went out and got what I needed," he explains, arguing that he really had no formal upbringing whatsoever. From the time he was ten he used to go off by himself—to steal whatever he could and to get away from the family—in the French Quarter of New Orleans, where he was introduced to crime and violence. He stayed there, living off the street, and was soon picked up by the prostitutes in the Quarter. He was eventually brought to the house of one of the more powerful madames in the area.

"I met Litha," Gervais remembers. "She was a beautiful woman who took me in when I was a street kid hanging out in the Quarter." Gervais also remembers a mysterious figure he calls "Danny," who, although he was a legitimate businessman of some repute, fenced stolen goods for local criminals. "I remember she and Danny gave me LSD and they taught me all about violence. They told me how important evil and the devil were." Danny, Gervais says, was also a loan shark in the area, and hired teenager and local thugs to collect on bad loans that were turned over to him. "This was where I learned about violence," Gervais says. "Not that I didn't have knowledge of it from home."

But the young Charlie Gervais soon learned that Litha was at the center of a group that was more than a criminal organization—it was a coven. She held rituals, Charlie says. She and Danny referred to themselves as priestess and priest. They wore robes and performed ceremonies with candles and incense. "They were a cult," Gervais explains. "Pure and simple. They were part of a cult that is based in San Francisco and Los Angeles. Charlie Manson was a member of this for a while." He says that this cult believed in dualism—either all good or all evil—and was quite visible in the Old French Quarter of New Orleans, where members would wear all-black costumes and walk their German shepherds along the narrow streets. Some of the cult members actually slept in coffins instead of beds, and the entire group wielded great power among the prostitutes and drug dealers in the area.

Gervais described the coven's rituals, which involved

drugs and desecration of graves. "We was doing rituals at the graveyard. The group was of about eight, nine, or ten, and we would all be high, an LSD high. And I would start telling them about death. I would tell them all sorts of things, but I was pretty loaded and so were they. Then we would run around the graveyards and yell. I'd even dig up graves. But most of all the coven was concerned with sex. Sex and more sex. The door was always open to sex and free love."

As Gervais grew older, the members of the coven in New Orleans learned to trust him more and sent him out on burglaries. They gave him money and drugs and introduced him to exotic forms of sex. They became Gervais's family. "I was far away from home," he says. "They had me stealing, doing burglaries every day, and bringing jewelry around, passing it out to different people. I just didn't give a shit. I was a kid. I didn't need money. I already had it. I was about fourteen."

The cult to which Gervais belonged was part of a network, he claimed, that stretched from Los Angeles to New York. They earned money through pornography, through prostitution, drug sales, trafficking in children, and from the sales of "snuff" videos. These were made-for-home video movies that depicted scenes of rape, torture, sadism, and murder. Despite many doubts about the authenticity of snuff videos, Gervais claims that they're real and depict actual events that take place.

"There's a whole bunch of them," he explains. "Not just two or three versions of this or that, but a whole lot of movies that are just pure brutal and bloody. Real movies. They aren't bullshit. They are made in hotel rooms and in the woods and places like that. In secluded areas. The groups earn their income from them." Gervais goes on to claim that he knows a judge in New Orleans who is a bisexual who is married, "but he'll pay to serve the members of the occult, to bring young boys to the courthouse and shit, and takes them in the judge's chambers and sucks their clicks. And he goes through the clubs where people drive around in their Mercedes and Jaguars."

From the time he was a teenager, Gervais was involved with prostitution rings, and procured children—young boys and girls—for members of a sex and pornography ring. Litha and Danny actively encouraged bisexual relations between the children that members of the group procured for them, forcing their younger members to sodomize the children. It was as a teenager in this group that Gervais witnessed the involvement of the New Orleans business community with the pornography ring.

He describes rituals in which robed cult members brutalized young children that had been abducted from homes or had been lured from the streets of the French Quarter, where they were literally starving to death, into the group with promises of food and shelter. There were many hungry children on the streets in the 1970s, Gervais remembers, and many families willing to sell children in order to get food for the rest of the family to eat. Though still a teenager at the time, Gervais says that he knew the group members had to be robed to protect their identities.

"Part of what was going on was that people needed to be depersonalized so they could be free of the responsibility they had every day. The robes hid what they were. They made them like everybody else. Then they were free." They used drugs, Gervais says. "They took LSD and other hallucinogens to loosen up, to put themselves into a state where they could do what they wanted to do without having their everyday lives weigh on them."

To be in a cult, according to Gervais, means that you have to be freed from the responsibility of behaving according to what society wants. "The whole point was to be free. You had to be free from all the conditioning you got from society. You had to be free to get involved in the rituals. You had to be free from yourself. You had to be free to kill the weak. The weak want to be killed. They put themselves in your power to be killed."

For Gervais, being in a cult meant being strong because the power of the cult flowed through him. It was all the family he had and all the family he knew. All his physical needs were fulfilled, and he saw that all the physical needs of the others were fulfilled as well. "There was nothing that anybody wanted that they didn't get," Gervais says. "Sex, drugs, money."

He explains that the cult gave him recognition. It gave him a sense that he was worth something. It protected him from the world of the streets. "For the first time I had acceptance," Gervais explains. "I was a kid. I had no home to speak of. I had no family. They made me do some terrible things, but it gave me power over others. I was sadistic. I was indulged in every drug fantasy you could imagine. They took my soul but they gave me life."

It was sex that got him into the cult, just as it was sex that took him off the streets. He remembers that when he was just nine or ten, he would wander through the French Quarter where the prostitutes would take a fancy to him. "I remember one of them was real young and she took me in. She was nothing more than a girl child, but she knew about sex like she was an old whore. She taught me all about sex when I was ten. I don't think I was actually raped, maybe I was. It was more like I was taught. But when I was fourteen I was having sex with Litha regular and with the other kids they'd brung in."

All of that came to an end when Gervais was arrested for burglary, convicted, and sent to prison. After he was released, he was arrested a short time later, this time on drug charges, and was sent back to jail. Gervais claims that he's spent eight years of his adult life in jail from the time he was eighteen. "I'm only twenty-six," he explains. "And I've been in jail most of that time, including reform school."

A BAGMAN FOR THE CULT

When Gervais was released in 1987, he sought out his friends in New Orleans, hoping to pick up where he'd left off before he was sent up. This time he wanted to run drugs for the group and procure women for the prostitution ring. Gervais had big plans. He was going to handle their money, that's what they'd told him while he was in jail. And now he was going to fulfill all of the sexual fantasies that had been haunting him while he was in jail. Now he was ready, he told himself; he was ready to move into the leadership of the coven.

He'd been out just a few days, he claims, when he approached Danny to move back to the French Quarter. But he was in for a shock. They let him handle some of the money, bringing the cash from drug scores back to the Quarter, but the police were following him. Danny let him down hard, Gervais says. The police knew who he was, Danny told him. He wasn't a kid anymore who could dart in and out of the narrow alleys that wind through the back streets of the French Quarter. His value to the cult when he was a kid had been his anonymity. Now that he was an adult and a convicted felon, every street cop in the Quarter knew who he was. He was a threat, and Litha threw him back onto the street.

Gervais had had delusions about establishing what he calls a "big-time" prostitution ring in Texas. Now he was free, he told himself. He would have his own cult. "We wouldn't be the Mafia or anything, but we would have girls and we would do drugs, and we would sell sex." And that was the reason, he claims, he sent Thelma out to find the johns whom they would kill and rob. "Once we had the money, we'd go straight to Texas." But they never dreamed they'd be caught by a psychic from southern California who had predicted a encounter between them and the brother of their very first victim.

TOXIC TIME BOMB

In some of the most critical areas of his background, Gervais's childhood resembles Charles Manson's. Perhaps that's one of the reasons he compares himself to Manson and even tries to show that his levels of violence exceeded those of Manson himself. In one specific area that I have been able to have him tested—Gervais's levels of lead and cadmium—his toxicity actually exceeds Manson's levels. In tests performed on Gervais's hair samples by Dr. William Walsh of the Health Research Institute in Chicago, toxicologists found that Charles Gervais had extraordinary high levels of lead and cadmium in his body. Most of the convicted time bombs who have been tested by Walsh, including serial killers Henry Lee Lucas, Bobby Joe Long, Arthur Shawcross, and Charles Manson, have also had abnormally high levels of lead and cadmium in their system.

William Walsh had said that similarities of lead poisoning and cadmium contamination among serial killers and other time bombs point out a type of condition in which their bodies are unable to process or expel the toxins as most normal physiological systems do. As a result, these individuals tend to lose their physical and emotional resiliency to stress: they develop hair-trigger reactions to the most minor of irritations; and they can even become almost delusional in their abilities to deal with the outside world. In Charlie Gervais's case, not only are his lead levels high enough to sap most of his physical resiliency, he is almost unable to differentiate between what he believes is real and the real world Angola State Prison. "When I am threatened or am in my zone of comfort, I go so crazy I can taste the blood," Gervais has said.

Gervais's system has been contaminated with lead for a long time, probably since he was a child. One of the physiological effects of that contamination may have been the slow deterioration of his kidneys. As he explains it, he has always had a problem urinating. He'd been catheterized off and on since childhood because of an inability to urinate naturally. Even now, he explains, he is confined to the prison hospital because of his need to catheterize himself every time he has to go the bathroom. Prison doctors even tried to operate on his kidneys to remedy the condition, but it did him no good.

"I've been in trouble most of my life with bad kidney problems," Gervais says. "I catheterize myself. It ain't even no bother or nothing. It hurt when they did it and when I did the first few times, but now it don't hurt or nothin'. I like to masturbate when I catheterize myself. Someone should take a picture of my penis sometime. It's a bloody scab."

Toxic retention and self-mutilation are two of the more important signs that an individual has a high potential for dangerousness. In fact, one of the symptoms that some specialists in the field of extraordinarily violent deviant behavior look for is biochemical imbalances. They have found that many people who commit violent acts, especially brutal violence, or people who obsess about death or violence, tend to retain their toxins. As a result, when they take drugs or drink heavily or even breathe fumes from factories or spent ammunition, the toxins from the chemical substances simply stay in their bodies, gradually poisoning them and impairing their neurological and biochemical functions.

THE EXORCISM OF CHARLIE GERVAIS

One of the lawyers consulting on the Gervais case, suggests that there isn't much of a chance that Gervais will ever get out of prison. "He was convicted of murder in the first degree and sentenced to life without the possibility of parole, which means just that in Louisiana. But he is only twenty-seven years old, and there is no reason he can't have a healing and a spiritual awakening at Angola. There is also no reason he cannot get an education. I find this case repelling, but if his coming forward to be tested medically and spiritually can help educate us in Louisiana, how to learn to prevent such violent behavior, I'll take this case *pro bono*," she says.

Now that he is in an institutional setting, Gervais claims that he has been having flashbacks to other crimes. These brief but vivid snatches of memory, Gervais says, are almost like images of faces that crop up in a dream. He thinks he may have committed crimes in other jurisdictions, and, he says, he wants to rid himself of the devils that have plagued him since his first introduction to the cult in New Orleans when he was a teenager.

Like other time bombs whose stories have made it to the media, Gervais claims he had a very unhealthy early family life. He says he was neglected and emotionally abandoned by his mother and left to wander on his own through the city streets. He learned to survive by creating his own family out of other street kids, prostitutes, pimps, and drug dealers. When he finally found a home, he became a child of a cult, and now he wants to discover what that meant.

One step the group is considering taking is an actual exorcism in combination with biopsychosocial research to try to retrieve the memories of previous crimes Gervais believes he may have committed. Combined with chemical tests to restore whatever imbalances are discovered, the exorcism and therapy might unlock some of the mysteries that seem to surround Gervais. As violent as he still is, what lurks below the very thin fabric of his resiliency might reveal more about the extraordinary violence that is growing with each generation than has been revealed in any other convicted killer.

From his hospital bed in the prison ward at Angola, processing the paperwork for each of his appeals, painting, Gervais lies there addicted to the catheter that drains the wastes from his body while it excites him sexually. There's nothing much for him to do these days except to wait for the answers to the hundreds of questions that have haunted him like demons since he was a teenager. He is still waiting.

10

CHARLES ANDREW WILLIAMS: DEATH IN THE SCHOOLYARD

His friends said they took him seriously enough to pat him down before he entered the school building on the Monday morning of his shooting assault at Santana High on March 5, 2001. But they forgot to search his backpack for his father's .22 ,which he'd stashed there. Nor did the friends who had searched his clothing report their suspicions about Charles Andrew Williams to the authorities at Santana High in Santee, California, or to the San Diego County Sheriff's Department. They simply satisfied themselves that Williams, who had been bragging for over a month that he was going to "pull a Columbine" to get even with the older kids who were beating him up every day, was just blowing off more of his hot air. He was just another Columbine wannabe—there were kids like him all over the Internet—who only succeeded in making his friends nervous for about thirty seconds.

Williams's friends had heard him making threats for about a month, and they searched him, they said, "just to make sure." They really didn't believe for a second that he'd go through with it, because they regarded him as just a punk who couldn't speak without stuttering and never, ever followed through on anything. After all, they said, he was nothing more than a wimp who took whatever the older kids dished out and then walked away. Even his friends described the timid Andy Williams as the runt of the litter who wouldn't defend himself, no matter how hard the abuse became.

Day after day, they would watch upperclassmen pick on Williams, beat him up, steal his lunch money, and even hold him down and pull the shoes and socks off his feet. From the very first day he arrived at Santana High School, the older students laughed at the skinny, undersized fourteen-year-old with big ears. They taunted him, and finally began hitting him and slamming him into walls just for fun.

One of Williams's friends told the newspapers that the abuse got so out of hand that upperclassmen would burn their lighters until they became almost too hot to hold, click them shut, and then press the hot metal into the soft skin of Andy's neck. This was not just bullying. It was a form of torture. There was nothing Williams could or would do about it. He was defenseless, and there was nobody who would stand up for him. He just took it as if he deserved it, tried to force a smile when it was all over, and even acted like he was ready for more. Maybe if he accepted the abuse and showed he could take it, the bullying would stop. But it didn't.

No matter how much abuse the students at Santana High dished out to him, Charles "Andy" Williams simply seemed to endure it. Maybe he was trying to fit in, thinking that if he took his licking, the upperclassmen would turn on someone else who would come along. Or maybe if he could just succeed at something, skateboarding or his music, maybe then he'd get enough respect that the beatings would stop. But, as the months of the school year went by, it looked like Williams wasn't going to succeed at anything. He only talked about forming his own heavy metal band. He only bragged that he would become a dazzling skateboard acrobat someday. In reality, he was only mediocre and never accomplished anything beyond talk. And it was the talk, the kids who knew him said, that only got the older kids mad and made no one believe him. So when he said he was going to turn Santana High into the next Columbine bloodbath, it was just an empty threat, they said.

Despite Williams's promises of retribution, the beatings continued. They even got worse. One of his classmates said that Williams seemed to fall right to the bottom of the pecking order. Santana High School sophomore Scott Wilk told reporters for local newspapers in a postshooting canvassing interview that it got so bad for Williams, "even the kids who got picked on the most picked on him." Whenever he tried to get inside a group, at least one of the kids would simply turn on him and Williams would simply take it. He wouldn't even defend himself verbally. To outsiders, it looked as though no matter what was dished out, Andy Williams would absorb it and move on. On the inside, however, he was a volcano waiting to erupt.

Things came to a head a week before Williams set up in the Santana High boys' bathroom, pulled his .22 out of his backpack, and began shooting at anyone he could find. At an ad hoc get-together among Williams's acquaintances at a local park, a couple of people accused Williams, who had begun using alcohol himself, of trying to get his twelve-year-old girlfriend drunk. Williams denied it at first. Maybe he was drinking a beer and she wanted to try a few sips, but he never tried to get her drunk. He said he wasn't trying to be funny, but his denials weren't enough. Kids, classmates that Williams thought were his friends, jumped on him, threw him down, and pounded him in the face so badly that Williams became shaken and simply staggered away when his friends lost interest in hitting him.

Williams had been making threats about seeking retribution from his tormentors for a month. The revenge he would exact, he promised, would turn the high school into a war zone. He could get his hands on a gun and he would use it, he warned. But because he had never followed through on any of his promises in the past, people who heard him laughed and said he was only blowing more hot air. His acquaintances derided him, called him a punk, and said that if he had a gun, he should use it. Some even taunted him to pull off the shooting. Evidently, after the beating he took from those whom he thought he could trust, Andy Williams got serious.

His friends who derided him did not know that Williams had already stolen his father's .22 Arminius handgun, a German-made collector's item, and had hidden it in the bushes in the park across the street from the school. Williams didn't worry about his father, who, he said, was rarely home and certainly wouldn't check the place where he kept the weapon. Now all he had to do was work himself up to carry out his threats. The beating that he had endured at the park a week before had been the final straw. It would take him a week of boasting and threatening before he would do anything.

He'd stepped up his warnings during that week, talking about his revenge so much that his friends thought maybe he'd gone over the edge. He was a braggart—something they already knew—but this time, maybe it was worth checking into, even if it meant egging him on. At least they'd know what he was planning. But, according to people who spoke to him, they all came away with a sense that he wasn't prepared to do anything. When he and one of his friends, Josh Stevens, talked about shooting up the school, another friend said that it was a deadly serious threat. But Josh Stevens told her that the two boys were just kidding with each other. On the Saturday before the shooting, however, as Williams and his group were hanging around Josh Stevens's apartment, Williams, at first, was oddly nonconversational, distant, as if he were lost in thought. Later, though, he began talking about "pulling a Columbine," a conversation that caught the ear of Chris Reynolds, Josh's mother's boyfriend. Reynolds told police and the newspapers that when he asked Williams whether he was serious about carrying out his plans, Williams told him he was just kidding. So Reynolds dropped the matter and nothing more was said about it until Reynolds learned what Williams had done.

On the Monday morning of the shooting, Williams was up early. He had already planted his gun at the park. He shared a joint with friends at an apartment complex near the school and then met up with other friends at a Jack in the Box restaurant across the street from the campus. They looked through his clothing, assuring themselves he wasn't carrying any gun, and then got back to joking. But Williams wasn't joking. He was serious. He wasn't stuttering. Then, alone, he got up to leave. First he went to the park to retrieve the gun he'd hidden. Then, just before 9:20 A.M., he headed toward the school.

His first stop was the boys' bathroom, where, hidden behind a stall, he pulled the eight-shot revolver out of his backpack, cocked it, and aimed at the students standing near the door. Then he started reeling off shots, almost at random. If there had been someone in particular he was after, you couldn't tell it by the way he was firing. He immediately shot two students in the bathroom and then stepped out into a narrow courtyard, where he aimed and fired at anyone in his line of sight.

"It didn't seem as if it mattered to him," one witness said. "He just had this smile on his face as he pointed the gun and fired."

Whatever caught his eye or moved across his range of fire became a target. He didn't know whether the two students he'd left on the bathroom floor were dead or wounded, but it didn't seem to slow him down. He'd already reloaded the revolver, fired off another eight rounds, and reloaded again. Now, as the students ran, he took just a bit more time to aim, then saw students drop to their knees as the bullets hit their marks. In only a couple of minutes, he'd shot thirteen more victims, who were now either lying flat out on the ground or trying to crawl away to safety as more bullets whizzed over their heads.

Students changing classes or on their way to school said they heard the light popping sounds of a small-caliber weapon and the wail of police sirens converging from different directions. They were in shock when they looked into the courtyard to see Andy Williams firing away. A girl who had seen Williams on Saturday night at Josh Stevens's house admitted that she had never thought Williams would do anything he'd said. But here he was carrying out the threat just as he had said he would. Nobody had taken him seriously. She was not the only student who had expressed surprise that Williams had actually carried through on something he had bragged about doing.

Now the campus was suddenly alive with the sound of blaring sirens welling up around the panicked students, the hard, protesting squeal of car tires, and the loud squawking and whistling of police radios. Students were still screaming as they ran. But the popping had stopped.

The shooting only lasted six minutes or so before fifteen victims were down, two fatally. By then, the San Diego County Sheriff's Department had arrived and begun to deploy around the school perimeter. Deputies with their weapons drawn swept the school corridors as students, still running from the small quad where the shooter's victims lay sprawled against the sides of buildings, pointed to the narrow courtyard where they'd seen Andy Williams firing away. Some of them said, "The bathroom" to one another as the deputies pressed closer to the knot of students fleeing the gunshots.

While the heavily armored SWAT units took up positions on the high school's athletic fields, the first students encountering deputies from the San Diego Sheriff's black-and-white units pointed to the small quad and the bathroom that opened onto it, shouting they saw a small kid with a handgun retreat into the bathroom. They didn't know it, but Williams had run out of bullets again and had gone back inside to reload. He was set to unleash another barrage when the deputies stormed through the door.

Confronting the tiny student with the small-gauge revolver, the deputies did not fire. Instead, they hollered at him to put the weapon down and surrender. As he lowered the nozzle, Williams surrendered to the police, who asked him if there were any other shooters.

"It's only me," the child whimpered as the sheriff's officers cuffed him and led him away.

With the shooter safely in custody, paramedic teams began evaluating victims at the scene and preparing them for transport to local hospitals. Bodies were strewn all over the courtyard and in the boys' bathroom, blood running in rivulets along the sides of the school walls. Some of the victims were treated right there at the scene for superficial wounds and interviewed by deputies. The more seriously wounded victims were stabilized and transported immediately. Two critically wounded victims died from the gunshots. They were fourteen-year-old Brian Zuckor, a skateboarder who told friends he wanted to be a stuntman, and seventeen-year-old Randy Gordon, who said he wanted to join the navy. It was ironic, friends of the two high-school students said, that they were well-liked individuals who excelled at the things they chose to do. Andy Williams, on the other hand, was not liked at all and rarely succeeded at things he said he wanted to do. It was part of the upside-down world that was suddenly created in the wake of what was, as Williams had threatened, America's next Columbine.

SPATE OF SHOOTING INCIDENTS: WILLIAMSPORT, PENNSYLVANIA

Whatever thoughts of premeditated violence were circulating through Andy Williams's brain in the weeks before the shootings, his actions had an immediate result. Just days after news on the Santee shooting broke, about twenty schoolchildren in different parts of the country, teenagers as well as preteens, were arrested in separate incidents, either on actual weapons or assault charges or for making threats against teachers or other students. A thirteen-year-old Catholic-school eighth grader, Elizabeth Bush of Pennsylvania, brought a .22 to school, followed the head of the cheerleading squad into the cafeteria, pulled out her weapon, and shot her in the shoulder. Like Andy Williams, Elizabeth Bush had made her intentions clear to friends and fellow students, and she repeated those intentions as she pulled the trigger. But no one had taken her threats seriously until she actually stood there, her fingers on the trigger, and shot the other girl who, she claimed, had betrayed her.

Also like Andy Williams, Elizabeth Bush claimed she had been tormented by other schoolchildren. Her parents said she had been ridiculed and made fun of throughout her school years, and that was the reason they had transferred her to the small Catholic school in Williamsport. But the ridicule continued, and Bush became as unhappy at Bishop Neuman as she'd been at her other school. Everything came to a head when she tried to befriend the head of the school's cheerleading squad, admitting private secrets about herself to gain the girl's confidence. But when she, too, began making fun of her, it was like an all-too-painful script that was played out again. Bush said she tried to make peace, e-mailing her tormentor and trying to find a way to reconcile. But, according to friends, when Elizabeth Bush's secret revelations about herself turned up as gossip among the very people making fun of her, she believed she had been betrayed, and that's what became the final straw. The Elizabeth Bush shooting was only one of many similar incidents around the country in the days after the Santana High School rampage that got people asking who these shooters were.

WHO WAS CHARLES ANDREW WILLIAMS?

In the aftermath of a major crime—such as a serial murder, mass murder, workplace or schoolyard shooting—among the first questions asked are "Who is he?" "What kind of person did this?" and always "why?" This is exactly what happened in the media's search for answers in the Andy Williams shootings. Friends described Williams as a docile kid, desperately seeking acceptance in different high-school cliques, but always facing rejection. He wasn't a jock and didn't fit in there. He didn't seek admission to the Mexican gangster wanna-bes or gang cliques, and he wasn't a skinhead. He bounced around during the first weeks of the new school year until he tried to squeeze himself into the skateboarder types, even though he was only a mediocre boarder himself. But at least he could claim that he had become an insider among a group of counterculture outsiders and had a crew he could say he hung out with on weekends. But the bullying that had dogged him his whole life soon picked up in California, right where it had left off in Maryland.

Called a "wimp" and a "pussy" by those who pushed him around every day at school, Williams, who wore a nickname necklace with the word "Mouse" on it, simply withdrew from confrontations rather than stand up for himself. It was his withdrawal, his refusal to defend himself, which made the bullying even worse. It was as if his tormentors were looking for the point at which the kid would fight back. Even if he took a licking, friends said, fighting back would have earned him at least some respect. As it was, the older students at Santee simply found new and more creative ways to make his life miserable.

Andy Williams was beyond timid. A horde of reporters descended upon Santana High School the day after the shooting, and everyone who knew Williams described incident after incident in which Williams seemed to absorb punishment from others as if it were his due. At the absolute bottom of the social pecking order at Santana High School, Williams, who boasted and bragged about the accomplishments he would someday achieve, seemed almost to be playing out a role.

In the ritual of the male-primacy dance, certain individuals seem to place themselves deliberately at the bottom of the order. Whether they make themselves into targets in order to be protected or kept around by members higher on the scale, or whether they are simply victims, there is a social basis to their position in the hierarchy. But in Andy Williams's case, he was not the clown, could find no one to take care of him, and endured particularly severe physical abuse. It is likely, therefore, that Williams was not trying to be a victim. Rather, he consistently sought out friends, sought to join groups as a member, and looked for those common interests that would assure him a slot in a group. But, in Santee, California, it was not to be.

Those people whom Williams thought would become his friends constantly taunted him and tried to provoke him. They challenged him when he bragged, even egging him on when he threatened to pull a Columbine at Santana; they also doled out physical retribution whenever they felt motivated to do so. Despite his attempts to make himself likable, newer members of whatever group Williams hung out with assumed primacy over him and joined in the bullying. This must have been particularly frustrating and demoralizing for Williams because it was within his peer group that he was seeking a replacement for the family structure he did not have at home.

Williams had moved to California with his father in 1999. They first settled in the desert community of Twenty-Nine Palms before moving to San Diego, where his father worked for the military. They had moved there from Maryland, where he and his father had lived for eight years after his parents divorced. Andy's older brother, Michael, had stayed with his mother, Linda Wells, when Andy went to live with his father. But even when they lived together as a family, Michael remembered that his younger brother was always picked on.

After the shooting, Michael told reporters that for as long as he could remember, Andy had been the target of schoolyard bullies. In an interview with the *Atlanta Journal-*

Constitution, Michael Williams said that because his brother was undersized and very odd-looking, with a skinny physique and too-large ears, he almost looked like Mickey Mouse. That resemblance made him the butt of every schoolyard joke. The jokes turned into taunting, and, as he grew older, the taunting turned into outright physical punishment. Kids got into the habit of using Williams as a punching bag, just because they felt like it. Andy felt there was nothing he could do about it. Other friends from his Maryland school days told newspapers that bigger children routinely picked on Andy because he was the smallest kid around and just never seemed to fit in.

Maybe it wasn't only that Williams was tormented at school. Although many might say that when the older students at Santana High burned his flesh with their lighters, it went beyond simple bullying into the kind of torture even the Geneva Convention governing the treatment of prisoners of war forbids. After all, other children are tormented and don't bring guns to school; so why did Andy Williams? And maybe it wasn't merely that Williams had begun drinking alcohol and smoking marijuana. Other adolescents also drink and do some drugs. But what was clear is that in the midst of his being subjected to sustained and increasingly brutal physical and psychological abuse by upperclassmen, he turned to alcohol and drugs and probably did not have a family support system at home to help him weather the emotional turmoil he was going through. He even told friends that getting high each morning helped him face what he knew he'd encounter each day from the kids who beat him up.

Michael Williams told reporters that he occasionally communicated with Andy via e-mail and saw him only twice a year when Andy visited with his mother. Andy's father seemed unaware of what was happening to his son. Andy's bragging that he had stolen a rare handgun from his father's collection weeks before the shooting seems to indicate that, at least, Andy believed his father was unaware of what was going on in his son's life or that he wasn't around enough to notice that one of his guns was missing.

Thus, with a long history of being bullied, an inability to find solace in his new school in California, a school administration that he felt he could not turn to, and with no one who took his threats seriously enough to get the school authorities to intervene, Andy Williams probably felt very much alone. And with what might have been an insufficient family support structure at home, Williams probably felt that as his life slipped away from him each and every day, he had nothing to lose and only a feeling of satisfaction to gain by seeking violent revenge. Maybe he wanted to commit suicide by his own hands or at the hands of the police and complete the arc of his own vision of self-destruction. His blood would be on the hands of others for the rest of their lives, just like Dylan Klebold and Eric Harris's apocalyptic visions that had been described on video and on the Internet in the weeks before the Columbine shooting. Maybe, in the seconds after the San Diego County Sheriff's deputies pushed through the door of the bathroom where Williams was trying to reload his weapon, Williams realized he couldn't shoot himself and was afraid to be shot down by the police. Maybe Andy Williams just didn't want to die. In his mind, perhaps, the statement of violence that he had made was enough to guarantee that he had made his mark. Only the Santee shooter knows for sure.

THE BENCHMARK OF COLUMBINE

The fifteen victims—including two fatalities, Brian Zuckor and Randy Gordon—had indeed made Santana High School the worst schoolyard mass-shooting-spree incident since Columbine, almost two years earlier. Williams's crime shocked a nation already inured to teenage violence in the halls and classrooms of high schools and middle schools.

But what was there about this shooting that made it different from the tragedy at Columbine?

In fact, there were a number of all-too-familiar circumstances between the two shootings that made comparisons between them inevitable, not the least of which was that the two sets of shooters were outcasts and the butt of jokes and taunts. However, where Columbine's Dylan Klebold and Eric Harris reinforced one another and were aggressive about promising revenge, Williams withdrew. Where Klebold and Harris stockpiled weapons and built homemade bombs in their houses (bombs they would detonate inside Columbine), Williams stole a single handgun out of his father's apartment. Finally, Klebold and Harris seemed to have visualized what strategy they were going to pursue to drive home their revenge. They based their attack on the video game Doom, in which the attacker moves down hallways and corridors, destroying everything in his path. Williams fired at the students closest to him inside the bathroom and then stepped outside to a narrow courtyard. He did not stalk students through the halls.

It was Klebold and Harris who, both by their aggressiveness and their suicides, helped create the model that Williams said he was following when he told friends he wanted to pull off a Columbine at Santana High School. Klebold and Harris, unlike Williams, were violence-prone students who announced what they wanted to do—using the Internet as their medium—then carried out their threats and became counterculture heroes in the process. These were the outlaws who lived out video-game fantasies and took down the jocks, the preppies, the bullies, the cheerleaders, and anyone else who either directly tormented them or, through neglect, cast them into their own perceived outer darkness. They were seeking more than revenge, and that's what frightened school boards, administrators, and parents; it's also what set off a wave of Columbine-like threats and copycat events. One of those influenced was Charles Andrew Williams.

Part of the problem Columbine presented to schools and parents was that the traditional response of law enforcement to the Klebold and Harris siege seemed insufficient to stop the bloodshed. Although the sheriff's department said they had been trained for mass-shooting incidents, victims and their families, as well as others at the scene, said that the response of the sheriff's department itself contributed to the amount of violence. The sheriff's deputies did not enter the school building while the shooting was going on. According to reports, as Klebold and Harris were moving through the school, shooting their victims and detonating bombs, the deputies were ordered to remain outside until SWAT teams arrived. No one went inside to stop the two high-school students who were on a rampage. In fact, even after SWAT teams took their positions, the deputies still remained outside the school. How many students' lives could have been saved, parents of Columbine victims are now asking, had the deputies entered the school building when they first arrived on the scene?

In the end, questions still remain about how Klebold and Harris met their final deaths. Did, as a forensic science professor Lawrence Koblinski at John Jay College of Criminal Justice in New York, Eric Harris shoot Dylan Klebold in the head? In gruesome crime scene photos printed in the National Enquirer, both Klebold and Harris are lying side by side in their respective pools of blood. Their rage now quieted by the sudden violence that ended their lives. But, Professor Koblinski told the Enquirer, from the blood spatter evidence around Harris, whose weapon is still near his hand, it looks as though Harris shot himself. Klebold body position tells a different story. Klebold's weapon is near his feet, too far away from hand for him to have shot himself in the head and dropped it. Also, the nature of the entry gunshot wound to Klebold's head suggests that it someone else fired the fatal shot. Professor Koblinski told the Enquirer that Harris might have shot Klebold and then turned the weapon on himself. Of course, without access to the actual autopsy itself and the photos taken by the medical examiner, all of which have been sealed, any judgments about how Klebold was shot are only speculative.

Nevertheless, if what Professor Koblinski says about the revelations in the crime scene photos of the two dead boys are true, it might suggest that the two of them did have a suicide pact in which, when the final moment came, one was charged with the task of killing the other before taking his own life. What does that say about the final apocalyptic vision of Klebold and Harris and who might have been the dominant figure in the diad? Whatever drove Klebold and Harris into their final psychological bunker is something that must be evaluated if school administrators and law enforcement ever hope to develop a preventive methodology when it comes to schoolyard shootings.

In response to demands for a complete investigation, Governor Bill Owens of Colorado formed a fifteen-member special commission to get some answers to the questions surrounding the incident and to make recommendations for the future. The Columbine Review Commission was a blue-ribbon panel chaired by former state supreme court justice William Erickson to investigate what happened at Columbine High, how it happened, why it happened, and what could have been done to prevent the shooting and the loss of lives. The panel also came up with a list of recommendations not only to assess the possibilities of mass shootings at schools, but also to determine what the appropriate law-enforcement response should be. Among the lingering questions for the panel:

1) Did the Jefferson County sheriff do the right thing by having his deputies wait outside the school while the shooting was going on until the SWAT teams arrived?

2) Should deputies have entered the school to locate and subdue the shooters?

3) Were the rumors true that Jefferson County sheriff

John Stone had failed to act on complaints against Klebold and Harris a year in advance of the shootings?

In fact, one of the Columbine panel's specific recommendations was that the first law-enforcement units on a scene should give the highest priority to stopping any ongoing assault. "First Responders" to a crime scene, the report says, whether they are school resource officers or deputies responding to an emergency call, should be "trained in concepts and skills of rapid emergency deployment, whether or not assigned as members of standing or reserve special weapons and tactics teams, and should have immediately available all weapons and protective equipment that might be required in a pursuit of active armed perpetrators." And in response to complaints that there was no immediate command and control setup at Columbine, even though deputies and SWAT team members were on-site, the report recommends that law enforcement personnel should be trained to take command from the very beginning of a crisis. This was not done at Columbine.

While both the sheriff's department and parents of the Columbine victims had complaints about the panel's report, the panel did highlight some of the main issues about the nature of the Columbine shooting and the shortcomings of the sheriff's criminal investigation and the response of the school itself to the underlying causes of the attack. First of all, what is clear from the report is that the attack should have come as no surprise to anyone who knew Klebold and Harris because the two boys announced their intentions via the Internet, where they had made their threats absolutely clear. If Web site visitors on the other side of the world were able to view what Klebold and Harris said they wanted to do, why couldn't school administrators in Littleton and deputies at the Jefferson County Sheriff's Department do the same thing? Klebold and Harris also recorded videotapes in which they displayed the weapons they had and set forth their plans for the attack in detail. It was as if the two shooters had constructed a video game both on VHS and on their Web site, complete with the names of those students they were targeting, and they did this well in advance of the actual shooting.

Parents Randy and Judy Brown, whose son Brooks had received specific threats from Klebold and Harris that he was one of their targets, had complained to Sheriff Stone and reported the threats posted on the Klebold/Harris Web site. The threats had been documented on the Internet as real, and certainly pointed to a possible violation of the law, at least insofar as the storage of weapons and threat to manufacture bombs were concerned. Yet, the Columbine Panel concluded, although the sheriff's office had begun the preparation of a search warrant, the warrant was never served. "If the search warrant that was originally proposed had been issued," Justice Erickson said, "this probably wouldn't have happened. As a result, we had one of the greatest school-shooting tragedies. We've had copycat incidents since then." One of those copycat incidents was the shooting at Santana High School.

THE NATION REACTS TO SCHOOL THREATS

The Santee shootings, which came less than two years after Columbine and seemed to inspire a round of schoolyard-shooting incidents in early 2001, made school officials, law enforcement, and parents even more sensitive to the issues that most likely prompted Charles Andrew Williams to bring a gun to school in the first place. In many ways, what the nation saw and eventually learned about Columbine awakened people to the pervasive reality that suburban schools, with their layers of administrators and psychologists, provided no insulation from the violence that occurred in inner cities.

Columbine also showed that even highly motivated local enforcement could provide only limited protection from students bent on violence.

The specter of other Andy Williams–like shooters turning other local schools across the nation into scenes of carnage, threatening students and teachers, drew instant and intense reactions from school administrators as well as parents. In light of reports that the authorities had dismissed threats made by the shooters, school boards suddenly began to take threats very seriously. Many school boards ratcheted up their zero-tolerance policy against threats to the point where mere ideations of anger by elementary students were enough to bring reprisals. Students who were alleged to have made threats were summarily suspended from school and reported to police.

Although many of the new zero-tolerance policies around the country were probably well-intentioned, they were also looked at as draconian by the parents of students on the receiving end of punishment. For example, a third grader who kissed the cheek of another student was suspended from school for sexual assault; elementary students who even expressed dislike toward teachers were accused of making threats and were suspended; at least one student, in response to a creative-writing exercise, turned in a fantasy story about violence and was suspended because of the tale and turned over to police.

The problem with the new get-tough policies on threats and ideations of violence was that it was a net administrators tried to stretch too wide so as to cover every perceived threat—even when there was no threat. As a result, innocent children were caught on the teeth of a policy that didn't allow for distinguishing real threats from simple expressions of feeling that did not indicate volition. School administrators reacted out of fear because there simply was no measuring instrument to predict violence. The incidents at Columbine, where even the Jefferson County Sheriff's Department had received criminal complaints from parents of one of Klebold's and

Harris's victims and still did not intervene to prevent the shootings, were simply too horrific for school boards to comprehend. They had to do something, even if that something meant barring a high-school student from graduation because authorities found a knife in her car—a knife that didn't belong to her, she said. Policy had overrun reality, and still, the real causes of schoolyard violence had not been addressed.

Parents themselves were conflicted between the need for zero tolerance of threats and weapons on school campuses and a realization that sometimes ideas expressed by children were not threats at all. Many young students had no idea of what the consequences were to the angry things they said. Ideations of violence may precede violence, but they may also be expressions of situational feelings rather than intent, feelings that need to be addressed without punishing the person expressing them. As parents, particularly parents of those children punished either too harshly or unfairly by schools, began to oppose school administrators, it was becoming clear that simply turning schools into mini penitentiaries where even the slightest expression of anger carried harsh reprisals was not working. And despite the statistics, which showed that school violence was sharply on the decline between 2000 and 2001, problems were still there, and there was no guarantee that incidents of violence would increase again. No matter how well-intentioned they were, school administrators had not found a solution to the problems of school violence.

RED-FLAG INDICATORS OF TEENAGE AND SCHOOL VIOLENCE

Although most teenagers from time to time express anger, rebellion, and dissatisfaction both with authority and with the status quo, there are certain red-flag indicators that can serve as a warning of dangerousness. When teenagers are especially alienated, have few or no friends, have little or no family supervision or support structure, or feel threatened or in danger, they may strike out. But before they do, they usually announce their intentions, sometimes as a threat to those around them, other times as a plea for help. Usually, their peers are unable to decipher the warnings, but teachers, parents, and school administrators should have a quick-response mechanism that, while not directly punishing potentially dangerous adolescents for the way they feel, addresses feelings of rage and provides a support system. Among the red-flag indicators are:

Alienation, Ideations of Hatred and Self-Destructiveness

Perhaps the most detailed pointers of possible violence, or "dangerousness," as professionals refer to it, come from the evaluations of Klebold and Harris that appear in the Columbine Panel's report. These descriptions of the pre-attack behaviors of Klebold and Harris, combined with the descriptions of what friends said about Charles Andrew Williams, provide a diagram of potential teenage schoolyard mass murderers.

In Dylan Klebold's journal, which the police released, he wrote, in 1997, about his feelings of depression, proclaiming, "I swear—like I'm an outcast. Is everyone conspiring against me? Fact: people are so unaware. . . . Well, ignorance is bliss, I guess . . . could explain my depression." These paranoid feelings were probably reinforced by his self-perception of being an "outcast," a pariah in the clique-oriented world of his high school where he lived as if in isolation from those around him. It's painful, any therapist will agree, for individuals to have to navigate through a well-defined and hierarchical social setting in which they are awash in feelings of depression and misery that they cannot share because those around them don't know or care to know. These kinds of ideations form the core of presuicidal feelings and, if unchecked, can result in some form of self-destructiveness or, turned outward into an apocalyptic statement of violence, mass murder/suicide.

Eric Harris had his own journal and a Web site in which he wrote statements of absolute hatred for those around him. He described his bomb-making activities as well as his suicidal and homicidal thoughts. He also felt isolated from those around him, an individual completely alone in a world that not only misunderstood him but simply did not care. He wrote of his fellow Columbine students: "I hate you people for leaving me out of so many fun things."

Similarly, Andy Williams, although he didn't confront those who taunted him, verbalized his ideations of violence when he told friends in Josh Stevens's apartment that he had a gun, that he would make good on the threats he'd been making for the past few weeks, and that he'd "pull a Columbine." When challenged about his threats, he pulled back and called them jokes, but, clearly, Williams already had the gun he would use and had been pushed to the brink, both by students who tormented him and his own feelings of hatred.

One of the first indicators of the potential for violence is the potential offender's own statements. The greater the detail of the violence described—and the more specific the threats with respect to individual students, teachers, or administrators—the more clearly thought-out the plan and the closer to its execution the child is. Free-floating ideations or nonvolitional statements about feelings might be indicators of future trouble and probably require at least some evaluation, but they really shouldn't be punishable as offenses. Direct threats, however, fall into a different category.

Direct Announcements of Threats

Ideations of violence can be an initial stage of planning for an act of violence. But the announcement of those threats in more formalized settings indicates that a potential offender has reached a stage where he or she is prepared to take responsibility for what the offender is about to do. The fact that Andy Williams announced his intentions was important and despite his denials should have been heeded. Klebold and Harris went even further. They formalized their plans and threats on the Internet and on videotapes. Harris made his intentions even clearer, according to the Columbine report, when he actually played portions of the videotapes that he'd made in the Columbine students' video studio in front of a small audience. In addition, Dylan Klebold had written an essay about perpetrating violence that had so disturbed a teacher, it led her to meet with Klebold's parents and a school counselor about what, in her words (quoted by the Columbine Panel's report), was a "ghastly" composition. The teacher did the right thing by alerting the school as well as the parents to the degree of dangerousness she perceived in the essay. Whether Dylan's parents, who, according to the panel's report of the police investigation, had actually discovered bomb-making ingredients in their son's bedroom, took any direct action to intervene to prevent violence is a matter still under investigation and, perhaps, will be part of the resulting civil litigation that is the fallout from the Columbine shootings. The direct threats against Brooks Brown were also an indicator of high dangerousness because of the specificity of the threats and the public forum in which they were made.

Encounters with Criminal Justice or Juvenile Justice System

Encounters with the justice system are usually strong indicators of dangerousness, whether the offender is an adult or a juvenile. In fact, many repeat offenders, mass murderers, serial or spree killers, or serial sexual predators have had previous and sometimes extensive encounters with justice systems in different localities. Except for very young offenders, encounters with juvenile and criminal justice systems usually provide one possible point of intervention before an offender commits an ultimate crime.

Klebold and Harris were no exception to this indicator, having been arrested by the Jefferson County Sheriff's Department for theft after breaking into an electrician's van. The pair stole about $250 worth of items. They also ran afoul of the law for having hacked their way into the Columbine High School computer system. Even though they were placed in a diversion program for first-time offenders, the two students still made threats against the school and went on to post threats against Brooks Brown on Eric's Web site. Because of a failure of communication between agencies, the Browns' complaint against Harris to the Jefferson County authorities did not reach County Magi-strate John De Vita. Despite the Browns' continued complaints, no action was taken.

Charles Andrew Williams might not have had the degree of contact with the local juvenile-justice system that Klebold and Harris had, but he was certainly at risk. Not only was he violating the law by his possession of alcohol, he was also giving alcohol to his twelve-year-old girlfriend. In addition, he was smoking marijuana in public and had stolen a weapon weeks before the day he planned to bring it to Santana High School. Andy Williams was at high risk for an encounter with his local juvenile-justice system.

Easy Access to Weapons

In almost every school shooting over the past five years, one of the standard indicators of dangerousness has been the easy access the offenders had to weapons. Most of the shooters simply stole weapons their parents owned, as was the case with Andy Williams. Even though the weapons may have been locked up, the shooters knew where to find the key and knew that their parents did not routinely check their weapons so as to discover if one was missing. In at least one case, shooters stole a weapon that they knew their grandfather kept in his truck. Klebold and Harris, for example, stockpiled shotguns, a 9mm semiautomatic rifle, and a 9mm assault pistol via friends and two adults who purchased the weapons for them. They manufactured the pipe bombs themselves and had brought jellied gasoline with them to school on the day of the massacre. The jellied gasoline was intended to explode like napalm.

The amassing or acquisition of one or more weapons is a red-flag indicator of dangerousness because it shows that the person has gone beyond ideations of violence into the reality of weapons possession. In cases of very small children, however, it's important to determine whether the child who brought it to school understands the seriousness of the weapon and comprehends or appreciates the damage it can do. That's why, people who own guns and have small children in the house must be held responsible not only for keeping their guns out of sight and locked, but also for making sure that they constantly monitor the security of their weapons to make sure that no guns are missing.

PREVENTION AND COUNTERMEASURES

School administrators now seem to realize that they have to be proactive in defusing threats of violence to other students and to teachers. As recently as five years ago, despite the number of schoolyard and mass shootings on school property, student shooters were considered isolated incidents. Even gang shootings, a threat since the early 1990s, seemed not to require school intervention as much as police intervention. But, since 1995, with the spate of non-gang-related shootings at schools, a new profile of a student shooter has emerged. In this profile, the student is seen to be suicidal or near suicidal, and, if the threats are not pure revenge directed against a single individual or a small group, his or her threats embody a general apocalyptic vision of destroying oneself amidst one's enemies. If a school psychologist or guidance counselor perceives this threat, no matter how unrealistic it may seem for a student to carry out, it nevertheless warrants an investigation so as to defuse the nature of the student's anxiety and feelings of self-destructiveness. This, at the very least, should be the platform on which all other countermeasures are based.

The Code of Silence

Within most middle schools and high schools, even those that have the most benign application of disciplinary codes, there is a natural sense of "we" versus "they" when it comes to the way student populations view teachers and the school administration. Such an adversarial view is almost natural, considering that the student population is asserting its own independence. Accordingly, it's not far-fetched to assume that students who run to the administration or to schoolteachers with the slightest possible rumors about potential crimes or discontent brewing within peer groups are considered snitches who rat out their friends. Thus, a code of silence develops in which students routinely avoid reporting others to the school administration. According to the Columbine Panel, this code of silence is one of the issues that has to be addressed so as to set limits on what constitutes loyalty to other students and what constitutes a legitimate threat that can put lives in danger. A school administration must find a way to communicate to the student body and to parents that threats, no matter how minor, may be calls for help as well as simple bragging and these outbursts may pose a real threat to the safety of the entire student population. Even jokes have a way of turning serious, as the friends of Andy Williams found out after he laughed off a threat as a joke and carried it out just two days later.

Tip Lines and Hot Lines

For those students conflicted about breaking the code of silence yet in possession of knowledge about a threat, an anonymous-tip line may be another mechanism. Handled correctly and sensitively, it is a way for school administrators to learn about potential threats before they become an immediate danger.

Bullying-Prevention and Investigation Programs

When people realize how many school-shooting incidents stem from student feelings of hopelessness and fear at being the target of bullies, one realizes this is not a simple schoolyard problem. There will always be bullies, and bullies will always have victims. But schools have to get involved when young people are subjected to serious abuse by other younger people who are inspired by violent video games, organized and staged bullying contests such as televised professional wrestling and other entertainment in which bullying is glorified. They especially have to get involved when this same culture of violence inspires the victims to seek lethal weapons to get revenge. First there has to be some way for younger children to put the violence they see on television and in video games into perspective. Many researchers have found that the constant repetition of violence, particularly violence in the professional-wrestling ring from which the contestants walk away with no lasting damage, creates a false perception among younger viewers that individuals can sustain blows from blunt objects, dropkicks, being hurled through the air, with no physical consequences. The professional-wrestling personalities themselves refer to what they do as entertainment and not real combat. But that doesn't stop young children from copying what they see on television and imitating the violence, for they are often unaware of the consequences of their actions.

People who are victims of bullies know what pain is and

feel the psychological damage. That's why reports of persistent bullying should require that the school investigate those incidents where students are taunted and bullied to see what the problems are and what help can be offered.

Many schools are adopting bullying-prevention programs in which codes of student behavior are set forth, conflict-resolution mechanisms are established, and enforcement and reporting processes are put into action so that children know there's a place they can get help and direction to defuse situations. Also, because of the violence culture young children are exposed to in the media, school districts should be encouraged to develop lesson plans for conflict resolution and bullying prevention.

Threat-Assessment Teams Inside School and in Law Enforcement

The Columbine Panel suggested that threat-assessment teams should be established at every Colorado high school to evaluate the potential of threats reported by students and other members of the school population. Such assessments should evaluate the kinds of threats that are made, Internet threats, hit lists of potential victims, and other factors that help school administrators and psychologists decide how to help the person making the threats. Psychologists should pay special attention to threats that appear to be made by a student contemplating or having ideations about suicide; these students who perceive they have nothing to lose, and only want to wreak revenge at the point of their own deaths, are probably closer to committing mass murder than other students.

Threat assessment should be approached from a strictly professional perspective that includes qualified psychological consultation, legal evaluation, law enforcement evaluation, and a kind of administrative ombudsman to make sure that the privacy and rights of all concerned are protected. The threat-assessment team should be tied in administratively with bullying-prevention programs, conflict-resolution specialists, and antiviolence programs so that students don't get lost in the administrative process and real problems are addressed and resolved. Additionally, parents have to be involved because, critical to any school programs, they provide the underlying support for problem resolution at home. At the same time, however, in order not to exacerbate problems with troubled juveniles, school officials and the law enforcement response teams that work with local schools have to know how to differentiate various levels of threats from actual weapons violations so as not to push juveniles into violence—and in so doing, become part of the problem rather than the solution.

Sharing of School and Law Enforcement Data

The Columbine Panel recommended specifically that all agencies, including schools, social services, and law enforcement, that collect information about individuals' encounters with the local juvenile-justice system, juveniles who have demonstrated threat potential, and juveniles at risk, share that information with each other in a way that does not violate rights of privacy or the rights of the juveniles' families. Tracking children at risk, particularly as they move from school to school, is important not only from the perspective of protecting other children and teachers, but because it gives local school and services officials that ability to offer help and support to troubled juveniles. In instances where that support is combined with offering special-education services, counseling, and other forms of outreach, students who have a high-threat-potential can be defused and violence can be prevented.

Police Response Teams to School Shootings

Among the major recommendations that school districts and law enforcement agencies are making all across the nation is requiring more specific training for police response teams to school shootings. In the wake of Columbine, where police teams waited outside the building while Harris and Klebold continued to shoot and harass their victims, school administrators realized that police had to have procedures that would enable them to go inside buildings to rescue victims and apprehend the shooters. The differences in the police responses in Santana High School and Columbine High School are instructive because the first sheriff's deputies on the scene at Santana went looking for Andy Williams instead of waiting for instructions from a SWAT command center. Accordingly, local police need to receive better preparation in the floor-plans of local schools and have school response officers with the latest information about school schedules and specific threats to the schools and their populations.

Substance-Abuse Intervention Training for Teachers

With students as young as twelve experimenting with alcohol and marijuana, teachers and school psychologists need to have specific types of training in recognizing symptoms and dealing with students and their families in coordination with local or county social-services personnel. Many times, as was probably the case with Andy Williams and certainly the case with Jeffrey Dahmer, parents don't know that their children are drinking alcohol. Dahmer, for example, confessed to police that he had begun drinking before he started high school, and even his friends knew how he used to sneak cans of beer into school in his oversized ski jacket. Andy Williams was drinking alcohol as well as smoking marijuana at fifteen. Teachers and school guidance personnel should be able to identify troubled students dealing with substance-abuse and be able to work with parents in addressing the behavior. This type of training probably requires the development of comprehensive in-school substance-abuse evaluation programs to help school personnel understand the symptoms of substance abuse even among preadolescent juveniles and elementary-school students.

Intervention Management and More Interaction with Parents

If schools are prepared to intervene in the lives of students who pose a threat, determine who is being bullied and who is bullying and why, and deal with those students who are abusing alcohol or drugs, administrators have to develop a management process for intervention in children's lives and coordinate that process with families and parents. In the overwhelming majority of schoolchildren's homes, all of the parents work. This is especially the case in the majority of families where there is only one parent with custody during the school week. Accordingly, most parents don't know that their children are having problems or posing problems to the school. Similarly, most parents can't get to school for daytime meetings or conferences.

If intervention in the lives of high-risk students is to work, schools have to deal with parents and families on their own schedules. They must recognize that parents in large metropolitan areas may work two or more hours away from where their child attends school. This requires a high level of communication with parents of children at risk, which may—if parents are unresponsive—force the school administration to work with county or local social services as well as the local police. Intervention has to be managed with a delicate balance because it offsets the juvenile's and his or her family's rights to privacy against the legitimate safety needs of the larger school population. Just where that line is drawn may well determine the degree of success of any school-based intervention program.

Provide a Psychological Support System for
At-Risk Students

In line with intervention techniques and different kinds of student risk-management programs is a level of psychological support services, sometimes in coordination with local social services, that helps both teachers and the students they deal with. Teachers, the front line in dealing with at-risk juveniles in classrooms and corridors, are often targets themselves, as school shootings have recently shown. In Columbine, because of a hesitation and confusion in the rescue of a wounded teacher, the teacher may have bled to death while police and medics tried to determine what to do.

How should teachers cope with at-risk students? What do teachers do when they are targets and at the same time have young children to protect? Are there specific things teachers can do to defuse potentially violent situations, particularly those involving the use of weapons? These are some of the questions training will answer. Supporting that training is also a level of psychological reinforcement that recognizes the danger teachers face, even from fifth and sixth graders, and helps them acknowledge and reconcile themselves to that danger.

Students, too, require a level of psychological support, particularly those who are identified at even low levels of risk. What might have happened had a guidance counselor or teacher recognized that Andy Williams was enduring severe physical abuse at the hands of older students? A teacher might have at least been able to communicate the situation to Williams's father. Maybe just by helping Andy Williams identify the types of behaviors that brought on bullying or put him at risk from older children might have been enough to release some of the tension, as if the process were a pressure safety valve, to allow Andy to reach a workable equilibrium that kept him from exploding. Similarly, perhaps a school administrator who recognized what was going on at the Eric Harris Web site might have been able to bring the parents to intervene in the lives of Harris and Klebold so as to short-circuit their plans to lay siege to Columbine High School from the inside.

These are all questions after the fact. But what is a fact is that the landscapes of elementary schools, middle schools, and high schools have changed. Students are now being left to the care of the schools for longer and longer hours; there's a climate of violence that pervades too many students' lives; frighteningly, there's an easy access to weapons, which even young elementary-school children have. The schools themselves have to adjust, both administratively and logistically, to compensate for the danger because it's clear that no matter how much professionals bemoan the new climate of violence in our nation's schools, the violence is preventable. When we look at what happened at Santana High School and Columbine High School, and contemplate statistics from a recent study that show 70 percent of boys between the ages of eight and twelve will find guns, even hidden guns, in a room and play with them, and that 48 percent of those boys will actually pull the trigger, we're immediately struck by the volatility within our schools. We're also struck by the preventability of school shootings.

There's nothing we really don't understand about school shootings because every time a student decides to bring a weapon to school and fire on other students and teachers, the reasons, in hindsight, are absolutely clear: The child had been pushed to the limit; there was little or no parental support system at home—even when both parents lived with the child, the child had easy access to weapons; the child had already vented his or her frustrations and no one either heard them or addressed them; the child may have been experimenting with alcohol or drugs; the school was unaware of the child's problems or did nothing to address them; the child felt alienated, isolated, threatened, and perceived he or she had nothing to lose. These are the profiles of the children shooting up our schools, and there is nothing we *don't* understand about their problems. It's simply a matter of addressing them.

Postscript

On August 15, 2002, Charles Andrew Williams was sentenced to fifty years to life in prison after he tearfully apologized for the shooting rampage. He didn't explain why he opened fire with his father's handgun at Santana High School in Santee on March 5, 2001, but said he felt "horrible about what happened."

"If I could go back to that day, I would never have gotten out of bed," the 16-year-old said, his voice breaking.

11

THE POTENTIAL FOR DANGEROUS BEHAVIOR

In the research I've been conducting over the past fifteen years, I've found that a great many people have a potential for violent behavior. More people than any of us realize may be closer to the edge than they may seem on the surface. Predispositions for violence may be right there, coloring thoughts and actions, but most people don't see it because they rarely understand their motivations. Whether that potential is ever actualized depends a lot upon the circumstances surrounding each person's individual situation, the levels of stress people endure, and the resiliency people tend to lose over the years. Even in everyday situations, many people are capable of the kinds of violence that cause them to lash out suddenly and irrationally and inflict harm on others around them. The time bombs in the preceding chapters were all individuals in whom violence was lurking but who were allowed to slip through the net undetected because few saw the warning signs. Recognizing warning signs, such as the ones each of the time bombs in the preceding chapters displayed, is sometimes the critical element in helping a person at risk to get help to protect himself and others. People who are not potential abusers themselves may inadvertently be enablers by allowing a potentially dangerous person to pursue a course of behavior that may lead to violence.

How do you know what's potentially dangerous behavior and what's not? Each one of the stories in the preceding chapters is complete with descriptions of interactions between abusers and bystanders who watched preventable violence take place. Had the players in the lives of these time bombs known what was dangerous, they might have acted to prevent it. The problem may lie in education. From having read the stories of some of the most notorious killers in recent years and witnessing the points at which intervention might have prevented their crimes, you can see that there *are* clear signs of danger. Based on these and hundreds of other stories of time bombs and people at risk, I have developed a questionnaire that I use in my own therapy to evaluate potentially violent individuals who have come into contact with the courts.

THE PREVALENCE OF VIOLENCE

Although recent U.S. Department of Justice surveys report that violent crime has decreased dramatically over the past decade and dropped 15 percent between 1999 and 2000, individuals are still victimized by violence at the rate of one person every five minutes. With the exception of those regions of the world torn by political violence or racial or ethnic strife, American still remains one of the most violent countries in the world. This should come as no surprise to the victims of violence or to people who live in violent communities. Gang violence, subway and street crime, drug-related crimes, and domestic violence are taking their toll on victims and in communities around the country. An entire generation of "crack" children is now entering the public school system. These children have already been compromised by being removed from their parents—some of them placed in institutions or welfare facilities—and in the process they have been deprived of the normal nurturing that children require in order to develop both a functional sense of self and adequate levels of social and emotional resiliency. Have we created a new generation of "walking time bombs"? Will we ultimately become the victims of our own social system? Have we, in fact, already "lost" the war against drugs because the casualties of that war will now turn upon the rest of society?

Drugs and substance abuse are only part of the problem affecting the coming generation of schoolchildren. Child abuse and ritualistic crimes may be even bigger problems. Special police investigative units warn their municipalities of another category of growing menace: domestic abuse, ritualistic crime, and cult-oriented violence. As the stories of Charles Manson, Henry Lee Lucas, and Charlie Gervais show, victims of ritualistic crimes often become violent offenders themselves. Victims of child abuse, as all of our stories have illustrated, have a very high probability of turning into child abusers. When children are abused under ritualistic circumstances, such as the practices of occult groups or covens referring to themselves as satanic, these children become adults who are predisposed to practicing ritualistic violence on others. Unless there is some form of intervention in their lives, these cycles can remain unbroken for years, ensnaring generation after generation in vicious webs of violence.

PREDISPOSITIONS TO VIOLENCE

Regardless of the category of killer—mass murderer, spree killer, serial killer, serial rapist, ritualistic murderer, and on and on—all of these individuals have sets of signs, symptoms, syndromes, and predispositions of actions that place him or her at risk. If the perpetrator is a spree killer or an episodically suicidal mass murderer, the pathology is more acute and more obvious. If the perpetrator is a long-term serial killer living behind the mask of normalcy for year after year, the pathology is probably more insidious and more difficult to identify. To make matters worse, almost all potential episodically violent individuals are living in states of denial even though they may be aware that they are sick inside. Bobby Joe Long, Florida's infamous Classified Ad Rapist, was one such individual. He has said that he stood in the doorway of a psychiatrist, struggling with a confession of his compulsive rape crime, before the fear of criminal prosecution finally overwhelmed him and led him to believe he could control his own passions. Had Long crossed that threshold before he killed even though he was already a serial rapist, his nine young victims would probably be alive today, and Bobby Joe Long would have probably served his time, been released and be raising his own son and daughter.

What are the components of this "walking time bombs" pathology? How can they be identified? Can other people recognize the symptoms of a potentially dangerous and violent individual who is in denial? Does everybody who shares even one of these components stand a good chance of becoming a multiple killer?

The answer to the final question is perhaps the most important and is a firm "No!" The presence of one or more individual symptoms does not automatically turn on a time bomb switch. It is the combination of symptoms, and the critical mass of these symptoms triggered by an inciting event, that can trip a high-risk individual into a killing spree or a mass murder. While no litmus test exists that can definitively test a person's potential for danger, there are a variety of trouble indicators, some of which have a high probability of accuracy.

Obviously there's no questionnaire with one hundred percent accuracy that can pinpoint potential serial killers or people likely to commit brutal homicides. And even if we had such a questionnaire, the use of such an instrument would require stringent controls so as not to violate anyone's civil rights. Historically, our entire legal system is premised on the prosecution of individuals for the crimes they've committed, not for the crimes they're likely to commit. Therefore, the use of a questionnaire or some sort of a "serial killer test" that would somehow redflag suspect individuals and track them through life would fly right in the face of the civil rights that most Americans correctly hold to be sacrosanct. However—and this is a big however—an instrument that would allow doctors, courts, or the child welfare system to intervene in certain "at risk" cases can be structured so that it would not compromise anyone's rights and might just save a few lives. Precedents for just this type of intervention already exist in the various federal educational entitlement programs.

Therefore the questions in this chapter are not a "serial killer test." By recognizing familiar patterns in the questions, you are not saying, "I will become a violent criminal." The questionnaire I've written to help me in my work with researching violent behavior, and which follows in part, is designed to identify certain factors that may contribute to a type of dysfunction that may ultimately predispose someone to certain patterns of violent behavior down the line. It suggests to people that they may be at risk. There are a variety of background components and issues that enter into the larger equation, but these issues help to identify the problems that may need intervention.

FOURTEEN ISSUES TO LOOK FOR

There are fourteen major issues that people looking for potential danger try to identify:

1. Intrusive and violent fantasies. Do you know anyone who has complained about having violent fantasies of brutal behavior or abusive sex against another person or type of person? Have these fantasies become

almost obsessive? There's nothing illegal about having fantasies, but when they become obsessive or dominate the person's waking moments, they can be dysfunctional.

2. Is someone sending out warnings to people that he or she is on the edge of committing violence against them? Almost every time bomb experienced a significant period of time during which he or she sent out warnings before actually committing a crime. These warnings are cries for help. The person may not want to hurt anybody, but may feel compelled to do so. The warnings are a way to call attention to the problem and get help. Too often, however, those responsible, such as the police, doctors, or family members, pay the warnings no heed and the person commits acts of violence. Listening to the warnings, no matter how bizarre, may protect potential victims.

3. Auditory hallucinations. Do you know someone who hears voices or messages urging him or her to kill? These are actively psychotic symptoms that may have a physiological basis, a neurological basis, or a purely psychological basis. Whatever the cause, eventually they can become so obsessive that the person is literally driven to kill. David Berkowitz complained of voice messages from the "Son of Sam." Henry Lee Lucas claimed that he heard the voice of his mother in his prison cell telling him to kill. Even Daniel Rakowitz claimed that he heard voices urging to commit violent acts. This is a high-risk warning.

4. Has the individual committed two or more previous acts of violence or sexual violence? People who have made two or more attempts at murder, rape, or brutal

assault are in the highest risk category. People who have committed or attempted two previous acts of violence are sixty percent likely to commit a third act.

5. Is the individual a chronic drug or alcohol abuser or a chronic user of cocaine or speed? Substance abuse can trigger violence by sapping an individual's resiliency and ability to cope. Substance abuse can also so physically diminish a person's cognitive capacity that he or she is unable to function. Chronic substance abusers are also subject to mental blackouts during which they may be unaware they have committed acts of violence. Finally, chronic substance abusers may have a history of mean, violent, or excessively cruel behavior after drinking or drugging.

6. Cumulative rage. Does the person have a rage that seems to grow and grow and have no outlet? Does the person seem unable to calm himself or herself down after a period of intense anger or rage? Sometimes this dysfunctional rage is camouflaged by a mask of normalcy, but it is nonetheless there. It is likely that people in this category will display extreme cruelty to inanimate objects or to defenseless individuals such as children, the elderly, women, or subordinates at work.

7. Tremendous mood swings. Does the person experience or evidence wide mood swings or dramatic changes in behavior after physical or emotional traumas or personal catastrophes? After a while, even those who have experienced some catastrophe in their lives tend to even out somewhat. People who do not may be in severe emotional distress and might require intervention to help them overcome the desire to commit violence upon others or themselves. Does

the person experience wide mood swings as a result of changes in prescribed medication or as the result of an injury, especially an injury to the head? These people may be at risk as well, because they may have become victims of brain or neurological damage.

8. Insatiable sex drives. Does the individual have an intense sex drive that cannot be satisfied and is coupled with violent sexual fantasies? It's one thing to have a large sexual appetite. It's quite another thing to have an appetite that cannot be satisfied and to have to go to greater and greater lengths to achieve sexual satisfaction. If the person believes that the only way to satisfy a sex drive is to perform violent sex on another individual, the person may be a potential time bomb.

9. Does the individual have an insatiable jealousy combined with rage and violent fantasies? Similarly, a jealous rage that cannot be satisfied and that had a violent bent can mean an individual in trouble.

10. Is the individual preoccupied with death, blood and gore, horror, terrorism, violent racism or homophobia, cannibalism, or vampirism? This is another prescription for impending violence if not dealt with, especially if the person is fixated on the physicality of the violence.

11. Does the person have a history of indifference to the life, the pain, or the suffering of other people or animals? Does the person like to torture animals? These are clear instances of people who may be predisposed to violence. Many people can lead apparently normal lives while they are fascinated by the torture, pain, and suffering of small animals. There are others for whom the torture, pain, and suffering of small

animals are stepping-stones to violence on other people. In either case, it's not healthy.

12. Does the individual have a history of repeated arson? Do fires excite the person sexually? Arson and fire-starting are clear warning signs.

13. Did the individual have a history of homicidal behavior as a child? Did he or she have a history of throwing rocks at other children with the intention of inflicting harm? Did the person use weapons such as pipes, sticks, or bats against others? Homicidal children require intervention or else they will grow up with an accumulated rage. Individuals with an accumulated rage that cannot be addressed through therapy will usually wind up working it out in some way, often by inflicting harm on others.

14. Is the individual actively gathering an arsenal of weapons? Is this arsenal coupled with suicidal rage or fantasy, or is the person actively talking about or making plans for hunting humans or a public suicide combined with mass deaths? This can be a penultimate stage of violence. It may be one of the final warning signs before the individual erupts.

BACKGROUND AND SECONDARY WARNING SIGNS

There is much more to the questionnaire beyond these fourteen points. Most of the remaining issues are divided into physiological questions, which ask about blood type and physical maladies that people you know and members of their families may have; family-history questions, to get them to think about what kinds of maladies may run in their families; behavioral questions, which get them to think about their habits and routines; and psychological questions, which get them to think about the ways people see and react to things.

Other questions ask who the primary caregiver of the individual was, whether the caregiver was changed frequently or whether the child was left to his or her own devices for long periods of time, and whether the primary caregiver abused or neglected the child. I try to find out whether the child was either emotionally, sexually, or physically abused by the caregiver, or all three in combination. These are primary questions designed to see how much, as a child, the individual being questioned was encouraged to develop a sense of self or a sense of trust in others or in the world. The weaker the sense of self or trust, the less compassionate or sympathetic the individual tends to be. The true loners, the ones who trust no one, usually don't trust in their own abilities, either. At the extreme edge of the scale, these individuals tend to be sociopathic and violent.

Food allergies, nutritional disorders or deficiencies, and reactions to prescription drugs comprise another large area of the questionnaire. People who have nutritional disorders and food allergies may have spent much of their young lives suffering from a variety of symptoms that could not be diagnosed as a disease. They may have been overweight despite diets and exercise programs, chronically listless or depressed because of vitamin deficiencies, or chronically agitated because of allergies to specific foods or to starches, dairy foods, or refined sugars. Behavioral problems that might have been the result of food or medication reactions can become way overblown by the time the subject reaches adolescence and sometimes may even put the person at risk in the juvenile and criminal justice system. If this person comes from a family with a history of eating disorders, nutritional deficiencies, food allergies, or reactions to contraindicated medication, the behavior might conform to a genetic road map laid out in previous generations.

I ask a large number of "environmental" questions in

order to find out the source of the subject's current and childhood water supply; whether the person was consistently exposed to toxic chemicals, lead, or cadmium; whether the person lived near a highway and was constantly inhaling carbon monoxide or other toxic substances; or whether the person worked or works in an environment in which he or she is exposed to toxic substances. These are important issues, because lead, cadmium, and cobalt poisoning can affect behavior; people exposed to toxins can develop severely psychotic symptoms; low-level carbon monoxide poisoning can diminish cognitive and intellectual capacities and render a person listless or violent; and low-level radiation can cause a person to feel consistently sick and nauseated, and can impair behavior in children. All of these are issues that come to bear when a chronically violent or antisocial child is brought into court for an evaluation or a pre-sentencing hearing. It is a time when intervention can become a real opportunity to remove the individual from the environmental poisons and get him or her adequate medical attention.

I ask a number of questions about stress-related issues, because how an individual reacts to stress, whether it's sudden and traumatic, catastrophic and life-threatening, or long-term, says a lot about how resilient that individual is. A person who has developed dysfunctional coping mechanisms because he or she grew up in a home typified by longterm abuse will be less resilient than a person from a more healthy environment. Because a person's resiliency enables him or her to cope with the natural catastrophes of life such as the breakup of marriages, accidents, and loss of jobs or financial reverses, the less resiliency a person has to begin with means the less cushion a person has when the going gets rough. Serial killers and homicidally violent individuals are usually nonresilient people who cannot cope with any reverses or frustration. Their first or only recourse is to violence.

A significantly large part of the questionnaire asks about perceptual, cognitive, and neurological issues, such as the highest level of schooling a person has achieved, whether the person is dyslexic or is easily confused by numbers or shapes, or whether the person has problems coordinating muscular activity with what he or she perceives. These types of issues bear a great deal on an individual's behavior. A person who is constantly frustrated by an inability to react appropriately or to process information at the same speed average students or coworkers process it might be accumulating rage that someday might spill over into violence. Almost every one of the time bombs I have studied has had some degree of neurological damage that may actually have been the cause if it contributed to other violent tendencies by reducing the person's resiliency to stress.

I also ask about neurological symptoms such as migraine headaches, extra-powerful sensory reactions, hypersensitivities to sound or to light, a chronic inability to remember numbers or letters or to confuse them, headaches that seem to move along one side of the head or the other, impaired speech after headaches, or stabbing bright lights that seem to emanate from behind the eyelids. These are all possible symptoms of cardiovascular problems that affect the neurological system and can impair a person's behavior over the long term.

The final two groups of questions ask about psychological symptoms and behavioral issues. These are obviously critical determinants of a subject's health and emotional stability. The psychological questions address standard issues of family history, history of mental illness in the family, delusional feelings, frequency or currency of hallucinations, feelings of paranoia, blackouts, anxiety, fear, and the like. The behavioral questions address habits and belief systems, ways the subject copes with negative feelings, feelings about sex and human relationships, and habits that the subject has developed for working out problems.

The wide range of questions I ask are designed to help people create a composite map of their physical, emotional, and social situations. I use it to find specific recurring patterns in an individual and in the individual's family. There are also a great number of questions dealing with emotional attitudes and reactions, mental blackouts, trancelike states, and issues surrounding periods of psychological disorientation. These are not necessarily absolute indicators of potential violence. However, they, like many behavioral questions, help to establish a pattern that may fit into what I call a composite violence-prone personality. It doesn't mean that the person you're concerned about will commit a violent act. It may only mean that there's a degree of risk. If you know, for example, that a person is prone to emotional blackouts after drinking, you're aware of a high-risk factor. If that person keeps on drinking, he or she is flirting with the dangers associated with that risk.

The insidious nature of most of these types of patterns that I identify in my questionnaire is that by themselves, the patterns are usually benign. However, in combination with one another, these patterns become progressively more dangerous and can compromise a person's ability to function in society. Violence feeds on itself. Once the boundary between fantasy and physical violence has been crossed, the next violent act may be easier to commit. Therefore, prevention of violence is the key once the patterns of dangerousness have been identified. That's why there are a number of questions dealing with criminal fantasies and overt criminal acts. They are designed to highlight the need for intervention as a person's propensity toward violence increases.

Another problem with many of the behaviors, neurological dysfunctions, or physical illnesses I attempt to identify concerns their tendency to put their victims at risk concerning authority figures, schools, and the courts. A problem such as dyslexia, which in itself is simply perceptual, may put a victim on a path of confrontations with parents, older family members, caregivers, teachers, and employers. As a result of these confrontations, the individual may internalize patterns of negative behavior and reactions. He may decide that it's all his fault. She may blame herself for always "screwing up" or always confusing left and right. These negative patterns build on themselves and become self-fulfilling. Eventually, what started out as a mild dyslexia becomes a full-blown learning disorder by grade five. The individual, who may be highly intelligent, is tracked out of the more challenging academic programs in his or her school system by high school and channeled away from a college degree. The level of frustration and resentment that might have built up at that point is literally boiling over. Imagine if you were told that you just couldn't succeed no matter what you did, yet you knew that someone inside you had the same abilities as anybody else.

As this resentment continues to build, as repeated failures are pyramided on top of one another, the person may travel along other antisocial paths. Channeled away from normal relationships, he or she may socialize with dangerous persons. He or she may develop drinking or substance-abuse problems. He or she may feel so ostracized by society that cults or other ritualistic groups provide the only sense of personal reinforcement or empowerment that the individual ever receives. The individual may feel that by committing crimes of personal violence, he or she can express the rage that's been building up over the years. The individual may be encouraged to commit these crimes by group members, or these crimes may be suggested by what a person sees on television. The individual may commit crimes copycatting what he or she has read in newspapers. The pattern of violence may escalate until the individual feels there's no turning back. However, had someone—a doctor, teacher, school guidance counselor, or even a family friend—suggested that the child was not stupid or "damaged goods" but merely suffered from a perfectly remedial perceptual difficulty, the entire course of that person's life might have been changed. I'm not being melodramatic. I'm looking at the hard, cold facts in hundreds of case studies that I've consulted on.

In most of the cases I've studied, if a critical pattern of dysfunction or a physical symptom had been picked up, the individual might have been treated medically. In those cases, the lives of many victims would have been saved. I called these instances "missed opportunities" because the authorities—be they family, medical, or legal—had the chance to intervene in the life of a potentially violent individual. Had the intervention taken place, lives might have been saved. Thus, the range of questions is premised on the need to determine patterns, and not necessarily on a desire to look for specific indicators of criminal behavior.

THE DEPRAVITY SCALE

Dr. Michael Welner, Associate Professor of Psychiatry at NYU's School of Medicine and Chairman of the Forensic Panel, has proposed a codification of depraved behaviors into a type of scale that can be applied to defining evil behaviors. Employed for the purposes of establishing a benchmark evaluation for courts, the Depravity Scale would apply common definitions and examples for different types of behaviors, relating them to the intent of the accused, the accused's behavior, and the facts of the case.

Although Dr. Welner disclaims any intent with his Depravity Scale to provide an indicator of potential dangerousness, it's hard to argue that in cases of repeat offenders, where crimes grow more serious with each occurrence, that the scale itself might have a predictor value, especially in cases of juvenile crime. If the crimes of repeat offenders were evaluated according to a Depravity Scale—even if the scale wasn't used as an arbitrary measure for sentencing purposes—schools, juvenile authorities, as well as parents, might have a means of gauging the direction of children's behavior and assessing whether the child was headed for a collision course with a violent or potentially fatal event.

CULT MIND-SETS

Finally, here is a short checklist I routinely use to determine whether an occult group has a potential for instigating violence or for hurting its members or the victims those members gather for the group's rituals. Many times, what cult members call "religious experience" is actually a type of mind-set that predisposes them to be influenced by a charismatic leader. As you will see, I make no determination with respect to the group's beliefs qua beliefs. This is still a free country, and if a bunch of people want to get together to worship a pagan deity, a wood nymph, or any supernatural force, for that matter, it's their right. What I'm looking for is the potential of that group to inflict harm on other people. Manson's family qualifies as a cult under these guidelines; so might "Christian" sects that require that their membership perform blood sacrifices on people they deem as infidels, and so might various satanic groups that practice ritualistic sacrifices on victims.

The group leader is able to exercise power over his or her followers by recruiting the most susceptible types of individuals who may share common dysfunctional personalities. Once recruited, the group empowers its members to take control of their own lives and the lives of others through adherence to the cult's principles. These are the most important ingredients of just such an organization:

A Charismatic Sociopathic Leader

The leader is an individual whose own aims and beliefs obliterates all personal boundaries and take precedence over the aims, beliefs, and goals of all other people.

The Need for a Dramatic
Explosive Outlet

The group members come together to seek a place where they can share and synthesize their individual dark impulses. The group provides an acceptable outlet for fantasies about death, blood, gore, pain, deviant sex, obsessive control, and other socially "unacceptable" attitudes.

Rage of a Cumulative Nature

People who join this group have been building up their individual anger for a long, long time. The group provides a way to share that anger and focus it toward others or a common enemy. Cumulative rage is also one of my fourteen major "red flags" of imminent violence.

Antisocial Personality Caused by Some
Form of Abandonment From a
Significant Other:

- Death of a mother, father, or loved one
- Rejection of a mother, father, or loved one
- Emotional or physical abuse inflicted by a mother, father, or loved one

Family Orientation Toward Rigid,
Unyielding, Fundamentalist Beliefs

- Zealous belief in the spiritual power of individual events
- Zealous belief in the spiritual power of individual objects
- Membership in hate groups (Nazis, Ku Klux Klan)
- Children of extreme radicals

Individual Need to Obtain Power in a Hostile World

Group members feel alienated and powerless, and use the group as a means to take power for themselves and exercise it through the group.

A Need for a Secure Environment to Share Drugs or Use Drugs Individually

Many groups form up specifically for the purpose of providing a secure drug haven. Group members usually use many different types of drugs at the same time as well as alcohol. Drug and alcohol abuse are one of the "givens" of group membership. From there they develop a "drug ethos" in which individual group members are empowered to control their own destinies. The groups find common enemies, formalize their entrance rituals, discipline wayward members, and evolve to a cultlike organization.

Need to Traffic Drugs

As the group becomes more sophisticated, it may engage in drug-trafficking transactions, it may fence stolen goods in order to generate cash, develop connections to other drug or underworld groups or secret societies, and become tied in to a network of underground criminal activity. Many times group members share individual prejudices and have common targets. Many times the group becomes nothing more than a gang whose members are from the same neighborhood and from the same racial or ethnic backgrounds.

Need to Practice Atypical, Antisocial, and Perverted Sexual Activity Including

Sadomasochism
Cannibalism

Ingestion of human and animal waste
Vampirism

Need to Vent Dark Creative Urges

Violence becomes an artistic expression for cult members. They see their expression of violence not only as a need to vent rage but as a need to be creative. This is why so many cult crimes take such bizarre twists and lead police off on wild-goose chases.

Lack of Hope in the Future

Occult group members share a profound lack of hope in what the future can bring. They see only death and destruction on the horizon, and join the group to tap into power during the coming chaos. Organized religions generally promise hope and hold out a vision of an optimistic future. Satanic groups paint a pessimistic future of violence and destruction.

Need to Deal with Internal Demons

Many group members suffer from hallucinations, chronic delusions, and obsessive fantasies. The group helps them live with their problems in ways similar to support groups of patients with a common disease.

Compulsive Rituals

As the group formalizes itself, individual fantasies might be expressed in ritualistic ways. These are usually "dark" rituals, expressing the hopelessness, futility, chaos, and violence that motivate the group members. These are compulsive rituals in that group members don't see themselves as having any choice but to perform them. They are compelled to participate in these rituals because the rituals become ends in themselves, losing all meaning except in their mindless repetition.

The Need to Be Guilt-Free

By the very nature of the group's formation, the membership is absolved of all personal guilt. Simply by joining the group, the members are made to feel that they are no longer guilty for their dark thoughts, their drug use, their antisocial habits, or their alienation from society.

The Need to Practice Magical Thinking

Magical thinking means that the members empower external objects with supernatural forces that fly in the face of all reality. Magical thinking informs many traditional religions as well, but religious leaders attempt to ground it in some sort of reality. In other words, miracles can take place, but they must be judged miracles only in the appropriate context and only by competent authorities empowered by the religious hierarchy to make those judgments. The magical thinking that informs most occult groups is nonresilient magical thinking, a type of perception in which the individuals have no way of making judgments about the world and, because they are powerless, impart powerful forces to seemingly inanimate objects or forces.

The Need to Associate with a Significant Other

This means that there are personal needs for brotherhood or sisterhood, for intimate companionship, or for sexual relationships with others dwelling in the same darkness as the rest of the group members. These may be victims sharing a common misery or abusers sharing a common habit.

Dramatic Change in Personality or Mood

Individual members experience a dramatic change in their personalities and moods upon joining the group. They become less spontaneous, lose their senses of humor, change the types of clothing they may wear, adopt a group uniform or common costume (all black, masks, brownshirts, all leather, "biker" costumes), they display group symbols (upside-down crosses, broken crosses, satanic symbols, swastikas), they withdraw from all positive activities, they withdraw from their individual families or groups of friends, they may isolate themselves within their old groups, they lose the ability to form new relationships, and they may openly flaunt taboo symbols.

Obsession with Death

Group members may become fixated on death and show a growing irreverence for life. This may include extreme cruelty to others or to animals.

Loss of Free Will

Once in the group, individual members lose their ability to make personal choices. They may even complain that the group that empowered them also sucked away their ability to be free. It's almost a kind of paradox, but it sometimes forces group members into conflict with the group's leaders.

Chronic Listening to Heavy Metal Music, Speed Metal, Death Rock, Industrial Music

Fascination with Occult
Reading Material

Chronic Involvement with Fantasy
Role-Playing Games in Which Group
Members Incorporate the Characters'
Roles Into Their Own Personalities

Extreme Identification with
Racial Supremacy

Aryanism
Nazism
Skinheads

Dramatic Change in Financial Situation

Individual group members may become unable to hold a job or they may suddenly have an unexplained amount of money.

Hatred for Christianity

Group members exhibit extreme blasphemy. In specifically non-Christian or satanic cults, members profess a hatred of Christianity. Thus, parents whose children are becoming extremely blasphemous and violently antagonistic toward society should look at the wide range of their behavior. If the child's anger and blasphemous attitude occurs with a dramatic change in daily habits, personal appearance, a loss of interest in previous hobbies or activities, his or her bonding with types of people that seem alien to the way you raised the child, and a profound change in physical behavior that leads you to suspect either drug or alcohol abuse, then you should confront the child. If the child denies that anything is wrong—in itself a form of denial—and refuses to discuss it, it might be worthwhile to speak to your doctor, a mental health professional or certified substance-abuse practitioner, or a community mental health group about an intervention. All of the mind-set attitudes that I have cited are also warning signs of impending dangerousness.

WHO REQUIRES INTERVENTION?

Everyone has feelings of rage, deep anger, or even violent or violently sexual fantasies from time to time. People who are under extreme provocation or stress experience moments of vividly emotional homicidal feelings, or who are just plain deep-down dog angry and fly off the tandle, needn't turn themselves in for prosecution. Having violent fantasies or increasingly violent sexual passions are not illegal. Acting out these fantasies is illegal. Therefore, people should talk to professionals about fantasies and escalating or episodic feelings of rage if they begin to recur frequently or if they become obsessive. People suffering from violent obsessions may feel ashamed about the way they feel. They may feel guilty about having violent thoughts about their loved ones or people they know. They may feel as if they're somehow not "whole," not "together," or simply not rational. These feelings can be dealt with by talking about them with a competent professional.

People who suffer from violent sexual fantasies usually feel a nauseating, skin-crawling, gutwrenching sense of shame at having been violated by someone when they were younger. They often feel a rage so overpowering that they want to go out and kill when they think about what's happened to them. Having those thoughts if you've been a victim is okay. In fact, these thoughts are a natural part of an emotional process that takes place after a trauma. Sometimes doctors call it posttraumatic stress.

But simply saying that we have those thoughts doesn't mean we should stop there. If a person keeps them bottled up, that person may explode, and sometimes hurt themselves and others before they are stopped. Rejecting one's guilt, shame, or rage is called denial—and, simply put, denial can kill. Feelings of guilt, shame, and rage and their accompanying fantasies, if any, have to be dealt with; they have to be talked about; they have to be integrated into your past, present, and future. This integration is a natural and necessary part of the healing process.

Healing can begin when we recognize unhealthy feelings about ourselves. Healing begins with acknowledgment and understanding. It begins with the taking of a "moral inventory" of your own life or the lives of people close to you and a willingness to admit that you or others around you may have problems. Any instrument that asks someone to look at his life honestly and forthrightly will help.

12

SOLUTIONS

We can find ways out of the problem. We can help potentially dangerous people and their families get help. Parents, doctors, teachers, professional counselors, and juvenile authorities can identify potential walking time bombs. Professionals can also identify the symptoms of profound unhappiness, incipient violence, obsessive sexuality or sexual fantasies, abuse of animals and small children, fascination with fires and fire-starting, and substance abuse among adolescent juvenile offenders. We can spot them in troubled children while they are still young enough to be protected from crashing into authorities. We can look for problem family histories and telltale medical evidence of first-time offenders and perpetrators of sex crimes. We must provide a humane and supervised program for all violent parolees that does more than simply monitor their whereabouts and comings and goings. We must look at their medical histories and see to it that they receive whatever treatment is necessary to keep them from falling back into abusive patterns that will lead to violence. We can flag the police records of individuals convicted of child abuse or molestation. In other words, when people pass through the system, we can identify them and require counseling and intervention for those at risk. We can also identify victims of child abuse in emergency rooms and in schoolrooms by making reporting requirements easier to fulfill and by encouraging teachers, doctors, and nurses to follow through on their hunches about the patients they treat. We must ask the professionals in the human-care systems to do more than process their clients; we must look at the human tragedies that pass before us on a daily basis and do something about them before too many years have worn away what was left of their ability to cope and they find their own solutions to dealing with the pain that has been building in them.

We must look at productive methods of controlling episodically violent criminals: criminals who have spent their lives in and out of police custody and in juvenile detention, in doctors' offices, or in emergency rooms; criminals who have so baffled us that many people have given up on learning about them; criminals who are so extraordinarily violent their actions are beyond the comprehension of those of us who lay any claim to normalcy. The criminal-justice system is only one component of this control, and we already know from our own observation that it is only marginally successful.

Too often, courts and prosecutors take an all-or-nothing approach to such individuals, prosecuting them on the most expedient of charges, allowing them to plea-bargain their way through the system. In this way, like Arthur Shawcross, they fall through the cracks from year to year; their potential dangerousness is never measured, nor is the likelihood that their crimes will escalate ever truly considered. Too often, we realize and act on the true nature of an individual's dangerousness only after it is too late. That is the nature of our current criminal-justice system. And the life and death of Laurie Dann shows what can happen when the criminal-justice system operates at its lowest possible level of energy and vigilance.

I believe we should have another set of criteria, as well as a different mind-set, which we can apply *before* and not *after* a terrible crime has been committed. And this is why I developed and now apply the sets of criteria to measure potential dangerousness. These criteria won't jeopardize the rights of the accused, but will help those at risk to get the health and medical treatment they need to prevent them from becoming serial killers and mass murderers who terrorize our communities and destroy the lives of our citizens.

The goal is to heal the pain and save lives. We can heal the pain. We can make a difference. We can protect generations of victims yet to come by steering potential time bombs away from high risk and into programs that will save their lives and ours as well.

POSITIVE STEPS

While violence is escalating in America, a growing number of experts from a wide variety of disciplines suggest that violent crime can be reduced through prevention. Even the former United States Surgeon General, C. Everett Koop, who has termed violence and domestic crime a public health issue that should be addressed by the medical community, has suggested that violence can be reduced in society. He and others promote identification of the causes of violence and a focusing of national and local resources on remedying those causes. Experts suggest the following steps:

1. Literature concerning the medical symptoms of violence—including alcohol and drug abuse and sexual abuse—should be distributed in schools and community health facilities. Primary and secondary school students should be encouraged to talk about drug and alcohol abuse as well as domestic violence issues. Victims of abuse as well as abusers should be encouraged to seek help and counseling.

2. High-risk individuals should be encouraged to seek help. These individuals should be forewarned that they are engaging in violent behavior or are fantasizing about violent behavior, and that they should talk to their lawyers, doctors, or psychological counselors about the symptoms or signs they believe they exhibit. People who are actively violent may be afraid—as illustrated in the Bobby Joe Long case—that in seeking help they may actually be waiving any constitutional rights they may have. Counselors advise individuals in these situations to talk to a lawyer or a member of the clergy about their problems. If people do not know an attorney, they can contact their local public defender or from the Legal Aid Society.

3. Enablers of potentially violent individuals or of abusers should seek help from lawyers, clergy, or their doctors, their counselors, or from community health organizations. These enablers may include parents, spouses, children, other family members or relatives, friends, and neighbors. Enablers should be encouraged to recognize medical and emotional symptoms, to understand what denial is and how it can be addressed, and to talk about their feelings and perceptions with qualified health care professionals. Enablers should also be encouraged to seek assistance from local chapters of such groups as Al-Anon or Alcoholics Anonymous to discuss family problems and abuse-related issues.

4. Community group and mental health organizations should be educated in violence-related issues so as to develop intervention and support-group techniques. These intervention techniques can be modeled after the intervention plans of drug and alcohol abuse treat-

ment. These techniques should, however, be focused on high-risk individuals and should ensure that civil liberties and individual rights are protected. Part of the irony concerning the prevention of violence is that potentially violent individuals may be under the care of counselors or therapists who are simply not aware of their patients' predispositions toward violence. By educating these groups, many experts feel, the warning signs of dangerousness can be more widely understood and applied in those instances where they can help protect potential victims.

5. Because a large percentage of abused and neglected children eventually turn on society, agencies at all community levels should actively shift their perceptions of violence as not only an issue of the criminal and juvenile justice system but as issues of public health also.

6. Old research on the causes of violence—including the genetic causes—should be reviewed and even resurrected. A startling number of career violent criminals are turning up with XYY chromosomal imbalances, once thought to be a prime cause of genetic predispositions to violence, and family histories of violence dating back two or three generations. The genetic components of other types of mental illnesses are being reviewed as well, including clinical depression and manic depression, schizophrenia, and paranoia. The genetic components of abuse-related syndromes such as alcoholism are also being reviewed. This new scrutiny on predisposed behaviors requires that children in families where there are multigenerational medical histories of emotional problems and substance-abuse problems should be evaluated very carefully by their doctors.

7. The clinical nature of violence needs to be studied by family-practice physicians, emergency-room personnel, and emergency-medical-service professionals as well as by psychologists, lawyers, and career professionals in the criminal and juvenile justice systems. In other words, while recognizing that violence must be punished, far too many professionals are unaware that violence can be prevented through medical intervention early enough to prevent it from turning victims into potential abusers. The only sure way to prevent the spread of violence is to break the cycle of violence that creates new offenders out of victims in each succeeding generation.

The key to containing violence is education. The more that professionals understand about the medical nature of violence, the better able they will be to identify those predisposed to commit it and those who are abused emotionally or sexually. Therefore, the government should provide incentive for ongoing training in the medical nature of violence, and incentives and training in violence prevention for those entering the health-care and helping professions. The government should also institute training for people either in law enforcement or entering law enforcement, to enable them to work with violent offenders or high-risk individuals already in the criminal and juvenile justice systems.

THE IMPORTANCE OF PARENTAL AFFECTION AND CAREGIVING

The ultimate hope for the prevention of violence lies in the vigilance with which our society addresses family issues and educates children about the critical seriousness of childraising. Too many adolescents and young parents—especially those who have been victims of abuse—do not understand what their responsibilities to their children are, and thus they contribute to a cycle of dysfunction. Parental neglect or indifference toward newborn babies is one of the more elementary components contributing to disturbed children and, ironically, is one of the easiest elements to understand and remedy.

People need to understand that the child's first year and the parents' reactions to that child during that first year are absolutely essential to the success of the child's later development. Child psychologist Eric Erickson describes the newborn's first year of development as critical to the establishment of trust and confidence. The child, by reacting to the nurturing of the parent/caregiver, is loving, caring, and friendly; the child learns to place trust in the world. The child accepts the basic positive nature of the world and ultimately develops confidence in it. If the world is hostile, the child withdraws and tends not to develop personal boundaries. In later life, the child will have a tendency to withhold trust. In the most extreme of situations—and this is the situation of the vast majority of dysfunctional individuals (not to mention almost every killer)—the child never makes the distinction between self and outside world. In many cases, it requires significant therapy to help a child adjust to the world if it has not received care, loving, and nurturing during this critical first year. The parent expresses this care and nurturing by touching, hugging, and responding to the child's needs. In studies where parental love and nurturing were withheld from baby chimps, the chimps became violent, attacked other chimps, and eventually destroyed themselves. These critical experiments helped establish the importance of parental fondling and nurturing during the critical months after birth.

To a lesser degree, the absence of parental love, fondling, touching, and caressing result in children who, as they grow older, may recognize intellectually, but have no emotional means of dealing with, boundaries between themselves and the outside world. They might become inordinately cruel to others, sexually abusive, chronically unsympathetic, or, in extreme cases, they might become sociopathic. Brutal politicians such as Hitler, Joseph Stalin, and Saddam Hussein had histories of deprivation of parental care and, consequently, were unable to sympathize emotionally with the levels of pain they inflected on their victims. In the worst cases, they took emotional pleasure from the torture of their victims, intellectualizing it as the furtherance of their political aims. In all cases, however, parental care had much to do with the establishment of personal boundaries.

The second major point here is that parental fondling and touching during the early months of a newborn's life also stimulates the brain to regulate an important neuropeptide— the hormone oxytocin.

Oxytocin is not limited to human beings; it is found in all mammals, where it governs the licking and nudging behavior of mothers toward their newborns. The mothers are stimulating their newborns, firing up the vast array of tactile sensors. The human equivalent of licking and touching is fondling and caressing. The critical hormone oxytocin, thus stimulated, plays a critical role in the ability of the individual to be affectionate and to respond appropriately to sexual stimulation. There is a vital link here between affection and sexual stimulation, almost as if one were an extension of the other. This link also helps to explain why most, if not all, lust killers and serial rapists evidence a pronounced disability to form normal affectionate relationships. Even the relationships they do have are far from intimate. They are marked by a serious withholding of ultimate affection by the abuser, a cloaking of the self from the significant other. The partner or enabler simply allows this withholding to take place without challenging it. Many traditional developmental psychologists have assumed that the withholding of affection has a lot to do with the abuser's inability to form trust-based relationships. The research currently being conducted on oxytocin might show that there are physiological and neurological bases for this dysfunction as well.

There is a third indicator of the importance of this hormone and the importance of parental touching and fondling as well. It concerns what I call "dysfunctional chronic autostimulation." This very fancy term describes a set of behaviors that range from obsessive masturbation through various degrees of self-mutilation to the life-threatening "head banging" response. I've seen all of these behaviors in convicted serial killers, and it's not a pretty sight. You see, absent any form of parental nurturing, touching, fondling, caressing, or simple affection, the developing newborn cannot become tactilely stimulated from the outside world. Without this tactile stimulation, the newborn learns to generate its own stimulation through childhood behaviors such as picking, poking, scratching, and rubbing. This is why puppies in a litter are always wrestling and nipping at each other, and why kittens in a litter dig into one another's fur even before their eyes open. As the child gets older, and normal preadolescent hormones begin their secretion sequences, this autostimulation becomes sexual and results in obsessive masturbation, and ultimately may result in more violent forms of self-stimulation such as gouging of the arms, inflicting pain, and raising all kinds of sores and welts. These wounds are almost too common among convicted serial killers. I've sat across from Arthur Shawcross and watched him gouge his own arms deeply with his nails and have seen Joe Fischer scratch himself until he opened old scars. This is a "chemical" reaction. It all has to do with tactile stimulation and may be affected by the regulation of oxytocin during the initial first few months of life.

It is important to remember that absence of parental care and nurturing does not automatically mean that one will become a criminal. It usually means, however, that in the more severe cases a child will require some form of intervention in order to become a normally well adjusted child. That being said, I want to flip the argument and suggest that parents, no matter how dysfunctional they believe they are, should make at least some rudimentary attempts to fondle and caress their newborns. The hormones thus stimulated will give the child what it needs and will probably even stimulate the parent's own affection-response mechanism. When you realize the inordinately high numbers of sensory receptors on the surface of the human skin, you can begin to understand the importance of tactile stimulation. Thus, in order to stimulate a chemical affection-response, parents should make it a point to touch their children in a loving and nurturing fashion. Touching is not a sin. Caregivers need to come into contact with newborns. The absence of this touching can ultimately deprive the newborn of the ability to experience normal affection. Am I suggesting that there is a chemical basis for what we call love? Yes! And love is a perfectly simple and healthy way to start breaking the chain of violence from generation to generation.

EPILOGUE: THE ARREST OF GARY RIDGWAY IN FOUR GREEN RIVER MURDERS

Sheriff Dave Reichert of King County waited nearly twenty years for the arrest of a suspect in the 1982 murders of Opal Mills, Marcia Chapman, and Cynthia Hinds, whose bodies were found in the Green River. Their cases and those of over forty-five other women, most of whom were linked to the red-light district frequented by prostitutes along Seattle's Sea-Tac strip, came to be known collectively as the Green River Murders, one of the country's longest ongoing serial homicide investigations. And from 1982, King County homicide detective Dave Reichert was the primary investigator on the case. Green River was his case, and when the investigation seemed to be going nowhere because there was no arrest—even as more bodies began turning up in the river—it was Reichert to whom people looked for answers.

In 1983, the Green River Task Force was assembled and other law enforcement agencies became involved, particularly the FBI. But still, in public, at least, there was no apparent solution to the case. By 1985, there were no new official Green River cases, even though from the 1980s to the present, women thought to have links to prostitution were still disappearing. But the investigation into the Green River homicides continued.

What the public did not know back in 1985, according to interviews that King County sheriff Dave Reichert has now given to the press, was that Gary Leon Ridgway, who was arrested in November 2001 for the Opal Mills, Marcia Chapman, and Cynthia Hinds murders, had been one of Reichert's top five suspects "all along." Ridgway's arrest was not the result of a chance encounter with a police officer on a deserted strip of highway or an instance where he was caught in the act of abducting a woman. His arrest was the result of enormous patience and restraint that kept police from jumping on a suspect too quickly, and a trust in forensic science that eventually provided investigators with a method to test all of the DNA they had assembled over the years.

Gary Ridgway had come to the attention of King County detectives in the 1980s because he turned up in a number of tips and leads. As in other serial homicide cases, if a name keeps turning up from a variety of different sources and keeps popping up in a database of tips and leads, police tend to give credence to that name, even though at first there may be no hard evidence connecting that name to a particular crime. Police contacted Ridgway a number of times, interviewed him, and, according to newspaper reports, "kept him in their sights." Their ongoing interest in Ridgway paid off years later when Tom Jenson, the sole detective who had remained on the vestigal Green River Task Force and who was monitoring the developments in forensic technology, believed he had a way to use the DNA samples that the police had collected from the victims over the years.

In 2001, after a reevaluation of the case, Detective Jenson said he believed that there might be a way to conduct advanced DNA testing on the samples from the victims. There was a new type of DNA analysis, a Polymerase Chain Reaction (PCR), that was able to utilize limited samples of

DNA in order to get a match. The problem with the amount of DNA material Green River investigators had been collecting over the years was that the samples were seemingly too small to be of any real use, because DNA testing in the early days of the procedure required large samples to get accurate comparison results. If the samples were too small, they couldn't be used for the test. However, a new method of DNA testing was developed by Nobel Prize–winning Kary Mullis, at Berkley, in which the DNA strands were broken apart and exposed to an enzyme solution that duplicated the DNA. As Dr. Beverly Himick, a forensic scientist at the Washington State Patrol Crime Lab, explained in an interview with the *Seattle Post-Intelligencer,* the enzyme solution "acts as a chemical photocopier" and creates exact copies of the DNA.

Finally, after years of waiting for a method to evaluate the samples of DNA they'd collected, King County police were able to use PCR testing. Jenson had done his research well and, because police had also collected a swab of saliva from suspect Gary Ridgway years earlier, they had a sample they could use to see if it matched the crime scene samples from Green River victims. After the tests were conducted, according to what Sheriff Reichert told newspaper reporters, Tom Jenson walked into his office one day, dropped the analysis of DNA from two of the victims on his desk, "and then he flipped over a sheet of paper and said, 'Sheriff, here is the DNA of the Green River Killer.'" It was a DNA match with one of their suspects, Gary Leon Ridgway. And shortly thereafter, King County Sheriff's homicide detectives put Ridgway under surveillance. Ridgway was finally arrested at his Renton, Washington, home and charged with the murders of Opal Mills, Marcia Chapman, Cynthia Hinds, and Carol Christensen.

THE INVESTIGATION OF GARY RIDGWAY

The Green River case was two years old when, in 1984, Gary Ridgway approached Green River investigators with an offer to help. He told them he'd met one of the victims. Although Ridgway had passed a lie detector test in 1984, detectives were taking a closer look at him by 1985, especially after police records showed that in 1980 Ridgway had been arrested for choking a prostitute. He had been released at the time after telling police that he was defending himself from the woman who had attacked him. The cops believed his story. But in 1982, Ridgway had been arrested for solicitation during a prostitution sting, and in that same year, he was reported to have been parked in his pickup truck with a woman whose body, years later, was recovered not far from where she'd been sitting with Ridgway. After her body was found, the woman's name was listed as one of the Green River victims. Ridgway had not only been contacted by the police in connection with having choked a prostitute, he was linked to one of the Green River missing and murdered victims.

There were other incidents as well that kept the investigators' attention on Ridgway. In 1983, according to an incident described in *The Search for the Green River Killer,* Ridgway was spotted picking up a prostitute named Marie Malvar at a bus stop on Pacific Highway South. Marie Malvar's boyfriend, Robert Woods, recently said in an interview with KOMO-TV in Seattle that he watched Ridgway pull up to the bus stop in his pickup truck, come to a quick stop, and then speed away with Malvar. "The way he sped up on her was what caught my eye more than anything," Woods told his interviewer. What struck him, he said, was how quickly the truck pulled up and drove away. Most johns, he described, drive away slowly. This truck was moving too quickly, and that made Woods nervous. Woods followed the truck in his car and pulled up alongside, trying to look inside to see what was going on. "All I seen was a lot of hand movements. Yeah, a lot of hand movements. I don't know if she was talking fast, if she was hysterical, or what," Woods said.

The truck got away, but three days later, after Woods told Marie's father, Jose, that his daughter had disappeared, Woods and Jose Malvar searched for the truck in the area. They found it parked in a cul-de-sac in a driveway that belonged to Gary Ridgway. It was that tip, which Malvar gave to officers in the Des Moines, Washington, Police Department that led detectives to Ridgway's house, where they questioned him. However, Ridgway denied that he knew Marie Malvar, and police didn't have enough evidence to hold him responsible for her disappearance. Woods told KOMO that he had only seen Ridgway's profile and couldn't make a positive ID. However, the lead that Jose Malvar gave the police prompted detectives to take a saliva swab from Ridgway in 1987, the swab that ultimately led to his arrest.

Although Gary Ridgway had passed, according to the police at the time, two lie-detector tests, they did not completely eliminate him from consideration. His vehicle was one of the suspect vehicles in the investigation and he was still in the database. They conducted interviews with Ridgway, maintained their contact with him, and in 1987, they executed a search warrant on Ridgway and obtained a saliva sample for DNA analysis. Also, police interviewed Ridgway's former wife, who then took them to areas she said her ex-husband had frequented. These areas were close enough to some of the Green River dump sites that police believed Ridgway had to have been familiar with the area. As a rule, serial killers will dump bodies in areas where they have a high comfort level, and that means areas they're familiar with and where they believe they won't be discovered.

But Ridgway, even though the circumstantial evidence seemed to be piling up, still wasn't arrested. Police didn't want to make an arrest on a case where they didn't have solid biological evidence to back them up, for fear that if the DA couldn't get a conviction, Ridgway could not be tried again on the same charges. Also, even if Ridgway were rearrested for different murders, his acquittal on some of the charges might weaken a case against him for subsequent charges. So they waited and waited until technology caught up with their suspect and allowed police to use the samples they had collected years earlier.

Coworkers and neighbors described Gary Ridgway as someone who desperately wanted to be liked by other people. His former wife also described him as having been dominated by his mother, a strong-willed woman who once broke a plate over Ridgway's father's head when they were sitting together at the dinner table. Ridgway was described as a "nice" guy who had worked as a truck painter for thirty years and a navy veteran who took care of his house and his yard. His former wives, however, told a different story.

In the affidavit police filed to support their request for a search warrant for Ridgway's home and work locker, detectives cited information from his former wives and girlfriends in which they said that Ridgway liked to have sex outdoors. Police noted that many of the places where Ridgway said he enjoyed having sex were near Green River body dumpsites. One spot in particular was a location along the Green River where police had previously recovered five bodies.

In February 1984, according to the police affidavit, a prostitute contacted the Green River Task Force and reported Ridgway as a Green River killer suspect. This contact triggered the interest of one of the detectives who discovered that, previously, Detective Larry Gross on the task force had interviewed Ridgway back in 1983 as a result of Ridgway's contact with the Des Moines Police Department over the disappearance of Marie Malvar. This discovery prompted the police to call Ridgway in for an interview in April 1984. During this interview, Ridgway disclosed that he dated or had contact with "numerous" prostitutes from the Pacific Highway South area. And seven months later, still another prostitute reported that Ridgway had asked her for a car date, drove her to a remote location, then took her into the woods, and attempted to choke her to death. The description in the affidavit reads like a chilling narration of a murder in progress, which might have been completed had not the victim managed to break free from her assailant and flee from the scene.

The woman told police that Ridgway told her he wanted to "walk her into the woods" for their "car date," a trick for which she was to be paid $20. "During the sexual act that ensued, Ridgway placed the female prostitute in a policelike chokehold, forcing her to the ground facedown. Ridgway released the chokehold with his arm and immediately placed his hands around the back of her neck while choking her. As the struggle continued, the woman managed to turn over onto her back, facing Ridgway, while he continued to choke her with his hands, which were now placed around the front of her neck. The female said at this time there was no doubt in her mind that he was going to kill her. The woman managed to break free from [him] and escaped. She ran to a nearby mobile home in a trailer park and has never seen Ridgway since the incident."

Ridgway told the police, who questioned him afterward, that the woman had actually attacked him during the sexual encounter and he was defending himself. But in a subsequent interview about this incident, Ridgway admitted to choking the prostitute and said that he was addicted to having sex with prostitutes in Seattle and Tacoma and that they "affect him as strongly as alcohol does an alcoholic."

In an earlier affidavit, filed in 1987 pursuant to a request for a judge to sign a search warrant for Ridgway's home, police revealed that a former Ridgway girlfriend had complained that he once took her to a campground, near Cle Elum, where he tied her to wooden stakes that he drove into the ground. He bound her wrists and ankles with nylon rope, but then let her go. And this was only one of many stories about Ridgway's sexual behavior that kept the police interested in him from 1987 through 2001.

Police kept Ridgway under surveillance during these

years, watching as he took a circuitous route to his job in Renton and slowing down as he drove past Pacific Highway South as if he were looking at women believed to be prostitutes walking the street. On another occasion, police watched as Ridgway slowed down along Pacific Highway South and made two "unexplainable" U-turns across the middle of the highway as if, according to the police description, he were "seeking something."

Finally, in 2001, the rape kit DNA samples from victims Opal Mills and Marcia Chapman, which back in 1983 were considered too small to be tested conclusively, were submitted to PCR amplification testing. The results that were returned indicated that DNA material in the test was consistent with Ridgway's DNA. Also in October, victim Carol Christensen's vaginal swabbing was sent in for testing, and the test pinpointed Gary Ridgway, or an identical twin if he had one, as the sole individual in the "world's population [who] would exhibit this DNA profile." Subsequently, on November 30, 2001, detectives contacted Ridgway at his job, and during the ensuing interview, Ridgway admitted knowing Christensen "but denied having any type of sexual relationship with her." With the DNA tests now part of the evidence in four of the Green River homicides, King County police arrested Ridgway at his home and filed charges against him in the murders.

WHO IS GARY RIDGWAY?

For the past seventeen years, Gary Ridgway has been subjected to search warrants, interviews, on-and-off surveillance, interrogations, polygraph examinations, and the retrieval of a saliva swab. For the past thirty-two years, he showed up for his night shift at Kenworth Truck Company, where he worked as a painter. His coworkers knew that the police were talking to Ridgway about the Green River killings because his name had been circulating as a result of his 1980 and 1982 arrests, the latter for soliciting a police-woman as an anticrime decoy in a prostitution sting. According to the newspapers, other workers at Kenworth Truck thought the police interest in Ridgway was kind of a joke and they called him "GR," not for Gary Ridgway, but for Green River.

Nobody at Kenworth truly suspected that Ridgway was the "Green River Killer," they told reporters, because the guy seemed too nice and not big enough to kill anybody with his bare hands. He'd come down the hall at night, very cheery, and give a "Hi, friend" to whomever he met. People he worked with and knew might have been aware that Ridgway had taken two lie-detector tests and was thought to have passed them both, even though police later deemed the tests inconclusive because they did not go far enough in clearing him. What his coworkers didn't know was that police had already compared Ridgway's work schedule with dates of the abductions of prostitutes and found that he couldn't be eliminated as a suspect. Police had also found that Ridgway had frequented the very areas from where bodies had been recovered, and this aroused their interest in him as a suspect. Perhaps his friends and coworkers were unaware that Ridgway had once choked his second wife, Marcia, after becoming very drunk at a party, a story she told to police along with descriptions of the nights her husband would come home soaking wet from being outside in the woods. Thus, even while Ridgway lived beneath the camouflage of a steady job, a home, and a marital relationship, police were looking for the one piece of biological labwork that could conclusively link Ridgway to one or more of the homicides.

It was a shock, indeed, to his neighbors in the Lake Geneva neighborhood when the police secured the suspect's home with crime tape and searched it for evidence. Ridgway and his wife, Judith, had moved to Lake Geneva from Maple Valley three years earlier, and they had befriended the neighbors around them. People remembered Ridgway chopping wood, something he said he loved to do, and had, what neighbors told the newspapers, was "a mammoth woodpile." He always kept his trees trimmed and his lawn cut, and was a friendly enough guy over the back fence. Judith Ridgway also made friends in the neighborhood and held garage sales.

Next-door neighbor Kim Straus told the *Seattle Times* that her dog would often stray over to the Ridgway property. But the Ridgways were "good neighbors," she said, and they never complained. "They were always very nice about it," Straus said. "They'd call us, and we would come get her." It was almost eerie, she thought, because she never suspected that Gary Ridgway would be arrested in homicides that were a part of one of the longest and most celebrated serial-murder cases in the United States. She said she was even embarrassed to tell her friends that the suspect lived on the same street. But Kim Straus and the other residents along Federal Way could only watch in shock as the police methodically moved back and forth from the house to their vans in the heavy December rain. And if, in fact, Ridgway turns out to be convicted for the homicides he is charged with, he will indeed have become the quintessential "killer next door."

ABOUT THE AUTHORS

The late **DR. JOEL NORRIS**, a clinical psychologist who founded the International Committee of Neuroscientists to Study Episodic Aggression, was a pioneer in the study of the constellation of psychological, biological, and social symptomology of serial aggressive behavior. He was a member of the board of directors of the Coalition of Victims' Equal Rights, a Los Angeles–based organization dedicated to studying the prevention of violence in the United States, founded by Doris Tate, mother of slain actress Sharon Tate.

New York Times best-selling author **DR. WILLIAM J. BIRNES**, Norris's coauthor on *Serial Killers* has also collaborated with Dr. Robert Keppel on *Riverman* and *Signature Killers*, and with Lieutenant Colonel Philip Corso on *The Day After Roswell*. He lives in Los Angeles with his wife, novelist Nancy Hayfield.